"Our People Die Well"

Glorious Accounts of Early Methodists at Death's Door

by

Joseph D. McPherson

To our special friends, Jim & Barb: May this book prove to be a blessing to you both.

Joe MᶜPherson

authorHOUSE®

AuthorHouse™
1663 Liberty Drive, Suite 200
Bloomington, IN 47403
www.authorhouse.com
Phone: 1-800-839-8640

First published by AuthorHouse 10/22/2008

ISBN: 978-1-4343-2981-3 (sc)

Library of Congress Control Number: 2007906587

Printed in the United States of America
Bloomington, Indiana

This book is printed on acid-free paper.

Dedication

This book I dedicate to my lovely wife, Margaret, sons Philip and Mark, daughter in law Candace and grandsons, Kevin, Kyle, Daniel and Stephen, who will always be warmly loved and cherished.

Contents

Acknowledgments

I would like to express my appreciation to the following people for their assistance in the writing of this book: Mrs. Philip (Lelia) Dawalt, long time instructor of English composition, and Mrs. Terry (Betty) Porter, Assistant Professor of English at Indiana Wesleyan University for the time and labor expended in proof editing this manuscript; Dr. Duane Thompson, one time Chairman of the Religion and Philosophy Department of Indiana Wesleyan University, Dr. Christopher Bounds, Associate Professor of Theology at Indiana Wesleyan University, and Dr. V. P. Reasoner, Academic Dean of Southern Methodist College, for their inspiring encouragement; Dr. Randall McElwain, missionary, musician, educator, and Charles Wesley scholar for his contribution to the content of the book; Mrs. John (Joy) Budensiek, educator and author, and Mr. Joseph Taylor, Director of Gospel Publishing Mission for their valuable and timely counsel. Last, but certainly not least, I would like to thank my dear wife, Margaret, for her unending support of my efforts to complete what had been a literary goal of many years.

Preface

There is an old story of someone approaching a religious leader and asking him why he never mentioned the subject of death. He replied, "I know that when I die I shall pass into eternal felicities, all pain and sorrow will be gone, I will be with my loved ones forever, and I shall never have to die again; but I just don't like to talk about such unpleasant subjects."

Not everyone is as obviously inconsistent as this. Indeed, we do like to think of heaven and all its glorious expectations, but most (at least many) of us do not like the thought of dying. Nevertheless, the prospects of heaven demand that our paths make their way through the gateway of death, the "valley of the shadow."

This book is all about just such experiences of the process of dying. And there is no better person to deal with this subject than Joseph McPherson. Early in his life he began a journey of delving into the writings of John Wesley and early Methodism. He diligently and systematically has read much from that era. His noteworthy insight gained in that study has made him an expert in the original writings. In the many conversations made possible by our friendship, I have become convinced that his own life and theological views have taken on the character of early Wesleyan Methodism.

Over a period of many years, Joseph McPherson has done exhaustive and dedicated research on a group of people who were so harmonious in their inner thoughts, prayers, beliefs, and actions that death was not such a gloomy prospect for them. They show us the way to live so that when we die we can die well. They show us that in the time of death we can be supported by such a sure foundation that death becomes a blessed entrance into abundant life with God.

You may have been afraid as you picked up this book that you were about to discover tragedy and sadness, but as you read it you may arrive at a fresh revelation of the power of faith to carry you safely through the transitioning of worlds. Since all of us will eventually face such a transformation, it is critical to know as early in life as possible just how the preparation for that change will make all the difference in it. If we are always ready for death, then life takes on new nuances and glory. To be ready to die well is to be ready to live to the fullest, for the future holds ultimate joy.

As the expression goes, "All's well that ends well." But these believers not only ended well; they believed that this was but a glorious beginning. These Christians found that the Apostle Paul's assertions were more than words; they were the reality that gave them a safe passage into another world:

> I have become absolutely convinced that neither death nor life, neither messenger of Heaven nor monarch of earth, neither what happens today nor what may happen tomorrow, neither a power from on high nor a power from below, nor anything else in God's whole world has any power to separate us from the love of God in Christ Jesus our Lord! (Rom. 8:38-39, Phillips)

If you picked up this book as a believer in Christ, you will find great encouragement as you read the final stages of these dying Christians. And if you are not one who has taken the Christian hope seriously, you may find that what early Christians called "The Way" you will also find as the Truth and the Life Everlasting.

R. Duane Thompson Ph.D.
One time Chairman of the Division of Religion
and Philosophy, Indiana Wesleyan University.

Introduction

Many years ago this writer was, by a chain of providential occurrences, led into an extensive study of early Methodist literature. One of the blessings received in such study was the reading of the many accounts and testimonies of dying Methodists of the eighteenth and early nineteenth centuries. Over and over these accounts reflected victory, unutterable happiness, and glory in those who were approaching death. Many of them were suffering extreme pain in their final days and hours, but in the midst of it all, they were able to give glorious expressions of praise, making known their possession of a heavenly peace and joy that words could not describe.

Capturing once again such scenes of heaven opening up to a host of early Methodists in their hour of death provides the reader no small confirmation of the truth of those biblical doctrines trumpeted by John Wesley and his preachers who ranged throughout the British Isles in revival effort. When heartily embraced, such truth was found able to bring any and all safely through "the valley of the shadow of death." The unprejudiced reader finds it convincing that if that which was preached and taught by the early Methodists proved so successful in bringing such a host of souls safely to paradise, then surely such truth can be just as effectual today when carefully and earnestly followed.

Under divine inspiration the psalmist assures us that "The death of his saints is precious in the sight of the Lord" (Psalm 116:15). This is doubtlessly one of the most touching and comforting verses in the Bible. As strange as it may seem, the Psalmist calls death "precious." It is a most unusual epithet for what is elsewhere identified as "man's last enemy."

God is intimately interested in all stages of a saintly life—not only in its beginning and its progress, but also in its earthly conclusion. This is the last step of the saint's earthly pilgrimage, and so this verse reveals something of that loving regard the Lord has for each of His saints as they depart from the company of friends and loved ones to enter with Him into paradise.

We know also that our heavenly Father feels deeply the loss suffered by those who are left behind. As R. Tuck beautifully expresses it, "He unveils a heart of infinite sympathy, who 'bears our griefs, and carries our sorrows.' How God feels toward us finds its illustration in the manifestation of God—Christ Jesus" (H. D. M. Spence and Joseph S. Exell, eds., *The Pulpit Commentary* III [London and New York: Funk & Wagnalls Company, nd], 82). How can we forget the compassion shown at Nain, when the Master stopped a funeral procession, touched the couch upon which the dead lay, raised to life the only son of a widow woman, and gave him back to his precious mother? Again, how can we forget the tears shed by the Master at Lazarus' tomb just before he raised him to life in Bethany? These accounts show us something of the sympathies of our God in times of loss due to death.

We may suggest several reasons why God counts precious the death of His saints. The first must be His loving and sympathetic nature. "His saints are dear unto Him." Because the living who are left are often overwhelmed with sorrow, He sympathizes. In that place of heavenly glory it is said, "And God shall wipe away all tears from their eyes" (Revelation 7:17). R. Tuck reminds us that the "tears [we shed] are precious ... to our heavenly Father, though, for the holiest ends, He may bid them flow on while we tarry here below" ("ibid., 82").

A second reason for God's counting precious the death of His saints may be observed in the fact that at the time of death, a saint often has a greater response of trust and an increased desire for the delights of God's presence. Whatever the degree of dependence upon God there may have been during life's passage, there is no time when dependence upon the merits of Christ's atonement is more fully exercised than in the hour of death's approach. The precious blood of Christ is then viewed with utmost value, for it is the object of all their trust. S. Conway reminds us that during life's tenure, we discuss all kinds of issues and questions, doctrines, and theological beliefs, but when we come down to the hour of death, our strongest desire is expressed in the words: "Thou, O Christ, art all I want!" ("ibid., 76"). It is that utter casting of the soul upon God that He delights. Such abandoned trust is precious to Him.

A third reason for the Almighty's looking upon the death of His saints as precious is found in the fact that they leave a wondrous witness of the mercies of God to others. This, of course, glorifies Him. The Apostle Paul could never forget the dying words and prayers of the saintly Stephen nor can we forget that the blood of the martyrs has ever been the seed of the Church. In less violent deaths than these, however, effective witness for God has been borne, and with power that was unknown in any other circumstances.

Finally, God considers precious the death of His saints because, as S. Conway assures us, "it is the moment of their safe in gathering. Till then, they have been, as the sheep in the wilderness, liable to wander, exposed to peril, [harassed by the wolves] of hell, and often all but lost." But death can be considered as God's means of "gathering them safe within the eternal sheep-fold" ("ibid., 76").

The future of the people of God is a glorious contemplation. Although there has obviously been a beginning of our existence, we are assured in Scripture that we shall have no end. And, in that sense we are eternal, never dying souls. Again, S. Conway reminds us that death cannot end it all. In fact, death could not be "precious" if it constituted the end of our existence. Nor can death introduce us into a state of unconsciousness. Death for God's saints is not a sleep, but rather an "entrance into the fullness of life with Christ" ("ibid., 76").

True, it is that the term "sleep" is used in the Scriptures to describe the state of the body while resting in the grave and awaiting the resurrection. But the unseen spirits of the redeemed enter immediately into the presence of Christ, where full enjoyment of paradise is experienced. "In thy presence," says the Psalmist, "is fullness of joy; at thy right hand there are pleasures for evermore" (Psalm 16:11). To the saint, therefore, death is a departing to be with Christ, which, as Paul says, is far better than remaining here. Surely, we may, as he admonishes us, "comfort one another with these words" (1 Thessalonians 4:18).

The death of a Christian, therefore, is not only precious in the sight of the Lord but has also proven time and again to be of indescribable blessing and happiness to the dying saint. The apostle John, while receiving the Revelation on the Isle of Patmos, "heard a voice from heaven saying ... Write, Blessed (or happy) are the dead which die in the Lord from henceforth: Yea, saith the Spirit, that they may rest from their labours; and their works do follow them" (Revelation 14:13).

According to Adam Clarke, these are they who "die under the smile and approbation of God, and they die to live and reign with God for ever and ever." He reminds us that they not only rest from the burdensome labors of this life but are released from all "tribulation and distress." Their works are even said to follow them, or "follow with them," as may otherwise be translated. We are to understand that the good works and sufferings of these dying saints are "represented as so many companions escorting them on their way to the kingdom of God" (Adam Clarke, *Clarke's Commentary* VI [New York & Nashville: Abingdon Press, nd], 1030).

According to Luke Wiseman, "It was the boast of the Wesleys that 'our people die well'—a fact, which they believed of great evidential value." A physician who had rendered medical assistance to several Methodists made the claim to Charles Wesley that "Most people die for the fear of dying; but," said he, "I never met with such people as yours. They are none of them afraid of death, but [are] calm, and patient, and resigned to the last" (Luke F. Wiseman, *Charles Wesley: Evangelist and Poet* [London: The Epworth Press, 1932], np).

Such evidence did indeed give ongoing support to the Wesleyan revival of the eighteenth century. That host of victorious saints in death proved to be a peculiar blessing to those who witnessed their final expressions of praise and their views of glory.

The following contents constitute but a sampling of the accounts one finds of early Methodist saints who died well. It is our prayer that those accounts shared herein will prove to be a special blessing to today's readers.

* Dates found below titles throughout this volume mark the time of death in each account. All accounts are then arranged in chronological order.

*All quotations cited in this volume are marked as found in original sources.

Rev. Samuel Wesley:

"The Inward Witness, Son ...
That Is The Strongest Proof Of Christianity."
(d. April, 1735)

The Rev. Samuel Wesley, father of John and Charles Wesley, was rector of the Anglican Church at Epworth, England for almost forty years. It is said that he "was distinguished for the zeal and fidelity with which he discharged his parish duties." He was known for his talents and learning of which his written works afford honorable evidence (Richard Watson, *The Life of the Rev. John Wesley, A. M.* [New York: W. Disturnell Publishers, 1834], 2).

He and his wife Susannah were the parents of nineteen children, several of whom did not survive infancy. These parents found it most difficult to provide their large family with the temporal necessities of daily life. Such were their financial hardships on occasion that Samuel was forced to spend several months in debtor's prison at Lincoln Castle. Because of the uncompromising manner of his preaching and his scriptural call for the repentance of his parishioners, the family suffered various forms of persecution, including setting fire to their rectory (parsonage), maiming their cattle, and destroying the family's food crops.

Below, we share the account of this good man's final hours and departure as provided by his wife Susannah and his sons John and Charles. To her son John, Mrs. Wesley writes: "Your father is in a very bad state of health; he sleeps little, and eats less. He seems not to have any apprehension of his approaching exit; but I fear he has but a short time to live." She then continues with further description of her husband's physical decline.

> "It is with much pain and difficulty that he performs divine service on the Lord's Day, which sometimes he is obliged to contract very much. Everybody observes his decay but himself. He acted on the maxim, 'Rather wear out than rust out;' and he sunk, fairly worn out with labors, old age, and infirmities, April 25, 1735, in the seventy-second year of his age." (Adam Clarke, *Memoirs of the Wesley Family* [New York: Lane & Tippet Publishers, 1848], 275-6)

Both of his sons, John and Charles, were at his bedside when he died. The former provides the following brief account by letter, dated, Dublin, March 22, 1747:

> "My father, during his last illness, which continued eight months, enjoyed a clear sense of his acceptance with God. I heard him express it more than once. 'The inward witness, son, the inward witness,' said he to me, 'that is the proof, the strongest proof, of Christianity.' And when I asked him, (the time of his change drawing nigh,) 'Sir, are you in much pain?' he answered aloud, with a smile, 'God does chasten me with pain; yea, all my bones with strong pain. But I thank him for all;

I bless him for all; I love him for all.' I think the last words he spoke, when I had just commended his soul to God, were, 'Now you have done all.' And with the same cheerful countenance he fell asleep, without one struggle, or sigh, or groan." ("ibid., 276")

In a sermon preached at Savannah, Feb. 20, 1736, Mr. John Wesley further adds, in giving an account of two persons "going out of this life, in what I call," says he, "a comfortable manner," the one, referring to the death of his father in England, the other to one at Savannah. "I attended the first (says he) during a great part of his last trial, as well as when he yielded up his soul to God. He cried out, 'God doth chasten me with strong pain; but I thank him for all; I bless him for all; I love him for all.' When asked, not long before his release, 'Are the consolations of God small with you?' he replied aloud, 'No, no, no!' Calling all that were near him by their names, he said, 'Think of heaven, talk of heaven; all the time is lost when we are not thinking of heaven.' Now this was the voice of love. And so far as it prevailed, all was comfort, peace, and joy. But as his love was not perfect, so neither was his comfort. He had intervals of fretfulness, and therein of misery; giving by both an incontestable proof that love can sweeten both life and death." ("ibid., 276-77")

"Mr. Charles Wesley's account, however, in a letter to his brother Samuel, is" according to Clarke, "the most circumstantial; and is as follows:--

"Epworth, April 30th, 1735.

"Dear Brother,--After all your desire of seeing my father alive, you are at last assured you must see his face no more, till raised in incorruption. You have reason to envy us, who could attend him in the last stage of his illness. The few words he uttered I have saved. Some of them were, 'Nothing too much to suffer for heaven. The weaker I am in body, the stronger and more sensible support I feel from God. There is but a step between me and death. To-morrow I would see you all with me round this table, that we may once more drink of the cup of blessing, before we drink of it new in the kingdom of God. With desire have I desired to eat this Passover with you before I die.' ("ibid., 277")

"The morning he was to communicate, he was so exceeding weak and full of pain, that he could not, without the utmost difficulty, receive the elements, often repeating, 'Thou shakest me! Thou shakest me!' But immediately after receiving, there followed the most visible alteration. He appeared full of faith and peace, which extended even to his body; for he was so much better, that we almost hoped he would have recovered. The fear of death he had entirely conquered; and at last gave up his latest human desires, of finishing Job, paying his debts, and seeing you. He often laid his hands upon my head, and said, 'Be ready. The Christian faith will surely revive in this kingdom; you shall see it, though I shall not.' To my sister Emily he said, 'Do not be concerned at my death; God will then begin to manifest himself to my family.' When we were met about him, his usual expression was, 'Now let me hear you talk about heaven.' On my asking him whether he did not find himself worse, he replied, 'O, my Charles, I feel a great deal. God chastens me with strong pain; but I praise him for it; I thank him for it; I love him for it.' On the 25th his voice failed him, and nature seemed entirely spent; when on my brother's asking, 'whether he was not near heaven?' he answered distinctly, and with the most of hope and triumph that could be expressed in sounds, 'Yes, I am.' He spoke once more, just after my brother had used the commendatory prayer. His last words were, 'Now you have done all.' This was about half an hour after six; from which time till sunset he made signs of offering up himself, till my brother having again used the prayer, the very moment it was finished he expired." ("ibid., 277-8")

Charles Wesley:

*Witnesses The Execution And Triumphant
Decease Of Converted Malefactors*

(d. July, 1738)

From his earliest days as a student at Oxford University, Charles Wesley not only studied religion but endeavored to put it into practice as well. He became the founder and first leader of the Holy Club whose members met several times a week to read and study the Scriptures and share the reading of religious literature. They also used their meager resources to help the needy, sponsor a school for poor children, and visit those in prison.

In his biography of Charles Wesley, Arnold Dallimore writes the following account of criminals who, being destined for execution, found their souls' salvation through the love, counsel, and prayers of their friend, Charles Wesley.

> Charles witnessed magnificent evidence of the power of the gospel as he ministered to the condemned men in London's Newgate prison. Being asked to do so by a fellow minister he reported, "I went with him ...

and preached to the ten malefactors, under sentence of death; but with a heavy heart. My old prejudices against the possibility of a death-bed repentance still hung upon me; and I could hardly hope there was mercy for those whose time was so short. But in the midst of my languid discourse a sudden spirit of faith came upon me, and I promised them all pardon, in the name of Jesus Christ, if they would then, as at the last hour, repent and believe the gospel.

"I visited one of them in his cell, sick of a fever; a poor black that had robbed his master. I told him of one who came down from heaven to save lost sinners, and him in particular; described the sufferings of the Son of God, his sorrows, agony, and death. He listened with all the signs of eager astonishment; the tears trickled down his cheeks while he cried, 'What? Was it for me? Did he suffer all this for so poor a creature as me?'"

When he visited the prison again three days later, Charles said, "I rejoiced with my poor happy black; who now believes the Son of God loved him and gave himself for him." As Charles declared the gospel's good news to the felons, even in what he called "the condemned hole," he saw its effect on them, one by one. But he also experienced its effect afresh within his own heart as, dealing with these pitiable individuals in this wretched place, he declared, "I had great help and power in prayer … I found myself overwhelmed with the love of Christ to sinners."

As the day of execution approached Charles increased his efforts. He and Bray allowed themselves to be locked in with the condemned men throughout the night; they "wrestled in mighty prayer" and saw fear and despair give way to peace and joy on one countenance after another.

On the morning of the hanging a boisterous crowd, intent on making sport of the event, gathered as usual at Tyburn, the place of execution. As the death cart drew onto the field, Charles and a few friends were there to meet it. "The black spied me, coming out of the coach," says Charles, "and saluted me with his looks. As often as his eyes met mine, he smiled the most composed, delightful countenance I ever saw."

Charles made his way through the crowd and climbed into the cart, but when the official chaplain tried to do the same, the prisoners begged he might not come; and the mob kept him down. There, in the death cart, disdainful of the jeers of the crowd, Charles again spoke words of scriptural comfort to the poor victims. He and his companions sang for all to hear a hymn that had been written by his father:

"Behold the Saviour of mankind Nailed
to the shameful tree!
How vast the love that him inclined
To bleed and die for thee!

Tis done! The precious ransom's paid;
'Receive my soul!' he cries;
See where he bows his sacred head!
He bows his head, and dies!"

A rope from an overhead scaffold was placed around the neck of each prisoner. Charles continued his ministrations, praying, giving encouragement and kissing whom he could. As the final moment approached he again broke into song:

"To the dear fountain of thy blood, Incarnate God, I fly;
Here let me wash my spotted soul,
From sins of deepest dye.

A guilty, weak and helpless worm, Into thy hands I fall;
Be thou my life, my righteousness, My Jesus and my all."

"When the cart drew off," says Charles, "not one struggled for life. We left them going to meet their Lord, ready for the Bridegroom.... I spoke a few suitable words to the crowd, and returned full of peace in our friends' happiness. That hour under the gallows was the most blessed hour of my life." (Arnold A. Dallimore, *A Heart Set Free,* I [IL: Crossway Books, 1988], 120-123)

Sister Hooper:
"I Shall Never Be Cast Down"
(d. No date)

From Charles Wesley's *Journal,* we share the following edited account. The exact date of the death of this saint is not known.

"I found Sister Hooper just at the haven …. The angel of death [had] come, and [there was] but a few moments between her and a blessed eternity. We poured out our souls to God for her, her children, ourselves, the church and ministers, and all mankind." Charles then expressed something of a perception of her joy. He confessed that he was "tenderly affected for her in her sufferings. And yet he was conscious of the fact that "joy swallowed up sorrow." The more she suffered, the more her consolations seemed to abound.

Later, she was again asked if she were not in great pain. She answered that she was but assured those around her that the joy she felt was greater than her pain. She said, "I would not be without either."

When asked whether she would prefer life or death, she replied, "all is alike to me, let Christ choose; I have no will of my own." Shortly before she died, Charles writes that he felt a mixture of grief and love that was quite overpowering. Then it was that her spirit ascended to God. "I felt our souls were knit together," says he "by the violent

11

struggle of mine to follow her. When I saw the breathless temple of the Holy Ghost, my heart was still, and a calm resignation took place. We knelt down," says he, "and gave God thanks from the ground of our heart" (Charles Wesley, *The Journal of Charles Wesley*, I [Baker House, 1980], 270-272).

Luke Wiseman has made the following comments in connection with the above account:

> It was the boast of the Wesleys that "our people die well"—a fact which they believed of great evidential value. Charles Wesley in one of his visits to this Mrs. Hooper, of Bristol, spoke with her physician, who said he had little hope of her recovery; "only," added he, "she has no dread upon her spirits, which is generally the worst symptom. Most people die for fear of dying; but I never met with such people as yours. They are none of them afraid of death, but calm, and patient, and resigned to the last." He had said to her, "Madam, be not cast down." She answered, smiling, "Sir, I shall never be cast down." Many had their periods of heaviness, struggle, and darkness, but Charles Wesley gives it as his experience that "all our people, without exception, be they ever so dark or weak before, when they come to die recover their confidence." The hour of last conflict was the time of final and triumphant victory. The house of mourning, therefore, became the temple of joy: "We sang a song of victory for our deceased friend; then went to the house, and rejoiced, and gave thanks." (Luke Wiseman, *Charles Wesley: Evangelist and Poet* [London: The Epworth Press, 1932], np.)

Sister Richardson:
A Joyful Funeral Attended With Persecution
(d. April, 1741)

The year 1741 marks an early time in the history of the Methodist revival. Only three years had passed since the evangelical conversion of both John and Charles Wesley in May of 1738. Numerous converts, however, were already being made in these early years. Likewise, victorious departures from this life were also being witnessed. Charles Wesley writes the following entry in his *Journal*, dated Sunday, April 19, 1741:

> Returning from Baptist-Mills, I heard that our Sister Richardson had finished her course. My soul was filled with strong consolation, and struggled, as it were, to go out after her, "as heavenward endeavouring." Jesu, my time is in thy hand: only let me so follow her, as she had followed Thee! The voice of joy and thanksgiving was in the congregation, while I spake of her death.
>
> Tuesday, April 21st. I hastened to the joyful funeral of our sister Richardson. The room was crowded within and without. My subject was, "I know that my

Redeemer liveth," &c. (Job xix. 25.) I spoke searchingly to the hearsay-believers; and then largely of her, whose faith they might safely follow. Great was my glorying and rejoicing over her. She, being dead, yet spoke in words of faith and love, which ought to be had in remembrance. Surely her spirit was present with us; and we were in a measure partakers of her joy, a joy unspeakable and full of glory.

The whole Society followed her to her grave. Through all the city Satan raged exceedingly in his children, who threw dirt and stones at us: but the bridle was in their mouths. (Charles Wesley, *The Journal of Charles Wesley*, I [Baker House, 1980], 268)

Reference above to the "whole Society" is to be understood as consisting of all the Methodist membership in that particular place. When John and Charles Wesley organized their followers, it was not with the intention of founding a new church denomination but rather the organizing of local societies within the governmental structure of the established Church of England. In this manner they hoped to revive the Anglican Church of which they were life long members and ordained clergymen.

The disrespectful and even violent treatment given these Methodist mourners by the rabble of that day was typical of the persecution they suffered in the early days of the Methodist revival. "Lewd fellows of the baser sort" were, in those days, known to go so far in their hatred of God's people as to destroy houses and places of business belonging to Methodists. Too often, Methodists suffered personal injury as well.

Jane Muncy:
"A Mother In Israel Hast Thou Been"
(d. July, 1741)

In the account shared below, Mr. Wesley makes reference to a time early in the formation of a Methodist society when there was some mixed fellowship with Moravians at a weekly meeting place called Fetter-Lane. The Moravians in their midst began to teach that saving faith must be received without using the means of grace; that before experiencing saving faith, seekers were not to attend church and sacrament; were not to pray nor read their Bibles. In their view, all of this activity was seeking faith by works. Instead, the seeker was to "be still" and wait, as it were, for faith to be given without any personal effort or activity (John Wesley, *The Works of John Wesley*, I [Grand Rapids: Zondervan Publishing House, 1958], 247).

To Mr. Wesley and his followers, this was unscriptural "enthusiasm," better known today as fanaticism. He maintained that using the means of grace, though meriting us nothing, was a necessary condition for becoming "workers with God" in the salvation of our souls. Attending church and sacrament, prayer and Bible reading were means ordained of God by which we receive saving faith and continued growth in grace.

Jane Muncy, as we see below, was one of those who gave her full support to Mr. Wesley's position in this debate.

> Hearing that one of our sisters (Jane Muncy) was ill, I went to see her. She was one of the first [to lead] women Bands at Fetter-Lane; and, when the controversy concerning the means of grace began, stood in the gap, and contended earnestly for the ordinances once delivered to the saints. When, soon after, it was ordered, that the unmarried men and women should have no conversation with each other, she again withstood to the face those who were "teaching for doctrines the commandments of men." Nor could all the sophistry of those who are, without controversy, of all men living the wisest in their generation, induce her either to deny the faith she had received, or to use less plainness of speech, or to be less zealous in recommending and careful in practicing good works. Insomuch that many times, when she had been employed in the labour of love, till eight or nine in the evening, she then sat down and wrought with her hands till twelve or one in the morning; not that she wanted any thing herself, but that she might have to give to others for necessary uses.
>
> From the time that she was made Leader of one or two Bands, she was more eminently a pattern to the flock: In self-denial of every kind, in openness of behaviour, in simplicity and godly sincerity, in steadfast faith, in constant attendance on all the public and all the private ordinances of God. And as she had laboured more than they all, so God now called her forth to

suffer. She was seized at first with a violent fever, in the beginning of which they removed her to another house. Here she had work to do which she knew not of. The master of the house was one who "cared for none of these things." But he observed her, and was convinced. So that he then began to understand and lay to heart the things that bring a man peace at the last.

In a few days the fever abated, or settled, as it seemed, into an inward imposthume; so that she could not breathe without violent pain, which increased day and night. When I came in, she stretched out her hand and said, "Art thou come, thou blessed of the Lord? Praised be the name of my Lord for this." I asked, "Do you faint, now you are chastened of him?" She said, "O no, no no; I faint not; I murmur not; I rejoice evermore." I said, "But can you in every thing give thanks?" She replied, "Yes; I do, I do." I said, "God will make all your bed in your sickness." She cried out, "He does, he does; I have nothing to desire; he is ever with me, and I have nothing to do but to praise him."

In the same state of mind, though weaker and weaker in body, she continued till Tuesday following; when several of those who had been in her Band being present, she fixed her eyes upon them, and fell into a kind of agonizing prayer, that God would keep them from the evil one. But in the afternoon, when I came, she was quite calm again, and all her words were prayer and praise. The same spirit she breathed when Mr. Maxfield called the next day; and soon after he went, she slept in peace.—"A mother in Israel" hast thou been, and "thy works shall praise thee in the gates!" ("ibid, 319-321")

Several days later, Mr. Wesley conducted the funeral service for this departed saint. He preached on those words, "Write, Blessed are the dead which die in the Lord from henceforth: Yea, saith the Spirit, that they may rest from their labours; and their works do follow them" (Revelation 14:13). From there, they all went to the grave site "in St. Giles's church-yard, where," he says, "I performed the last office in the presence of such an innumerable multitude of people as I never saw gathered together before." He then ends his comments with these words: "O what a sight it will be when God saith to the grave, 'Give back;' and all the dead, small and great, shall stand before him!" (Wesley, *The Works of John Wesley*, I, 319-321").

Sarah Whiskin:
Claimed Death To Be "Nothing"
(d. January, 1742)

Mr. Wesley records his conducting of a burial service for a young woman by the name of Sarah Whiskin, late of Cambridge. The account of her final days, her seeking for a personal revelation of God to her heart and her death are taken from the *Journal* and shared below in edited form.

Sarah had attended the preaching of Mr. Wesley and "was not disappointed. From that time she seemed quite taken up with the things above, and could willingly have been always hearing, or praying, or singing hymns." She gave evidence of being spiritually awakened and was found to be exceedingly careful in the making of all her daily decisions that they might be made in accordance with what she was persuaded to be God's will, even though she had not yet an assurance that all her sins were forgiven her.

It was said that, "she was almost continually praying to God that He would reveal himself to her soul." On one occasion her friend observed her "in tears and asked what was the matter. She answered, 'The devil is very busy with me.' On asking, 'Who condemns you?' She pointed to her heart,' and said, 'This; and God is greater than my heart.'"

A couple days later "after [a] Mr. Richards had prayed with her, she was much [more cheerful], and she could not doubt but God would fulfill the desire which he had given her." It was evident at this time that she was physically ill and that her health was declining rapidly. Nevertheless, in the midst of her physical weakness, she sought God with renewed effort. "Though God," said she, "has not yet revealed himself to me, yet I believe, were I to die this night, before to-morrow I should be in heaven." "I hope," said her sister, "God will restore you to health." Her response was, "Let Him do what seemeth Him good."

The next day, she said, "I saw my mother, and brother, and sister, in my sleep; and they all received a blessing in a moment." A friend asked her "if she thought she should die; and whether she believed the Lord would receive her soul. Looking very earnestly, she said, 'I have not seen the Lord yet; but I believe I shall see Him and live: Although these are bold words for a sinner to say. Are they not?'"

The following morning she was asked how she had rested. "She answered, 'Very well; though I have had no sleep; and I wanted none; for I have had the Lord with me. O let us not be ashamed of him, but proclaim Him upon the house-top; and I know, whatever I ask in the name of Jesus, according to his will, I shall have.'" It wasn't long before "she broke out into singing," being now delivered from all her fears. "Now it is done"; said she, "I am assured my sins are forgiven."

One who was present expressed the thought that "Death is a little thing to them that die in the Lord." She strongly replied, "A little thing! It is nothing." Soon after, her speech began to fail and she made signs for her sister to come near. She affectionately "kissed her and smiled upon her. She then lay about an hour without speaking or stirring; till about three o'clock [in the morning], she cried out, 'My Lord and my God' fetched a double sigh, and died" (John Wesley, *The Works of John Wesley,* I [Grand Rapids: Zondervan Publishing House, 1958], 354-356).

Mary Whittle:
"I Shall Go To My Lord Tomorrow"
(d. January, 1742)

"I again visited many that were sick," writes Mr. Wesley, "but I found no fear either of pain or death among them. One (Mary Whittle) said, 'I shall go to my Lord to-morrow; but before I go, He will finish his work.' The next day she lay quiet for about two hours, and then opening her eyes, cried out, 'It is done, it is done! Christ liveth in me! He lives in me:' And died in a moment" (John Wesley, *The Works of John Wesley,* I [Grand Rapids: Zondervan Publishing House, 1958], 352-353).

To find "no fear either of pain or death" among the sick visited by Mr. Wesley is truly a wonderful testimonial to the power of Christ whose Spirit inhabits those who are His. We are again reminded that "There is no fear in love; but perfect love casteth out fear; because fear hath torment. He that feareth is not made perfect in love" (1 John 4:18).

How do we account for Mary Whittle's assurance that she would "go to [her] Lord tomorrow?" From what might we suppose such a premonition originates? The hearing of such cases, however, is not as uncommon as some might think.

What work was it that Mary expected the Lord to finish in her before going to Him? Could it be that she expected Him to finish His work of heart perfection? In his *A Plain Account of Christian Perfection,* Mr. Wesley shows that though a regenerated believer has an assurance that he or she is "an heir of God, a joint heir with Christ," there may yet be "an inexpressible hunger after a full renewal in His image, in 'righteousness and true holiness'" (John Wesley, *The Works of John Wesley,* XI [Grand Rapids: Zondervan Publishing House, 1958], 381).

John Woolley:

*A Wayward Boy, Found Of The Good Shepherd
Before Dying Gloriously*
(d. 1742)

Mr. Wesley was called upon to preach a funeral service for a thirteen-year-old boy. In his sermon, he "explained," as he said, "the 'exceeding great and precious promises' which are given us." He then read "a plain artless account of a child, whose body then lay before [them]," and spoke of this account as "A strong confirmation" of those "promises." The following is the account read by Mr. Wesley in that service:

> "John Woolley was for some time in your school [Mr. Wesley's school in Kingswood]; but was turned out for his ill behaviour: Soon after he ran away from his parents, lurking about for several days and nights together, and hiding himself in holes and corners, that his mother might not find him. During this time he suffered both hunger and cold. Once he was three whole days without sustenance, sometimes weeping and

praying by himself, and sometimes playing with other loose boys.

"One night he came to the new-room [Methodist chapel in Bristol]. Mr. Wesley was then speaking of disobedience to parents. He was quite confounded, and thought there never was in the world so wicked a child as himself. He went home, and never ran away any more. His mother saw the change in his whole behaviour, but knew not the cause. He would often get up stairs by himself to prayer, and often go alone into the fields, having done with all his idle companions.

"And now the devil began to set upon him with all his might, continually tempting him to self-murder: Sometimes he was vehemently pressed to hang himself; sometimes to leap into the river: But this only made him the more earnest in prayer; in which, after he had been one day wrestling with God, he saw himself, he said, surrounded on a sudden with an inexpressible light, and was so filled with joy and the love of God, that he scarce knew where he was; and with such love to all mankind, that he could have laid himself on the ground, for his worst enemies to trample upon.

"From this time his father and mother were surprised at him, he was so diligent to help them in all things. When they went to the preaching, he was careful to give their supper to the other children; and when he had put them to bed, hurried away to the room, to light his father or mother home. Meantime he lost no opportunity of hearing the preaching himself, or of doing any good he could, either at home or in any place where he was.

"One day, walking in the fields, he fell into talk with a farmer, who spoke very slightly of religion. John told him, he ought not to talk so; and enlarged upon that word of the Apostle, (which he begged him to consider deeply,) 'Without holiness no man shall see the Lord.' The man was amazed, caught the child in his arms, and knew not how to part with him.

"His father and mother once hearing him speak pretty loud in the next room, listened to hear what he said. He was praying thus:--'Lord, I do not expect to be heard for my much speaking. Thou knowest my heart; thou knowest my wants.' He then descended to particulars. Afterward he prayed very earnestly for his parents, and for his brothers and sisters by name; then for Mr. John and Charles Wesley, that God would set their faces as a flint, and give them to go on conquering and to conquer; then for all the other Ministers he could remember by name, and for all that were, or desired to be, true Ministers of Christ.

"In the beginning of his illness his mother asked him if he wanted any thing. He answered, 'Nothing but Christ; and I am as sure of him as if I had him already.' He often said, 'O mother, if all the world believed in Christ, what a happy world would it be!—And they may; for Christ died for every soul of man: I was the worst of sinners, and he died for me. O thou that callest the worst of sinners, call me! O, it is a free gift! I am sure I have done nothing to deserve it.'

"On Wednesday he said to his mother, 'I am in very great trouble for my father; he has always taken an honest care of his family, but he does not know God; if he dies in the state he is in now, he cannot be saved. I have prayed for him, and will pray for him. [His father died not long after.] If God should give him the true faith, and then take him to himself, do not you fear, -- do not you be troubled: God has promised to be *a father to the fatherless, and a husband to the widow.* I will pray for him and you in heaven; and I hope we shall sing Hallelujah in heaven together.'

"To his eldest sister he said, 'Do not puff yourself up with pride. When you receive your wages, which is not much, lay it out in plain necessaries. And if you are inclined to be merry, do not sing songs; that is the devil's diversion; there are many lies and ill things in those idle songs: Do you sing psalms and hymns. Remember your Creator in the days of your youth. When you are at work, you may lift up your heart to God; and be sure never to rise or go to bed without asking his blessing.'

"He added, 'I shall die; but do not cry for me. Why should you cry for me? Consider what a joyful thing it is, to have a brother go to heaven. I am not a man; I am but a boy. But is it not in the Bible, *Out of the mouths of babes and sucklings thou has ordained strength?* I know where I am going: I would not be without this knowledge for a thousand worlds; for though I am not in heaven yet, I am as sure of it as if I was.'

"On Wednesday night he wrestled much with God in prayer. At last, throwing his arms open, he cried, 'Come, come, Lord Jesus! I am thine. Amen and Amen!' He said, 'God answers me in my heart, *Be of good cheer, thou hast overcome the world';* and immediately after, he was filled with love and joy unspeakable.

"He said to his mother, 'That school was the saving of my soul; for there I began to seek the Lord. But how is it, that a person no sooner begins to seek the Lord, but Satan straight stirs up all his instruments against him?'

"When he was in agony of pain, he cried out, 'O Saviour, give me patience! Thou hast given me patience, but give me more. Give me thy love, and pain is nothing: I have deserved all this, and a thousand times more; for there is no sin but I have been guilty of.'

"A while after he said, 'O mother, how is this? If a man does not do his work, the masters in the world will not pay him his wages. But it is not so with God; he gives me good wages, and yet I am sure I have done nothing to gain them. O it is a free gift; it is free for every soul, for Christ has died for all.'

"On Thursday morning his mother asked him how he did; He said, 'I have had much struggling to-night, but my Saviour is so loving to me, I do not mind it; it is no more than nothing to me.'

"Then he said, 'I desire to be buried from the Room; and I desire Mr. Wesley would preach a sermon over me, on those words of David, (unless he thinks any other to be more fit,) *Before I was afflicted I went astray; but now I have kept thy word.*'

"I asked him, 'How do you find yourself now?' He said, 'In great pain, but full of love.' I asked him, 'But does not the love of God overcome pain?' He answered, 'Yes! Pain is nothing to me: I did sing praises to the Lord in the midst of my greatest pain; and I could not help it.' I asked him, if he was willing to die: He replied, 'O yes, with all my heart.' I said, 'But if life and death were set before you, what would you choose then?' He answered, 'To die, and to be with Christ: I long to be out of this wicked world.'

"On Thursday night he slept much sweeter than he had done for some time before. In the morning he begged to see Mr. John Wesley. When Mr. Wesley came, and, after some other questions, asked him what he should pray for; he said, that God would give him a clean heart, and renew a right spirit within him. When prayer was ended, he seemed much enlivened, and said, 'I thought I should have died to-day: But I must not be in haste; I am content to stay. I will tarry the Lord's leisure.'

"On Saturday, one asked, if he still chose to die: He said, 'I have no will; my will is resigned to the will of God. But I shall die: Mother, be not troubled; I shall go away like a lamb.'

"On Sunday he spoke exceeding little. On Monday his speech began to falter: On Tuesday it was gone; but he was fully in his senses, almost continually lifting up his eyes to heaven. On Wednesday, his speech being restored, his mother said, 'Jacky, you have not been with your Saviour to-night:' He replied, 'Yes I have.' She asked, 'What did he say?' He answered, 'He bid me not be afraid of the devil; for he had no power to hurt me at all, but I should tread him under my feet.' He lay very quiet on Wednesday night. The next morning he spent in continual prayer; often repeating the Lord's Prayer, and earnestly commending his soul into the hands of God.

"He then called for his little brother and sister, to kiss them; and for his mother, whom he desired to kiss him: Then (between nine and ten) he said, 'Now let me kiss you;' which he did, and immediately fell asleep. "He lived some months above thirteen years." (John Wesley, *The Works of John Wesley,* I [Grand Rapids: Zondervan Publishing House, 1958], 358-361)

Having several times visited the New Room or Methodist chapel in Bristol, England, this writer could not help imagining the scene as it must have appeared on the day of John Woolley's funeral, particularly during Mr. Wesley's reading of this touching account.

Susannah Wesley:
"Children, As Soon As I Am Released, Sing A Psalm Of Praise To God"
(d. July, 1742)

The mother of John and Charles Wesley, sometimes referred to as "the mother of Methodism," received the witness of the Spirit that her sins were forgiven in a way that was common during the rise of the Wesleyan revival in the eighteenth century. Under the date of September 3, 1739, John Wesley records in his *Journal* his mother's testimony, made known in the following conversation with her. The reference to "my son Hall" is to Mrs. Wesley's son-in-law, a minister husband to one of John Wesley's sisters.

> I talked largely with my mother, who told me, that, till a short time since, she had scarce heard such a thing mentioned, as the having forgiveness of sins now, or God's Spirit bearing witness with our spirit: Much less did she imagine that this was the common privilege of all true believers. "Therefore," said she, "I never durst ask for it myself. But two or three weeks ago, while my son Hall was pronouncing those words, in delivering

the cup to me, 'The blood of our Lord Jesus Christ, which was given for thee,' the words struck through my heart, and I knew God for Christ's sake had forgiven me all my sins."

I asked, whether her father (Dr. Annesley) had not the same faith: And, whether she had not heard him preach it to others. She answered, he had it himself; and declared, a little before his death, that for more than forty years he had no darkness, no fear, no doubt at all of his being "accepted in the Beloved." But that, nevertheless, she did not remember to have heard him preach, no not once, explicitly upon it: Whence she supposed he also looked upon it as the peculiar blessing of a few; not as promised to all the people of God. (John Wesley, *The Works of John Wesley*, I [Grand Rapids: Zondervan Publishing House, 1958], 222-223)

One holiness preacher and teacher of theology was lately heard to respond to this account by stating, "We wouldn't try to lead one into a conversion experience by such means today." "And why not?" we might ask. Could it be because we do not expect God to reveal Himself by those means He alone has ordained? Is there insufficient faith to believe God for the healing of a soul by means of His own sacrament? How easy it is for man to prefer his own ritual and methods of doing God's work.

The following is John Wesley's personal account of his mother's departure to her heavenly home:

I left Bristol in the evening of Sunday, 18, and on Tuesday came to London. I found my mother on the borders of eternity. But she had no doubt or fear; nor any desire but (as soon as God should call) "to depart, and to be with Christ."

Fri. 23.—About three in the afternoon I went to my mother, and found her change near. I sat down on the bed-side. She was in her last conflict; unable to speak, but I believe quite sensible. Her look was calm and serene, and her eyes fixed upward, while we commended her soul to God. From three to four, the silver cord was loosing, and the wheel breaking at the cistern; and then, without any struggle, or sigh, or groan, the soul was set at liberty. We stood round the bed, and fulfilled her last request, uttered a little before she lost her speech: "Children, as soon as I am released, sing a psalm of praise to God."

Sun. August 1.—Almost an innumerable company of people being gathered together, about five in the afternoon, I committed to the earth the body of my mother, to sleep with her fathers. The portion of Scripture from which I afterwards spoke was, "I saw a great white throne, and him that sat on it, from whose face the earth and the heaven fled away; and there was found no place for them. And I saw the dead, small and great, stand before God; and the books were opened: And the dead were judged out of those things which were written in the books, according to their works." It was one of the most solemn assemblies I ever saw, or expect to see on this side of eternity. We set up a plain stone at the head of her grave, inscribed with the following words:--

Here lies the Body
Of

Mrs. Susannah Wesley,

THE YOUNGEST AND LAST SURVIVING DAUGHTER OF DR. SAMUEL ANNESLEY.

In sure and steadfast hope to rise,
And claim her mansion in the skies,
A Christian here her flesh laid down,
The cross exchanging for a crown.

True daughter of affliction, she,
Inured to pain and misery,
Mourn'd a long night of griefs and fears,
A legal night of seventy years.

The Father then reveal'd his Son,
Him in the broken bread made known;
She knew and felt her sins forgiven,
And found the earnest of her heaven.

Meet for the fellowship above,
She heard the call, "Arise, my love!"
"I come," her dying looks replied,
And lamb-like, as her Lord, she died.

(John Wesley, *The Works of John Wesley*, I [Grand Rapids:
Zondervan Publishing House, 1958], 383-384)

Elizabeth Marsh:
"Her Mind Was Never Clouded"
(d. September, 1744)

Mr. Wesley "committed to the dust the remains of Elizabeth Marsh, a young woman who had received a sense of the pardoning love of God about four years before her death, and had never left her first love." Although her health was poor and her body in physical pain, "she never murmured or repined at any thing."

The founder of Methodism speaks of visiting her often from the time she became "confined to her bed." He says that he always "found her quiet and calm, always cheerful, praising God in the fires, though longing to depart and to be with Christ." In all of his visits with Miss Marsh, he could not find that "her mind was ever clouded, no, not a moment, from the beginning of her illness." A short time before her departure, however, she told Mr. Wesley that she was "concerned," that she had spoken "a hasty word" that day. Someone in her presence had said to her: "You shall recover within ten days." She responded, "I don't want to recover."

When visiting her for the very last time, Mr. Wesley "prayed with her ... commending her soul to God." And though she could no longer speak,

Her eye dropp'd sense, distinct and clear

As say Muse's tongue could speak.

"It said, To me 'to die is gain.' 'I walk through the valley of the shadow of death,' and 'fear no evil.'" He says that he "could only speak a few words at her grave, but when [he] returned to the Foundery (the first place of worship for Methodists in London), God made his word as a flame of fire." He took his text and preached from Revelation 7:13-14, "And one of the Elders said unto me, What are these who are arrayed in white robes; and whence came they? And I said, Sir, thou knowest. And he said unto me, These are they which came out of great tribulation, and have washed their robes, and made them white in the blood of the Lamb" (John Wesley, *The Works of John Wesley*, I [Grand Rapids: Zondervan Publishing House, 1958], 470-471).

The reader is asked to notice Mr. Wesley's reference in the above account to Elizabeth Marsh's experience of faith, wherein it is said that she "never left her first love" from the time of her conversion until her death four years later and that "her mind was [never] clouded, [for even a] moment from the time of her illness." To have a continual consciousness of the "love of God shed abroad in the heart by the Holy Ghost given," is considered by some to be unrealistic.

Once referring to a sermon he had just preached, Mr. Wesley says: "From the words of our blessed Lord, 'He that followeth me shall not walk in darkness,' I largely showed that God never deserts any man, unless he first deserts God; and that abstracting from the bodily disorders on the one hand, and violent temptations on the other, every believer may be happy as well as holy, and walk in the light all the days of his life" (John Wesley, *The Works of John Wesley*, III [Grand Rapids: Zondervan Publishing House, 1958], 271).

Servant To Mrs. Clark:
"For God's Sake, Pray For Me!"
(d. September, 1744)

The following account shared by Mr. Wesley from his *Journal* illustrates well the dilemma in which many find themselves when death of a sudden stares them in the face. They quickly become panic stricken, aware that their soul is yet undone and their condition desperate.

A young man, servant to Mrs. Clark, of Newington, went home [from the funeral of Elizabeth Marsh] deeply affected. The next day he was taken ill, and every day grew worse; so that when I came to the house on Monday the 10th, (though I knew nothing of him, or of his illness before) he was just gasping for breath. It was a melancholy sight: Both his words and his eyes "witnessed huge affliction and dismay." Death stared him in the face, and he knew not God. He could but just say, "For God's sake, pray for me!"

John Nelson coming in, we asked life for our brother, in full confidence of the promise. All this day, as his illness so his terrors increased. But the next day, God gave him life from the dead. He told me, "Now I am not afraid to die; for I know God loves me. I did not use to love you or your people; but now I love you as my own soul. I love you all: I know you are the people of God; and I am just going to him." He continued praising God as long as he could speak; and when he could not, his eyes were fixed upwards. Between one and two on Wednesday morning he cried out, "I have lost my God! Where is he? I cannot see him." But he soon recovered himself and said, "Now I have found him; and I shall lose him no more." About seven I prayed with him, and praised God on his behalf.

Fri. 14.—I performed the last office (according to his desire) over his body, which was interred in the presence of a vast multitude of people, at a small distance from that of Elizabeth Marsh. (John Wesley, *The Works of John Wesley*, I [Grand Rapids: Zondervan Publishing House, 1958], 471-472)

John Evans:
Met Both God And Death On The Battlefield
(d. December, 1744)

Is it possible for one to participate actively in warfare and possess at the same time a conscious love for God, together with fervent love for the enemy of his country; the enemy of all he believes to be included in a righteous cause? Can a soldier actively seeking the destruction of the enemy in defense of his nation and people have the hope of sustaining God's peace and joy in his heart? These questions may be answered to our satisfaction as we read the following letter to Mr. Wesley, written by a young English soldier who, while in bloody combat against the French, experiences God's dealings. Since he later died in battle from a most grievous wound, Mr. Wesley adds a short account of the final moments of his life. This letter was written from the battlefield in Flanders during a mid-eighteenth century conflict.

"Rev. Sir,   Ghent, Nov. 12, O.S. 1744.

"We made bold to trouble you with this, to acquaint you with some of the Lord's dealings with us here. We have hired two rooms; one small one, wherein a few of us meet every day at one o'clock; and another large one, for public service, where we meet twice a day, at nine in the morning, and four in the afternoon; and the hand of the Omnipotent God is with us, to the pulling down of the strong-holds of Satan.

"The seventh instant, when we were met together in the evening, as I was at prayer, one that was kneeling by me cried out, (like a woman in travail,) 'My Redeemer! my Redeemer!' which continued about ten minutes. When he was asked what was the matter, he said he had found that which he had often heard of; that is, an heaven upon earth: And some others had much ado to forbear crying out in the same manner.

"Dear Sir, I am a stranger to you in the flesh. I know not if I have seen you above once; when I saw you preaching on Kennington-Common: And then I hated you as much as now (by the grace of God) I love you. The Lord pursued me with convictions, from my infancy; and I often made abundance of good resolutions: But finding, as often, that I could not keep them, (as being made wholly in my own strength,) I at length left off all striving, and gave myself over to all manner of lewdness and profaneness. So I continued for some years, till the battle of Dettingen. The balls came then very thick about me, and my comrades fell on every side. Yet I was preserved unhurt. A few days after this, the Lord was pleased to visit me again. 'The pains of hell gat hold upon me, the snares of death encompassed me.' I durst no longer commit any outward sin; and I prayed God to be merciful to my

soul. Now I was at a loss for books: But God took care
for this also. One day, as I was at work, I found an old
Bible in one of the train wagons. To read this, I soon
forsook my old companions, all but one, who was still
a thorn in my flesh: But, not long after, he sickened
and died.

"My Bible was now my only companion; and I
believed myself a very good Christian, till we came to
winter-quarters, where I met with John Haime: But I
was soon sick of his company; for he robbed me of my
treasure; he stole away my gods, telling me, I and my
works were going to hell together. This was strange
doctrine to me, who, being wholly ignorant of the
righteousness of Christ, sought only to establish my
own righteousness: And being naturally of a stubborn
temper, my poor brother was so perplexed with me,
that sometimes he was resolved (as he afterwards told
me,) to forbid my coming to him any more.

"When the Lord had at length opened my eyes,
and shown me that by grace we are saved through faith,
I began to immediately to declare it to others, though I
had not as yet experienced it myself. But, October 23rd,
as William Clements was at prayer, I felt on a sudden
a great alteration in my soul. My eyes overflowed with
tears of love. I knew I was, through Christ, reconciled
to God, which inflamed my soul with fervent love to
Him, whom I now saw to be my complete Redeemer.

"O the tender care of Almighty God in bringing up
his children! How are we bound to love so indulgent a
Father, and to fall down, in wonder and adoration of his

great and glorious name, for his tender mercies!—Dear
Sir, I beg you will pray for him who is not worthy to be
a door-keeper to the least of my Master's servants,

"John Evans"

"He continued both to preach and to live the Gospel, till the battle
of Fontenoy. One of his companions saw him there, laid across a
cannon, both his legs having been taken off by a chain-shot, praising
God, and exhorting all that were round about him; which he did till
his spirit returned to God." (John Wesley, *The Works of John Wesley*, I
[Grand Rapids: Zondervan Publishing House, 1958], 476-478)

Isaac Kilby:
A Suffering But Joyful Saint At Death
(d. June, 1745)

In a *Journal* entry, dated August 12, 1745, Mr. Wesley writes: "I had now leisure to look over the letters I had received this summer; some extracts of which are here subjoined." One of those letters is shared below. We are not informed who wrote the letter, nor are we provided with the identification of Isaac Kilby. We do know that Mr. Wesley enjoyed receiving news of departing saints who had left a vibrant testimony. The reader is asked to take notice of the glory this man was enjoying inwardly while at the same time suffering great bodily pain.

"Dear Sir,   June 27, 1745

"I sat up with Isaac Kilby three nights, and being greatly comforted by many of his expressions, I believed it would not be losing time to set a few of them down.

"On Wednesday, June 18, when I came into the house, he was supposed to be near his end. His body was in great pain, and just gasping for breath: But his mind was in perfect peace.

"He had little strength to speak; but when he did, (which was now and then on a sudden, as if immediately

43

supported for that purpose,) his words were strangely powerful, just as if they came from one who was now before the throne of glory.

"When he had just drunk something, I said, 'All may drink of the water of life freely.' He lifted up his hands in great love, and said, 'Yes, all, all; all the world.'

"After long silence, he suddenly asked me, how I felt myself: I replied, 'I find great consolation from the Lord.' He said, 'How strange it is, that such a rebel as I should bring glory to God!'

"When dozing, his mind would rove; but even then his discourse consisted chiefly of strong exhortations to some of his acquaintance, to repent, and persevere in the ways of God.

"On Friday I called, and found him in the same spirit, full of pain, yet full of joy unspeakable. I could not forbear sitting up with him again. All his words were full of divine wisdom, expressing a deep sense of the presence and mercy of God, and of his own unworthiness.

"Mention being made concerning his burial, (in the beginning of his sickness, he had desired, that Mr. Wesley might bury him, and preach a sermon from the text, 'Remember thy Creator in the days of thy youth,') he said, 'Now I do not think of such things; bury me as you will; yet I should be glad to have a sermon preached: But just as Mr. Wesley pleases.'

"He said to me, 'O go on, and you will rejoice as I do, in the like condition.' He prayed, that he might die before the morning; but added, 'Not as I will, but as thou wilt.'

"Thus he continued till Wednesday, June 25, when I sat up with him again. Being now much weaker, he roved more than ever. Yet when I asked, 'Isaac, how do you find your soul?' he answered, 'I rejoice in God my Saviour. I am as clay in the hands of the potter.' And about half an hour after twelve, he went to sing praise to God and the Lamb for ever." (John Wesley, *The Works of John Wesley*, I [Grand Rapids: Zondervan Publishing House, 1958], 511-512)

"We have this treasure in earthen vessels," writes the Apostle Paul (2 Cor. 4:7). The treasure of a soul that has been renewed in the image of Him who created it, is made to lodge in a poor earthen vessel; a mortal, corruptible body, subject to sickness, pain and death. How often have we been witness to the truth that the "corruptible body presses down the soul." Nevertheless, the children of God are gainers, seeing "our light afflictions, which are but for a moment, worketh for us a far more exceeding *and* eternal weight of glory!" (2 Corinthians 4:17).

"The heavenly treasure now we have
In a vile house of clay!
Yet He shall to the uttermost save,
And keep it to that day."

(John Wesley, *The Works of John Wesley*, VII [Grand Rapids: Zondervan Publishing House, 1958], 344-348)

Molly Thomas:
"I See The Towers Before Me"
(d. August, 1745)

By letter from Bristol, Mr. Wesley was informed of the victorious passing of another Methodist to realms of glory. From the content of the letter's first line, we may assume that Sarah Colston, who wrote the letter, was the leader of a band or class of women in which Molly Thomas was a member.

How important is the "constant use of all the means" of grace! Yet one may live above reproach, be very faithful in outward duties of religion, and continue quite content therein without any consciousness of the life of God within. This seems to have been the case with Molly Thomas until she began to look death in the face. Sarah Colston shares her story below.

> "I have delivered another of my charge to the Lord. On Saturday night Molly Thomas was taken home. She was always constant in the use of all the means, and behaved well, both at home and abroad. After she was taken ill, she was distressed indeed, between the pain of her body, and the anguish of her soul. But where is

all pain gone when Jesus comes?—when he manifests himself to the heart? In that hour she cried out, 'Christ is mine! I know my sins are forgiven me.' Then she sung praise to Him that loved her, and bought her with his own blood. The fear of death was gone, and she longed to leave her father, her mother, and all her friends. She said, 'I am almost at the top of the ladder: Now I see the towers before me, and a large company coming up behind me: I shall soon go. Tis but for Christ to speak the word, and I am gone: I only wait for that word, Rise up, my love, and come away.'

"When they thought her strength was gone, she broke out again:-

Christ hath the foundation laid,
And Christ shall build me up:
Surely I shall soon be made
Partaker of my hope,

Author of my faith is he;
He its finisher shall be:
Perfect love shall seal me his
To all eternity.

"So she fell asleep. O Lord, my God, glory be to thee for all things! I feel such desires in my soul after God, that my strength goes away. I feel there is not a moment's time to spare; and yet how many do I lose! Lord Jesus, give me to be more and more diligent and watchful in all things. It is no matter to me how I was an hour ago.

Is my soul now waiting upon God? O that I may in all things, and through all things, see nothing but Christ! O that when he comes he may find me watching!

"Sarah Colston"
(John Wesley, *The Works of John Wesley*, I [Grand Rapids: Zondervan Publishing House, 1958], 510-511)

Mary Cook:
With An Inward Glory, She Was Not Afraid To Die
(d. August, 1745)

In one of the letters Mr. Wesley received in the summer of 1745, an account of the glorious departure of Mary Cook was inserted. While reading this young woman's experience below, the reader is asked to take notice of the means or process by which she found her peace and happiness in God. Take notice also that once her soul was set free, she had no fear of death. The Apostle John assures us that perfect love casteth out that fear that hath torment.

> "Mary Cook, who had been ill for above six months, grew much worse a week or two ago. She had been long remarkably serious, and greatly desirous of knowing her interest in Christ; but then her desires were much increased, and she had no rest in her spirit, but cried unto him day and night. On Monday last, she mourned more than ever, and would not be comforted. Then she lay still a while, and on a sudden broke out,
>
> *Praise God, from whom pure blessings come!*

"Her mother asked her the cause of this. She said, 'O mother, I am happy, I am happy: I shall soon go to heaven:' And many more words she spoke to the same effect. I called upon her a few hours after, and found her still in a settled peace. She told me, 'I am assured of God's love to my soul. I am not afraid to die. I know the Lord will take me to himself: Lord, hasten the time! I long to be with thee.' On Tuesday and Wednesday she spoke little, being exceeding weak; but continued instant in prayer. On Wednesday, about noon, she desired her mother to get her up into the chair, which she did. A little before three, her mother holding her in her arms, she desired her to let her go. Then, placing herself upright in the chair, with her hands laid in her lap, and a calm majesty in her countenance, she said, 'Lord, receive my soul,' and expired." (John Wesley, *The Works of John Wesley*, I [Grand Rapids: Zondervan Publishing House, 1958], 509-510)

It is recorded above that Mary was "greatly desirous of knowing her interest in Christ." In other words, she desired to have an assurance given her by the Spirit's witness that her sins had been forgiven and that she was now a true child of God. We are not informed just how long she sought this inward witness but as her desires increased we notice that she ceased not to cry to God day and night and would not be comforted until she heard from Him.

Too often the time constraints felt by seekers and those praying with them at the mourner's bench are such that the following words of the Prophet Jeremiah are sadly and repeatedly fulfilled: "For they have healed the hurt of the daughter of my people slightly, saying, Peace, peace; when there is no peace" (Jeremiah 8:11).

Francis Coxon:
A Reawakened Backslider Made Ready For Heaven
(d. March,1747)

In the following story shared by Mr. Wesley in his *Journal*, dated March 30, 1747, an illustration can be seen of what may happen to the strongest of believers. The reader is asked to observe, (1) the subtle means by which this man lost his faith, (2) the way God reawakened him, (3) how he sought God anew in a state of spiritual darkness, and (4) the mercy of God who healed his backslidings and once again gave him to rejoice in Christ his Savior before departing this life.

> I had leisure to reflect on the strange case of Francis Coxon, who was at first the grand support of the society at Biddick. But after a time he grew weary of well-doing; complaining that it took up too much of his time. He then began to search after curious knowledge, and to converse with those who were like-minded. The world observed it, and courted his company again. Now he was not so precise; his school was filled with children; money flowed in, and he said, "Soul, take thy ease for many years." He came to Newcastle with John Reah the

Saturday after I came; but had no leisure to call upon
me. At night they set out homeward. He was walking
a little before his companion, about three miles from
Newcastle, in a way he knew as well as his own house-
floor, when John heard him fall, and asked, "What is
the matter?" He answered, "God has overtaken me:
I am fallen into the quarry, and have broke my leg,"
John ran to some houses that were near, and, having
procured help, carried him thither. Thence he was
removed to another house, and a Surgeon sent for, who
came immediately. He soon recovered his spirits, and
asked how long it would be, before he could be in his
school again. And on Sunday, Monday, and Tuesday,
was full of the world, nor was God in all his thoughts.
On Wednesday, the Surgeon told him honestly, he
thought he could not live. Then he awoke out of sleep.
The snares of death came about him, the pains of hell
overtook him. He continued all Thursday and Friday
in the lowest pit, in a place of darkness and in the deep;
warning all to beware of drawing back unto perdition,
and calling upon God with strong cries and tears. On
Sunday he found a little dawning of hope; this gradually
increased all the day. On Monday, he knew God had
healed his backsliding, and sorrow and sighing fled
away. He continued all day in fervent prayer, mingled
with praise and strong thanksgiving. "This night,"
said he, "will be a glorious night to me; my warfare
is accomplished; my sin is pardoned." Then he broke
out again into vehement prayer. About eight he left off
speaking; and soon after, without any struggle or groan,

gave up his soul to God. (John Wesley, *The Works of John Wesley,* II [Grand Rapids: Zondervan Publishing House, 1958], 50-51)

In his sermon entitled, "A Call to Backsliders," Mr. Wesley draws a contrast between the mercy often found illustrated among children of men and that mercy found in a truly compassionate God. He says, "What is their mercy compared to his mercy? Hence that comfortable word, 'I am God, and not man, therefore the house of Israel is not consumed.' Because he is God, and not man, 'therefore his compassions fail not'" (John Wesley, *The Works of John Wesley*, VIII [Grand Rapids: Zondervan Publishing House, 1958], 519).

The Glorious Deaths
Of Condemned Felons
(d. November, 1748)

In his *Journal,* dated November, 1, 1748, Mr. Wesley writes:

"Sarah Peters, a lover of souls, a mother in Israel, went to rest. During a close observation of several years," he writes, "I never saw her, upon the most trying occasions, in any degree ruffled or discomposed, but she was always loving, always happy." He says that her "particular gift, and continual care, [was] to seek and save that which was lost; to support the weak, to comfort the feeble-minded, to bring back what had been turned out of the way." While being involved in this manner, "God endued her, above [others] with the love that 'believeth, hopeth, endureth all things.'"

In the following incredible account, it is revealed just how Sarah Peters was used as an instrument of God in the salvation of several young men who were all condemned to be soon executed for crimes committed.

On Sunday, October 9, she went, with one more, to see the condemned malefactors in Newgate. They inquired for John Lancaster, in particular, who had sent to desire their coming. He asked them to go into his cell, which they willingly did; although some dissuaded them from it, because the gaol distemper (a kind of pestilential fever) raged much among the prisoners. They desired he would call together as many of the prisoners as were willing to come. Six or seven of those who were under sentence of death came. They sung a hymn, read a portion of Scripture, and prayed. Their little audience were all in tears. Most of them appeared deeply convinced of their lost estate. From this time her labours were unwearied among them; praying with them and for them night and day.

John Lancaster said, "When I used to come to the Foundery every morning, which I continued to do for some time, I little thought of ever coming to this place. I then often felt the love of God, and thought I should never commit sin more. But after a while, I left off coming to the preaching: Then my good desires died away. I fell again into the diversions I had laid aside, and the company I had left off. As I was one day playing at skittles with some of these, a young man, with whom I was now much acquainted, gave me a part of the money which he had just been receiving for some stolen goods. This, with his frequent persuasion, so wrought upon me, that at last I agreed to go partners with him. Yet I had often strong convictions; but I stifled them as well as I could.

"We continued in this course till August last. As we were then going home from Bartholomew-Fair, one morning about two o'clock, it came into my mind to go and steal the branches out of the Foundery [the place serving as a chapel for Methodists in London]. I climbed over the wall, and brought two of them away; though I trembled and shook, and made so great noise, that I thought all the family must be dead, or else they could not but hear me. Within a few days after, I stole the velvet; for which I was taken up, tried and condemned."

Some being of opinion it would not be difficult to procure a pardon for him, S. Peters, though she never mentioned this to him, resolved to leave no means unattempted. She procured several petitions to be drawn, and went herself to Westminster, to Kensington, and to every part of the Town where any one lived who might possibly assist therein. In the meantime, she went constantly to Newgate, sometimes alone, sometimes with one or two others, visited all that were condemned in their cells, exhorted them, prayed with them, and had the comfort of finding them, every time, more athirst for God than before; and of being followed, whenever she went away, with abundance of prayers and blessings.

After a time, she and her companions believed it would be of use to examine each closely, as to the state of his soul. They spoke to John Lancaster first. He lifted up his eyes and hands, and, after pausing awhile, said, "I thank God, I do feel that He has forgiven me my sins: I do know it." They asked how, and when, he knew it first. He replied, "I was in great fear and heaviness, till the very morning you came hither first. That morning I was in earnest prayer; and just as St. Paul's clock struck five, the Lord poured into my soul such peace as I had never felt; so that I was scarce able to bear it. From that hour I have never been afraid to die; for I know, and am sure, as soon as my soul departs from the body, the Lord Jesus will stand ready to carry it into glory."

The next who was spoken to was Thomas Atkins, nineteen years of age. When he was asked (after many other questions, in answering which he expressed the clearest and deepest conviction of all his sins, as well as that for which he was condemned) if he was not afraid to die; he fixed his eyes upward, and said, in the most earnest and solemn manner, "I bless God, I am not afraid to die; for I have laid my soul at the feet of Jesus." And to the last moment of his life, he gave all reason to believe that these were not vain words.

Thomas Thompson, the next, was quite an ignorant man, scarce able to express himself on common occasions; yet some of his expressions were intelligible enough. "I don't know," said he, "how it is: I used to have nothing but bad and wicked thoughts in me, and now they are all gone; and I know God loves me, and He has forgiven my sins." He persisted in this testimony till death, and in a behaviour suitable thereto.

When John Roberts came first into John L's cell, he was utterly careless and sullen. But it was not long before his countenance changed: The tears ran down his cheeks, and he continued, from that hour, earnestly and steadily seeking repentance, and remission of sins. There did not pass many days, before he likewise declared that the burden of sin was gone, that the fear of death was utterly taken away, and it returned no more.

William Gardiner, from the time that he was condemned, was very ill of the gaol distemper. She visited him in his own cell, till he was able to come abroad. He was a man of exceeding few words, but of a broken and contrite spirit. Some time after, he expressed great readiness to die, yet with the utmost diffidence of himself. One of his expressions, to a person accompanying him to the place of execution, was, "O Sir, I have nothing to trust to but the blood of Christ! If that won't do, I am undone for ever."

As soon as Sarah Cunningham was told that the warrant was come down for her execution, she fell raving mad. She had but few intervals of reason till the morning of her execution. She was then sensible, but spoke little; till, being told, "Christ will have Pity upon you, if you ask him," she broke out, "Pity upon me! Will Christ have pity upon me? Then I *will* ask him; indeed I will;" which she did in the best manner she could, till her soul was required of her.

Samuel Chapman appeared to be quite hardened. He seemed to fear neither God nor devil. But when, after some time, Sarah Peters talked with him, God struck him down at one stroke. He felt himself a sinner, and cried aloud for mercy. The gaol distemper then seized upon him, and confined him to his bed, till he was carried out to die. She visited him frequently in his cell. He wept much, and prayed much; but never appeared to have any clear assurance of his acceptance with God.

It was the earnest desire of them all, that they whom God had made so helpful to them might spend the last night with them. Accordingly she came to Newgate at ten o'clock, but could not be admitted on any terms. However, six of them were suffered to be in one cell. They spent the night, wrestling with God in prayer. She was admitted about six in the morning. As soon as the cell was opened, they sprang out, several of them crying, with a transport not to be expressed, "O what a happy night have we had! What a blessed morning is this! O when will the hour come that we long for, that our souls shall be set at liberty!" The turnkey said, "I never saw such people before." When the bellman came at twelve o'clock, to tell them, (as usual,) "Remember you are to die to-day," they cried out, "Welcome news! Welcome news!"

John Lancaster was the first who was called out to have his irons knocked off. When he came to the block, (at which this is done,) he said, "Blessed be the day I came into this place! O what a glorious work hath the Lord carried on in my soul since I came hither!" Then he said to those near him, "O my dear friends, join in praise with me a sinner! O for a tongue to praise him as I ought! My heart is like fire in a close vessel. I am ready to burst for want of vent. O that I could tell the thousandth part of the joys I feel!" One saying, "I am sorry to see you in that condition;" he answered, "I would not change it for ten thousand worlds." From the press-yard he was removed into a large room, where he exhorted all the officers to repentance, till Thomas Atkins was brought in; whom he immediately asked, "How is it between God and your soul?" He answered, "Blessed be God, I am ready." An officer asking about this time, "What is it o'clock?" was answered, "Near nine." On which Lancaster said, "By one I shall be in Paradise, safely resting in Abraham's bosom." To another prisoner coming in, he said, "Cannot you see Jesus? I see him by faith, standing at the right hand of God, with open arms to receive our souls." One asking "Which is Lancaster?" he answered, "Here I am. Come, see a Christian triumphing over death." A by-stander said, "Be steadfast to the end." He replied, "I am, by the grace of God, as steadfast as the rock I am built upon, and that rock is Christ." Then he said to the people, "Cry to the Lord for mercy, and you will surely find it. I have found it; therefore none should despair. When I came first to this place, my heart was as hard as my cell-walls, and as black as hell. But now I am washed, now I am made clean by the blood of Christ."

When William Gardner came in, he said, "Well, my dear man, how are you?" He answered, "I am happy, and think the moments long; for I want to die, that I may be with Him whom my soul loves." Lancaster asked, "Had we not a sweet night?" He said, "I was as it were in heaven. O, if a foretaste be so sweet, what must the full enjoyment be?" Then came in Thomas Thompson, who with great power witnessed the same confession. The people round, the mean time, were in tears; and the officers stood like men affrighted.

Then Lancaster exhorted one in doubt, never to rest till he had found rest in Christ. After this he brake out into strong prayer, (mingled with praise and thanksgiving,) that the true Gospel of Christ might spread to every corner of the habitable earth; that the congregation at the Foundery might abound more and more in the knowledge and love of God; that he would, in a particular manner, bless all those who had taken care of his dying soul; and that God would bless and keep Mr. W.s, that neither men nor devils might ever hurt them, but that they might, as a ripe shock of corn, be gathered into the garner of God.

When the last prisoner came into the room, he said, "Here is another of our little flock." An officer said tenderly, he thought it was too large. He said, "Not too large for heaven: Thither we are going."

He said to Mr. M., "O Sir, be not faint in your mind. Be not weary of well-doing. You serve a glorious Master; and if you go on, you will have a glorious reward."

When the officers told them, it was time to go, they rose with inexpressible joy, and embraced each other, commending each other's soul to the care of Him who had so cared for them. Lancaster then earnestly prayed, that all there present might, like him, be found of God, though they sought Him not.

Coming into the press-yard, he saw Sarah Peters. He stepped to her, kissed her, and earnestly said, "I am going to Paradise to-day; and you will follow me soon."

The crowd being great, they could not readily get through. So he had another opportunity of declaring the goodness of God. And to one in heaviness he said, "Cry unto the Lord, and he will be found. My soul for thine, he will have mercy upon thee." Then he said to all, "Remember Mary Magdalene, out of whom the Lord cast seven devils. So rely ye on him for mercy, and you will surely find it."

As they were preparing to go into the cart, he said, "Come, my dear friends, let us go on joyfully; for the Lord is making ready to receive us into everlasting habitations." Then turning to the spectators, he said, "My friends, God be your guide. God direct you in the right way to eternal glory. It is but a short time, and we shall be 'where all sorrow and sighing shall flee away.' Turn from the evil of your ways; and you also, with us, shall stand with the innumerable company on Mount Sion."

As they went along, he frequently spoke to the people, exhorting them to repentance. To some he said, "Ye poor creatures, you do not know where I am going. See that you love Christ; see that you follow Christ; and then you will come there too." He likewise gave out, and sung, several hymns; particularly that, with which he was always deeply affected,--

Lamb of God, whose bleeding love

65

We still recal (sic) to mind,
Send the answer from above,
And let us mercy find.
Think on us, who think on thee,
And every struggling soul release:
O remember Calvary;
And let us go in peace!

All the people who saw them seemed to be amazed; but much more when they came to the place of execution. A solemn awe overwhelmed the whole multitude. As soon as the executioner had done his part with Lancaster, and the two that were with him, he called for a hymn-book, and gave out a hymn with a clear, strong voice. And after the Ordinary had prayed, he gave out and sung the fifty-first psalm. He then took leave of his fellow-sufferers with all possible marks of the most tender affection. He blessed the persons who had attended him, and commended his own soul to God.

Even a little circumstance that followed seems worth observing. His body was carried away by a company hired of the Surgeons: But a crew of sailors pursued them, took it from them by force, and delivered it to his mother; by which means it was decently interred, in the presence of many who praised God on his behalf.

One thing which occasioned some amazement was, that even after death there were no marks of violence upon him. His face was not at all bloated or disfigured; no, nor even changed from its natural colour; but he lay with a calm, smiling countenance, as one in a sweet sleep.

He died on Friday, October 28, and was buried on Sunday, the 30th.

S. Peters, having now finished her work, felt the body sink apace. On Wednesday, November 3, she took to her bed, having the symptoms of a malignant fever. She praised God in the fires for ten days; continually witnessing the good confession, "I have fought the good fight; I have kept the faith; I am going to receive the crown:" And a little after midnight, on Sunday, the 13th, her spirit also returned to God. (John Wesley, *The Works of John Wesley*, II [Grand Rapids: Zondervan Publishing House, 1958], 119-125)

Francis Butts:
Snatched From Despair
(d. December, 1748)

In a *Journal* entry dated December, 8, 1748, Mr. Wesley mentions a "poor mourner [who] found peace." When she was in the midst of relating her experience to him, he "told her, 'If you watch and pray, God will give you more of his love.' She replied, 'More! Why, is it possible I should feel more love to God than I do now?' the natural thought of new-born babes, who feel as much as their hearts will then contain."

"In the evening," writes Mr. Wesley, "I saw one in a far different state.

> He was crying out, (in a high fever,) "O Sir, I am dying without God, without Christ, without hope!" I spoke strongly of the mercies of God in Christ, and left him a little revived. The next night he told me, "For some time after you [were] here, I was—I know not how; so light and easy! I had no doubt but God would have mercy upon me; but now I am dark again: I fear lest I should perish at the last." He then broke out into prayer. I left him a little easier, beginning again to cast his care upon God.

Three days later, "Several of our brethren called upon him, and found his hope gradually increasing." The next day, "he expressed a strong confidence in the mercy of God, and said, he feared nothing but [the possibility that] he should live and turn back into the world."

> Before noon he was a little delirious; but as soon as any one spoke of God, he recovered himself, and prayed so vehemently as to set all that heard him in tears. I called once more about six in the evening, and commended his soul to God. He was speechless, but not without sense, as the motion of his lips plainly showed; though his eyes were generally fixed upwards, with a look which said, "I see God." About half an hour after I went away, his soul was set at liberty.

In a final note, Mr. Wesley writes: "Thus, in the strength of his years, died Francis Butts, one in whose lips was found no guile. He was an honest man, fearing God, and earnestly endeavouring to work righteousness."

"Is it possible that I should feel more love for God than I now do?" Such was the question of the new-born babe in Christ whom Mr. Wesley mentions above. Notice his comment. This is "the natural thought of new-born babes, who feel as much as their hearts will then contain." Some have taught that being "filled with the Spirit" applies only to those who are entirely sanctified. It should be remembered, however, that there can be many fillings experienced during the Christian pilgrimage. New converts may experience their hearts full of love in the initial experience and later, because of an enlarged capacity, experience their hearts full of "more love." (John Wesley, *The Works of John Wesley*, II [Grand Rapids: Zondervan Publishing House, 1958], 126, 127)

John Nelson:

Shares Several Beautiful Accounts Of Dying Saints
(d. 1750)

John Nelson was a stone mason by trade, whose quality work was well known among those involved in the construction trades of mid-eighteenth century England. He tells of the first time he ever heard Mr. Wesley preach. It was in an open area of London, known as Moorfields. "Oh," says he, "that was a blessed morning to my soul! As soon as he got upon the stand, he stroked back his hair, and turned his face towards where I stood, and I thought fixed his eyes upon me." His appearance and "countenance struck such an awful dread upon me, before I heard him speak, that it made my heart beat like a pendulum of a clock." Once Mr. Wesley had begun speaking, "I thought," said he, that "his whole discourse was aimed at me." Upon the conclusion of the sermon, the poor awakened hearer thought to himself, "This man can tell the secrets of my heart; he hath not left me there: for he hath showed the remedy, even the blood of Jesus. Then was my soul filled with consolation, through hope that God for Christ's sake would save me." Sometime later, while in private prayer, he experienced in an instant, his heart "set at liberty from ... guilt and tormenting fear, and filled with a calm and serene peace" (John Telford, ed., *Wesley's Veterans.*

Lives of Early Methodist Preachers Told by Themselves, III [Salem: Schmul Publishers, 1976], 11-16).

Eventually, Nelson answered a higher calling and became one of Mr. Wesley's staunchest and most effective preachers. For his fearless preaching against notorious sins and his warfare against Satan's strongholds, he would suffer severe persecution, including impressments into the army and dungeon imprisonment. During his tenure as a preacher, God used him to call many from the bondage of sin to a life of righteousness. In the following letter John Nelson shares with Mr. Wesley several accounts of dying saints within the region he was then laboring.

"Dear Father in the Lord,

"My most earnest prayers (with my best love) for you and your brother are that God may prosper His work in your hands more and more, and make your souls as a watered garden. His right hand hath done great things in these parts, both in converting and finishing the work of faith in triumph, since I gave your brother the last account. The first was of Baidon society, who had been in a justified state about three years: she was very exact in observing all meetings as long as she was able. Her disorder was a consumption; in the beginning of which she had many conflicts and temptations; but for about ten weeks before she died, she was a monument of wonder to all that beheld her, for she did nothing but praise God and tell what He had done for her soul, and exhorted all she saw to seek the Lord while He may be found, and went praising Him out of this howling wilderness.

"The next was one of Halifax: several of our people were with her when she died who had attended her in her illness, and said she was as great a witness for God as ever they saw in that place. She had enjoyed a sense of pardon about two years.

"The next was Mr. Farray, who died the 17th inst., in the seventy-third year of his age. He was a man of unstrained character, and looked upon, by priest and people, to be the best Christian in that parish before he heard us. The minister of the chapel-of-ease often slept at his house, and strove to prejudice him and his family against the Methodists; and this he had done so effectually that when Mr. Ellison was buried he would not come to his funeral because I was to preach, though he was his brother-in-law. But it pleased God to strike with convictions all of his family that were at the funeral; and afterwards his wife. His two sons and his daughter prevailed upon him to hear for himself, as they had done. The first time he came, I was preaching from blind Bartimeus. When I had done, he cried, and said, 'I have been blind for threescore and ten years, and knew not but I was right till this day.' From that time he and all his house attended the word at all opportunities. As Mr. Merrick was preaching, he received a sense of God's love, and ever since had been steadfast, full of good works, ready to confess his blindness by nature, and the riches of God's love to him and to his house, in what company soever he came. He had three weeks' illness, which ended in his death, during which time I often visited him, to the satisfaction of my own soul;

for he was praising God in the midst of racking pain. At one of my visits, two of his brothers came to see him; and he declared to them he had lived to the age of man before he knew for what end he was born, and why Christ was sent into the world. Then he broke out in tears of joy, and said, 'What could God have done more for me and my family than He hath done? For He hath not left an hoof of us in Egyptian darkness. We are all His witnesses that He is a forgiving God. O my brothers, seek that you may find Him to be so to you!' He desired me to preach over him when he was dead; and said it might be a means to stir up some soul to seek salvation. This I did to a great multitude, from 'Blessed are the dead that die in the Lord.' It seemed to be a glorious season. Oh may we all praise God in behalf of His glorious witnesses, and tread in their steps, that our last end may be like theirs! …

"My grand-daughter, about sixteen years of age, rejoiced in the Lord about six weeks before she died. Her last words to her father and mother were, 'Fret not; for I am going to Jesus, and to help the angels to praise God.'

"Sarah Schools had been a steady follower of the Lord about twenty years. I visited her several times in her illness, and always found comfort to my own soul. The morning she died, she said to her son, 'I have had a glorious night, and now I am ready to go to my dear Redeemer. In the fore part of the night, there was a cloud between Him and my soul; but I cried, 'Lord, hide not Thy face from me!' and immediately the cloud dispersed, and the glory of God shone bright on my soul.' When Miss B. had prayed with her, she said, 'Hold on in the way thou art in, and we shall meet again in glory.' Having said this, she fell asleep in the arms of Jesus.

"S. H. [of Hanging-Heaton] falling into a kind of trance, when she came to herself she told her husband she had been both in heaven and hell. When she was in the latter, she said, she saw several there whom she had known on earth. As she came out, she said, she saw one she knew (whom she then named) tumbling in, head and heels together. As soon as she came to herself, she sent her husband to see whether he was dead or not. When he inquired of the family, they had no thought of his death, seeing he was quite well when he went to bed. But, on going to see, they found him dead, with his head and heels together, as she had seen him before. On this, she gave some account of what she had seen in heaven. Among others, she saw Paul Greenwood, who shone like a sunbeam, together with many more whom she knew on earth. Moreover, she saw the place she was to go to. She then told them when she was to die, and accordingly died exactly at that time. When these things were noised abroad, many hearts were filled with fear; and perhaps a few more stirred up to seek the Lord with great earnestness.

"N. B. This woman had known the Lord, and adorned the gospel, twelve years.

"Mrs. Crowder had adorned the gospel about six years, and was a great pattern both of charity and piety.

She laboured under a lingering illness, and was worn almost to a skeleton. The last time I visited her she seemed like a bride adorned for the bridegroom. I found the Lord was very present with her. The last words she spoke were, 'All is well! For I have neither doubt nor fear.' Then, with a smiling countenance, she fell asleep in the arms of Jesus, while many cried out, 'Oh let me die her death!'

"J. B. [of Kirkheaton] was awakened about thirty-one years ago, and soon received a sense of the love of God; but, marrying, the cares of the world so beset him that he walked in heaviness some time. When Mr. Wesley came first to Birstall, the Lord again revealed Himself to him, and in such a manner that he never lost His presence after for a single week. From that time, he adorned the gospel in the whole of his behaviour; though for ten years he laboured under a very sore disorder. In the midst of his suffering he mightily praised God, and exhorted the class, which he met for twenty-eight years, to keep in the way they were then in. He said, 'God will give you strength for your day, as He hath enabled me to fight the good fight of faith. Through Him I am more than conqueror; and there is a crown of glory prepared for me. I have no doubt or fear; for perfect love casteth out fear. Tell John Nelson to preach over my corpse.' So saying, he resigned his soul to Jesus, and left a good savour behind him.

"H. BOOTH [of Cleckheaton] was converted one-and-thirty years ago, and retained a sense of the goodness of God a great part of that time, though she had many trials in her family. The first two years her husband strove to provoke her; but, coming to hear Mr. Charles Wesley, he was convinced that she was right and he was wrong. He then sought the Lord, and found Him. Since then he has been a class-leader twenty-seven years; all which time he has also had the gospel preached in his house. His wife was quite happy in her last illness, and finished her course with joy. Thus is the Lord giving both living and dying witnesses of His grace, that the saints may be encouraged to go on, and that sinners may be without excuse.

John Nelson."
(John Telford, ed., *Wesley's Veterans. Lives of Early Methodist Preachers Told by Themselves,* III [Salem: Schmul Publishers, 1976], 185-192)

Richard Hutchinson:
A Child Who Wished Earnestly To Go To His Heavenly Home
(d. May, 1750)

In his *Journal,* dated Tuesday May 29, 1750, Mr. Wesley mentions an interest in hearing more concerning Richard Hutchinson, a boy just above four years of age. Upon inquiry, his mother informed Mr. Wesley that several months before, the boy "began to talk much of God, and to ask abundance of questions concerning him." His whole deportment from that time was serious. "He constantly reproved any that cursed or swore, or spoke indecently in his hearing, and frequently mourned over his brother, who was two or three years older, saying, 'I fear my brother will go to hell; for he does not love God." His mother continued as follows:

> "About Christmas I cut off his hair; on which he said, 'You cut off my hair, because you are afraid I shall have the small-pox; but I am not afraid; I am not afraid to die; for I love God.' About three weeks ago he sent for all of the society whom he knew, saying he must take his leave of them; which he did, speaking to them, one by one, in the most tender and affectionate manner.

Four days after he fell ill of the small-pox, and was light-headed almost as soon as he was taken: But all his incoherent sentences were either exhortation, or pieces of hymns, or prayer. The worse he was, the more earnest he was to die, saying, 'I must go home; I will go home.' One said, 'You are at home.' He earnestly replied, 'No; this is not my home; I will go to heaven.' On the tenth day of his illness he raised himself up, and said, 'Let me go; let me go to the Father; I will go home: Now, now I will go to my Father.' After which he lay down and died." (John Wesley, *The Works of John Wesley,* II [Grand Rapids: Zondervan Publishing House, 1958], 190,191)

How amazing it is that a child so young is found capable of responding in a positive manner to the gracious overtures of God. It goes to prove that God, who is love, works even in the hearts of children so as to reveal Himself in a most gracious manner.

John Dudley:
The Subject Of A Bizarre Anecdote
(d. June, 1750)

Those who choose to read John Wesley's *Journal* in its entirety will come across some very strange and yet interesting anecdotes. The following is very bizarre, so much so that it raises more questions than can be answered this side of eternity.

Recorded in his *Journal,* June 24, 1750, Mr. Wesley says that he had preached in the evening at Mount-Mellick. He was to go from there to Roscrea and be shown the way by two gentlemen. "One of them gave us so strange a relation," says Wesley, "that I thought it worth while to set it down, as nearly as might be, in his own words." He goes on to affirm that "The strangest part of it rests not on his testimony alone, but on that of many of his neighbors; none of whom could have any manner of temptation to affirm either more or less than they saw with their eyes." The father's story, in his own words, is as follows:

> "My son, John Dudley, was born at Roscrea, in the year 1726. He was serious from a child, tender of conscience, and greatly fearing God. When he was at school, he did not play like other children; but spent his whole time in learning. About eighteen I took him

home, and employed him in husbandry; and he grew more and more serious. On February 4, 1747, just as I was laid down in bed, he cried out, 'My dear father, I am ready to be choked.' I ran, and took him in my arms; and in about a minute he recovered.

"The next morning he cried out just as before; and continued ill about two minutes. From this time he gave himself wholly to prayer; laying aside all worldly business.

"Saturday, February 7. He did not appear to have any bodily distemper, but desired to make his will. I said, 'My dear child, I do not see any signs of death upon you.' He seemed concerned, and said, 'You don't believe me; but you will soon see what I say is true.'

"About noon, some neighbors condoling with me, on the loss of my wife, who died a few days before, when he saw me weep, he laid his hand upon my knee, and said, 'My dear father, do not offend God. Your late wife is a bright saint in heaven.'

"Before ten we went to bed. About twelve he came to my chamber door, and said, 'My dear honored father, I hope you are not displeased with me for disturbing you at this time of night; but I could not go into my bed till I brought you these glad tidings: I was this morning before the throne of grace, and I pleaded innocence; but my heavenly Father answered, that would not do; on which I applied to our blessed Redeemer, and now he hath, by his precious blood and his intercession, procured my pardon; and my heavenly Father hath sealed it. Everlasting praise is to his holy name.

"'I presumed to ask, how it was with my deceased mothers and sisters; on which they all six appeared exceeding glorious: But my last deceased mother was brightest of them all; fifty times brighter than the sun. I entreat I may be buried by her.'

"Sunday, 8.—I went early in the morning to his chamber, and found him at prayer, which was his constant employment. He asked if he should go with me to church. I said, I thought he had better read and meditate at home. As soon as I was gone, he began exhorting the servants and his younger brother. He then went into his chamber, where he continued upon his knees till I came home, crying to God with many tears, and sweating much, through the agony of his spirit.

"When we were set down to dinner, I desired him to eat. He said, 'I have no appetite; but to please you, I will.' He then ate two little bits; and, as soon as thanks were given, went to his chamber. He continued there in prayer about an hour, and then came out, and said, with a cheerful voice and countenance, 'I never knew the Holy Ghost until now: now I am illuminated with him. Blessed be my great Creator!' He returned to prayer, and continued therein till he came to family duty. In this he joined with an audible voice; and, commending us to God, retired to his room: Yet he did not sleep, but continued in prayer all night and all the next day.

"Tuesday, 10.—About three in the morning he put

off all his clothes, even his shirt, and laid them in order on the bed, and his Prayer-Book in the window; then, having opened two doors, he came to the outward door. I called, 'Where are you going?' He said, 'I am going out of doors.' I said, 'You need not go at this time of night.' He replied, 'I must go.' I said, 'Then make haste in again.' To which he gave no answer; but unlocking the door, and pulling it leisurely after him, said, 'My dear father, farewell for ever.'

"As soon as the day dawned, finding he was not returned, I went with several of my neighbors to seek him. We found his track at a stile near the house, and followed it as close as we could; but it was not possible to follow him step by step, for he had gone to and fro above three miles, through shrubs, and thick quickset hedges, and over deep ditches full of water. One mile of the three was all a bog, full of sloughs, and drains, and trenches, and deep holes, with hardly one foot of firm ground between them. Eighteen or twenty of us being together, about nine o'clock found him by the side of a lake. He was lying on the grass, stretched out at length, with his face upward: His right hand was lifted up toward heaven, his left stretched upon his body: His eyes were closed, and he had a sweet, pleasant, smiling countenance. What surprised us most was, that he had no hurt or scratch from the crown of his head to the sole of his foot; nor one speck of dirt on any part of his body, no more than if it had been just washed. On Thursday he was buried as he desired, just by my wife, whom he survived fourteen days." (John Wesley,

The Works of John Wesley, II [Grand Rapids: Zondervan Publishing House, 1958], 195-197)

Many of the details of this story are seemingly without reason or meaning. Why would a young man be taken out of the world while in seeming health and without accident? Could it be that it was the only way God, in His wisdom and providence, saw fit to secure his eternal salvation? Did the all-knowing Almighty foresee that had he lived longer, would have turned apostate, finally losing his soul? One can only agree with Mr. Wesley when he refers to it as a "strange relation."

Elizabeth Walcam:
A Teenager Who Panted For A View Of Jesus
(d. June, 1751)

John Wesley was intensely interested in all accounts of those who, under his leadership, preaching and pastoral care, were converted to God, made partakers of the Divine nature and who finally died in the triumph of faith. We are not informed who it may have been that provided Mr. Wesley with this report but it is interesting to keep in mind that the subject of this account was a sixteen year old English lass. On June 1 of 1751 he writes in his *Journal:* "I went down to Bristol, where I procured a particular account of one that went to rest some months before. Part of it was as follows:--

> "Elizabeth Walcam was born in March, 1733. From her infancy she was mild and affable. When she was about six years old, she was much in private prayer; and often called her brother and sister to join with her. If she was in any trifling and laughing company, she seldom went farther than a little smile. In the whole course of her life she was remarkably dutiful to her parents, and loving to all; mostly in an even frame of spirit; slow

to anger, and soon pacified; tender-hearted to all that were distressed, and a lover of all that was good.

"From the time she joined the society, she was a true lover of her Ministers and her brethren; not suffering any to speak evil of them, particularly of her Ministers: And, if her innocent answers did not stop them, she left their company.

"In the beginning of December last she was indisposed; and on Saturday, 8, took her room. In the afternoon she broke out, 'When shall I see my Jesus? I want to know that He has taken away my sins.' After a while she cried, 'He does love me. I know Jesus loves me. My Father! He is my Father and my God.'

"Yet on the Wednesday following she was in deep distress. I found her, says one who then visited her, crying out, 'O that I was washed in the blood of the Lamb! Pray for me, that I may know my sins are forgiven.' I prayed with her several times, and stayed all night. She did not sleep at all; her pain of body, as well as mind, being exceeding great. She was almost continually in prayer, crying for mercy, till I went away about eight in the morning.

"About nine in the evening I came again. She was still in violent pain, but did not seem to regard this in comparison of her soul. Her continual cry was, 'I do not know Christ: I want an interest in Christ. O that I might know Him! O that He would forgive my sins; that He would wash me whiter than snow!' She had never any ease but while we were at prayer, with which she was never satisfied; but held me, and would not let me rise from my knees, sometimes for an hour together. I was praying with her about twelve o'clock, when she called out, 'Help me to praise the Lord. I feel my sins are forgiven. I am washed and made whiter than snow.' She spent the remainder of the night in praise and prayer. About eight in the morning I went home.

"On Sunday evening I found her much weaker in body, but her soul was full of life and vigour. When I came in, she said, 'I am exceeding glad you are come. Now let us rejoice together. We shall meet together in heaven. I am washed in the blood of the Lamb: I know God is my Father. I know my name is written in heaven: There we shall all rejoice together.' She was never satisfied with giving thanks; not suffering me to rise from my knees, but holding me by my hands when I wanted to rise.

"About eight Mrs. W--- came in, and told us Mr. C--- W--- was come to town. She then broke out into prayer for him, for Mr. J--- W---, and for the society. Afterward she prayed for the Q—rs, that God would deliver them from all darkness of mind, covetousness, pride, and the love of the world. She continued praying till near twelve o'clock, speaking with a clear, strong voice; although whenever she ceased speaking, she seemed just dying away. About twelve she cried out, 'Lord, forgive me! What shall I do to be saved?' I was astonished to hear her voice so changed; and asked, 'My dear, what is it distresses you?' she answered, 'I feel anger toward Peggy.' (That was the maid's name.)

'Lord forgive me! Lord, lay not this sin to my charge!' We went to prayer together; and, after a time, she said, 'Help me to bless and thank the Lord. I find sweet refreshments from Him. He is reconciled again.' And from that hour she found no more darkness.

"She then began praying for her parents, her sisters, and brother; adding, 'Do pray, that God would restrain him from the evils of this world. I have been restrained from a child. I never could play, as other children did.' Towards morning she dozed a little; but all the intervals she spent in praise and thanksgiving, still speaking with as clear and strong a voice as if she had been in health.

"One day as she was praising God, one desired her brother to take pattern by her. She immediately answered, 'Not by me; take pattern by Jesus,--take pattern by Jesus!'

"About twelve at night, as I came into the room, she said, 'My heart is blessed of the Lord; and by the strength of the living God I speak. Come, let us go to prayer; let us praise the living God once more in this world; the Lord ever---.' Here her breath failed. But soon after, she sung with us,

Come, let us join our cheerful songs;

adding, 'I am more afraid to live than to die; but whether I live or die, I will praise the Lord.'

"On Sunday morning she said, 'Jesus loves me; he has been always with me; he is a merciful God; he is indeed. I shall go to glory, to glory. Come, O Lord Jesus, and make my passage easy to eternal glory! I long to be with Jesus. I could grasp him!' (stretching out her arms!) 'O give me an easy passage!—We shall soon meet again, to sing praises unto the Lord for ever.'

"At another time she said, 'Let others do what they will, we will praise the Lord. I am happy, I am easy; if he raises me or not, I shall praise the Lord.'

"She said to her father, 'I asked to drink of the bitter cup; but I knew not what I asked. But yet, if it is an hundred times more, I desire to drink it all.'

"As she grew weaker, she was seized with strong convulsions, which followed close one upon another. But the moment the fit ceased, she always began to speak, praying and praising God; nor was her understanding, or even her memory, either disordered or weakened thereby: Nay, her understanding remained even during the fit; so that she heard and knew all that was spoken near her; and when she recovered her speech, repeated as there was occasion, and remarked upon it.

"When Mr. C--- W--- and two others came to pray with her, she was exceeding low. After they were gone, she said, 'My spirit joins with them: They are the people of God; I know they are. How sweet they look! Don't they look different from other people? Come, mother, let us praise God: I am always better after prayer. O for a thousand tongues to sing my dear Redeemer's praise! O how great is my rejoicing! I shall be whiter than the driven snow.'

"Soon after, she said, 'I am refreshed; indeed I am. We shall see him on his great white throne. There we shall see him face to face. My dear Jesus! Praise Jesus: Why don't you praise Jesus? Praise my God: He is making intercession for me; He *is*: The Lord loves me; I *know* he does.'

"To her mother she said, 'What a blessed thing it is, that you have brought up a child for the Lord!'

"She continued praying and praising God till the 25th, when her breath was so short, that she could say nothing but 'Jesus.' This she uttered continually as she could, till, about six in the evening, she resigned her spirit, without any sigh or groan, or alteration in her countenance, which had the same sweetness as when she was living. She lived on earth sixteen years, nine months, and eighteen days." (John Wesley, *The Works of John Wesley*, II [Grand Rapids: Zondervan Publishing House, 1958], 232-235)

From the description given us of this young person, most would not hesitate to say that she was a model child from her earliest years. Having been "much in prayer from the time she was six years old ... remarkably dutiful to her parents and loving to all ... slow to anger ... tender-hearted to all that were distressed, and a lover of all that was good," ("ibid., 232") many would conclude that she needed no more of religion than what she had, but was already a good Christian.

God, however, was faithful to reveal to her consciousness the true state of her heart. To know one's own heart as God knows it is a necessary ingredient of repentance. Because this young lady came into a true knowledge of the state of her own heart she was in distress. How fortunate she was that there were no self-appointed counselors around who should attempt to "heal slightly" the "hurt" and sore of her heart "saying, Peace, peace; when there [was] no peace" (Jeremiah 6:14). How fortunate she was that no one persuaded her to believe she was safe before she had the Spirit's assurance and witness that her sins were forgiven. The experiential reality of heart religion as believed by early Methodists is underscored in this account.

Catherine Whitaker:
Announces Her Going To Christ
(d. March, 1752)

In April of 1746, Catherine Whitaker heard the preaching of John Nelson, one of Mr. Wesley's lay preachers. She was previously convinced of the truth by her reading, and "grew more and more serious" concerning eternal matters. Sometime later John H___ made her a visit and as he was leaving, said, "You must believe, whether you can or no." As soon as he had departed, "she began crying to God, and ceased not, till she knew she did believe in Christ." It is said that "She never afterward lost the sense of his love, nor could she rest, if she found the least cloud, till it was wholly removed, and the clear light shone again upon her soul."

By May, 1750 she appeared to be ill with consumption (tuberculosis). This, however, did not hinder her from continuing to rise early "to teach her scholars." In December of 1751 "her bodily strength failed, though she did not keep her room till March." For a time she became "afraid lest she should live to be a burden to her relations, but this fear soon vanished away, and she said, 'Now I can leave it all to God. Let me die sooner or later, it is all one.' But she had still some struggle concerning her husband, before she was thoroughly willing to give him up."

A little more than a week "before she died, one of her sisters, sitting by her, began singing,

> O happy, happy day,
> That calls the exiles home!

She immediately joined with her, and sung on to the end of the hymn. The Thursday after, she looked round upon us, and said, "O how I love you all! I am all love. I love every soul God has made." Her husband asked, "Are you happy?" She said, "O yes:

> I cannot fear, I cannot doubt,
> I feel the sprinkled blood:

Sing on, sing on,

> Let every soul with me cry out,
> Thou art my Lord, my God."

At breakfast she desired a little cold water; on receiving which, she looked up and said, "In a little while, I shall drink new wine in the kingdom of my Father." About ten o'clock she broke out,--

> My God is reconciled,
> His pard'ning voice I hear,
> He owns me for his child,
> I can no longer fear.

One asking her how she did, she said, "I long to be with Him whom my soul loveth." One Friday and Saturday, being extremely weak, she spoke very little. On Sunday morning she said, "So the Lord hath brought us to another Sabbath, 'Vouchsafe, O Lord, to keep us this

day without sin.'" She then partly sung, and partly
repeated, that hymn,--

> O when shall I sweetly remove,
> O when shall I enter my rest!
> Return to the Sion above,
> The mother of spirits distress'd!

She then asked, "Who is in the house? O, I do not
love the staying at home on a Sunday! Desire them all
to go to church. When I was most diligent in going to
church, I always found the greatest blessings." At night
she said, "Swelled legs! For a little time: There will be
no swelled legs in heaven." About five on Monday
morning, March 23, her husband asked, "Do you know
me?" She said, "Yes, I do;" and putting her arm round
his neck, quickly began to slumber. Waking soon
after, she said, "I must make haste, and dress myself for
the Bridegroom." She then dozed afresh; but waking
in a few minutes, said, "I am going to Christ;" and
fell asleep. (John Wesley, *The Works of John Wesley*, II
[Grand Rapids: Zondervan Publishing House, 1958],
266-267)

Rose Longworth:
"I See The Lamb In Glory"
(d. August, 1752)

"**I** learned from her husband," writes Mr. Wesley, "that Rose Longworth found peace with God in June, 1749. This she never lost, and often rejoiced with joy unspeakable. From that time she was always remarkably serious, and walked closely with God."

Around Easter of 1751, she became conscious of a great loss in physical strength, but never did it bring a complaint from her lips. She was "only concerned lest her soul should suffer loss."

In the following July, she went into the country, yet continued to walk in the light, cleaving by faith close to her Saviour. Near the end of the month, she realized that her time was short and wished to return to Athlone. Upon her return she was "extremely weak," but continued praising God. The whole following week she expressed a strong "desire to depart and be with Christ."

The sacrament was administered to her on the following Sunday and although she could speak very little, she made it known that "she had no doubt of her salvation." The clergyman in attendance "was deeply affected, and said he believed her, but could scarce speak for tears. When she could not be heard, she had her eyes constantly fixed upward, and her lips moving." Later in the day she fainted away. After a time she came to herself and said,

> "Ah! I was disappointed, I thought I had escaped." She then prayed for her husband, for her parents, for the society, the Church, and whole world. Fainting again, and coming to herself, she cried out, "See my Redeemer! See my Redeemer! See how his blood streams! I see the Lamb in glory. I see the Lamb in glory. Fare ye well. God be with you. Fare ye well." She then ceased to speak, and went to God. (John Wesley, *The Works of John Wesley,* II [Grand Rapids: Zondervan Publishing House, 1958], 272-273)

Mr. Stuart:

Doubts And Fears Vanished
(d. February, 1753)

"This day Mr. Stuart was released. For two or three years he had been 'instant in season, doing the work of an Evangelist, and making full proof of his ministry.' Three or four weeks ago he fell ill of a fever, and was for a while in heaviness of soul. Last week all his doubts and fears vanished; and as he grew weaker in body, he grew stronger in faith. This morning he expressed an hope full of immortality, and in the afternoon went to God" (John Wesley, *The Works of John Wesley*, II [Grand Rapids: Zondervan Publishing House], 280).

In his sermon entitled "Heaviness Through Manifold Temptations," Mr. Wesley makes it clear that there is a difference between spiritual heaviness on the one hand and spiritual darkness on the other. One may enjoy the love and peace of God and still suffer heaviness. Darkness, however, "implies a total loss of joy in the Holy Ghost." Again, darkness is caused by a grieving of God's Spirit and a loss of the inward life of God in the soul.

Heaviness is altogether different. Causes of heaviness, according to Mr. Wesley, include bodily disorders, poor health and pain, poverty, death of loved ones, "the unkindness, ingratitude, wickedness and apostasy of those who are united to us in the closest ties."

It has been frequently supposed, that there is another cause, if not of darkness, at least, of heaviness; namely, God's withdrawing himself from the soul, because it is his sovereign will. Certainly he will do this, if we grieve his Holy Spirit, either by outward or inward sin; either by doing evil, or neglecting to do good; by giving way either to pride or anger, to spiritual sloth, to foolish desire, or inordinate affection. But that he ever withdraws himself *because he will*, merely because it is his good pleasure, I absolutely deny. There is no text in all the Bible which gives any colour for such a supposition. Nay, it is a supposition contrary, not only to many particular texts, but to the whole tenor of Scripture. It is repugnant to the very nature of God: It is utterly beneath his majesty and wisdom, (as an eminent writer strongly expresses it,) "to play at bo-peep with his creatures." It is inconsistent both with his justice and mercy, and with the sound experience of all his children. (John Wesley, *The Works of John Wesley*, VI [Grand Rapids: Zondervan Publishing House, 1958], 91-103)

According to the above teachings of Methodism's founder, it would be fair to conclude that Mr. Stuart's "heaviness" was due to an ill state of health. "The corruptible body was, as it were, pressing down the soul." Such physical suffering may tend to sew seeds of doubt concerning God's providences and spawn a questioning of God's purposes. It is, nevertheless, encouraging to know that, as in the case of Mr. Stuart, fears and doubts can be vanquished and a strength of faith restored that is found working by a true and fervent love to God.

The Victorious Departure
Of Ann Beauchamp

(d. August, 1753)

The substance of the following account was given to Mr. Wesley by one of the sisters of this dying woman.

Ann Beauchamp had been ill for about a week when she was visited by this sister who "asked her in what state she found her soul." She replied in the following words:

> "I am quite happy. I know that my Redeemer liveth, and has taken away all my sins. And my heart is comforted with the presence of God: I long to die, that I may be with Him." I asked, "But are you resigned, either to live or die, as he shall see fit?" She answered, "I cannot say I am willing to live: It would go hard with me to live now. Pray that the Lord may perfect his work of sanctification in my soul."
>
> Being asked, if she could freely part with all her friends, she said, "Yes: And as to my children, I have cast them upon the Lord. I know he will take care of them; and I give them freely up to him, without one

anxious thought." She then prayed for her friends and acquaintance one by one, and afterwards, fervently and with tears, for each person in her band: Then for Mr. John Wesley, desiring she might be found at his feet in the day of the Lord.

Soon after she called her mother, desired forgiveness for any thing wherein she had ignorantly offended her and exhorted her not to grieve; adding, "God will comfort you, and give you strength to bear your trial. It is your loss, but it is my everlasting gain; and I am going but a little before you." She then prayed over her, and, kissing her, took her leave. In the same manner she took leave of all about her, exhorting, praying for, and kissing them, one by one: Afterward she called for, and took her leave of, her servants.

Seeing one of her neighbours in the room, she called her and said, "O Mary, you are old in years, and old in sin. The Lord has borne long with you, and you know not the day or hour when he will call you. I am young, and he is calling me away; and what should I do without an interest in Christ? Was my work now to do, it would never be done: But, blessed be God, it is not. I know the Lord hath washed me from my sins in his own blood, and is preparing me for himself. O fly from the wrath to come, and never rest till you rest in the wounds of Jesus! I am almost spent: But had I strength, I could exhort you all till morning."

To another she said, "'Martha! Thou art careful and troubled about many things; but one thing is needful;' and this one thing you have neglected. O seek God, and he will supply all your wants. It is time for you to begin: Your glass is almost run; and what will all your toil profit when you come to be as I am now? Find time for this, whatever goes undone. My neighbours used to wonder how I could find time, and think me foolish for spending it so; but now I know it was not foolishness. Soon I shall receive an exceeding great reward."

She continued to exhort all that were around her to "seek the Lord while he may be found," warning them that excuses in that day would be vain. "God," says she, "will have his witnesses; and I shall appear as a witness against you. If you repent not, these my dying words will rise up in judgment against you."

To one who was standing nearby, she expressed herself thus: "I forgive you all that you have done against me; and I have prayed the Lord to forgive you: Return to him now, and he will receive you; for he desires not the death of a sinner." She said, "I am a witness of this; for he has forgiven all my sins. O! I want strength to sing his praise! But I am going where I shall sing his praise for ever."

She then called her husband and said, "My dear, God has given you many calls, even in dreams: And when we will not hear his call, it is often his way to make us feel his rod by removing our darling from us." Continuing her words of admonition, she said, "I was your darling, and, seeing you refused the many calls of God, he is now taking me away from you, if, by any means, he may bring you to himself." She then prayed for, and took her leave of him.

The next day she was asked how she then found herself. She made answer in words of praise. She blessed God that she was "very well" in her soul. She said, "I know that my Redeemer lives: He is dear to me, and I am dear to him: I know he is preparing me for himself, and I shall soon be with him."

> She then prayed earnestly for entire sanctification; till a friend coming in, she said, "The Lord has brought you, and all my dear friends, to my remembrance: I have not forgotten you in my prayers. You must come and pray my last prayer. When you see me near my deliverance, go all to prayer, and continue therein till my spirit is gone. Let there be no crying over me; but all of you sing praises and rejoice over me."

Some will be amazed to read that this saint, on her deathbed, was heard praying for entire sanctification. It has been well observed that while those in today's holiness movement are quick to testify to entire sanctification, early Methodists were quick to seek but slow to claim the experience.

We are told that this blessed but suffering soul, "never once complained of her pain; but behaved from the beginning with that patience, sweetness, and love to all, that bespoke a soul which knew herself just entering into the joy of her Lord. Thus she died the next morning ... after crying out as in ecstasy,--

> Bold I approach th' eternal throne,
> And claim the crown through Christ my own."

(John Wesley, *The Works of John Wesley*, II [Grand Rapids: Zondervan Publishing House, 1958], 370-372)

Ephraim B---:
A Backslider Mercifully Restored Just Before Death
(d. July, 1755)

In his *Journal* entry dated July, 1755, Mr. Wesley mentions the burial of Ephraim B---. He describes this man as having "once been a pattern to all that believed." According to Mr. Wesley, his spiritual decay came about when "he left off fasting and universal self-denial." In these practices, "none" had formerly been "more exemplary for some years" says he. He sank lower and lower spiritually "till he had neither the power, nor the form of religion left."

Bodily illness later overcame him and he found himself "in black despair." Then it was that "much prayer was made for him" by those who truly cared for his soul.

Near to the close of life, "it pleased God to restore to him the light of his countenance. So," writes Mr. Wesley, "I trust, his backsliding only cost him his life, and he may yet live with God for ever" (John Wesley, *The Works of John Wesley*, II [Grand Rapids: Zondervan Publishing House, 1958], 337).

This last comment of Mr. Wesley is best understood in the light of his sermon entitled, "A Call to Backsliders." Therein he applies St.

John's reference to the "sin unto death" as possibly meaning "sin that God is determined to punish by the [physical] death of the sinner that the soul may escape destruction and be saved" (John Wesley, *The Works of John Wesley*, VI [Grand Rapids: Zondervan Publishing House, 1958], 520-21).

Christopher Hopper And His Wife:
Their Lives And Victorious Departures In Death
(d. August, 1755)
(d. March, 1802)

The following account of the suffering, temptations, and death of Christopher Hopper's wife were written by Mr. Hopper in a letter to the Rev. George Whitefield. He, as it turned out, lived and remained faithful in his labors and ministerial calling almost 47 years beyond the inexpressible loss of his dearest companion. He wrote as follows:

> "Friday, August 15, 1755, my dear and most loving wife took a violent nervous fever, at the Hagg, in Derwent-water, the place of her nativity; and on the 25th died in perfect peace, in the glorious arms of the dear Redeemer. On the 27th her funeral sermon was preached at the same place, to a large auditory, who came from every quarter; and that evening she was interred in Ryton church, amongst the dry bones of her dear ancestors, where her body shall sweetly rest till the morning of the general resurrection.
>
> "But perhaps it may be more agreeable to you still if

I give you a more particular account of God's gracious dealings with her in her sickness, more especially in the solemn article of death. In the beginning of her illness, Satan endeavoured by his infernal insinuations to make her give up her shield, and cast away her confidence, by suggesting, 'You are built upon the sand, you have laid a wrong foundation; all you have to trust in, after twelve years' progress in the Christian religion, are only false imaginations, a feigned castle in the air, or a mere chimera in your head; therefore you must lie down in sorrow, and be miserably disappointed in the end.'

"When this violent storm came upon her so near the haven, she immediately fled to the throne of grace, the rock of Israel; for it was now high time to cast anchor on that sure bottom, to examine her faith and the ground of her eternal hopes. She therefore entreated the almighty God of Jacob to discover her real state that she might see and know whether her condition was so melancholy in reality, or whether it was only a flood of temptations or the voice of the enemy. She had no sooner supplicated the Friend of sinners but the cloud broke and the glorious sun of righteousness began to shine, the old subtle tempter fled, and God filled her with joy and peace in believing.

"After she had spoken a few words to me concerning some temporal affairs, she gave up this world, her dear friends and relations, and the dearest part of herself, cheerfully. She patiently endured all her afflictions, and drank the bitter cup without complaining; nay, not so much as desiring the least abatement of her pain, or mitigation of her trouble. Her only request was for patience and resignation to bear and suffer all her heavenly Father's will. She expressed her firm trust and confidence in the Lord several times, without fear or doubt, as her wisdom, righteousness, sanctification, and redemption, as long as she could speak; and after that useful organ was silent, she manifested her inward joy, and the peace she felt, by her patience and heavenly looks. During this time I prayed with her twice; and was enabled in confidence to commit her body to the earth from whence it came, and her precious soul to the dear Redeemer who bought it with His most precious blood. Near the time of her happy departure, I took her in my arms, and said, 'Farewell! farewell! farewell! my dear wife, and most loving companion! The Lord receive thy spirit!' When death, that long-desired and long-expected friend, was executing his last office, and drawing the last pin of the poor earthly tabernacle, she looked up, and gave me a parting smile, and then calmly and sweetly fell in the arms of Christ, without a struggle, sigh, or groan.

"Now, my dear friend, what shall I say? I soon shall close my weary eyes in peace, and stretch composed upon my dusty bed. O death! thy quiet and refreshing shade shall yield a long, an unmolested rest from all our fruitless toil and vanity below the sun. May we love the dear Redeemer! and may we live in Him, and die in Him! is the sincere prayer of your afflicted friend, C. H." (John Telford, ed., *Wesley's Veterans. Lives of Early Methodist Preachers Told by Themselves,* I [Salem: Schmul Publishers, 1976], 168-170)

Christopher Hopper was known as "one of the first Methodist preachers," having been one of the first of many laymen to labor with Mr. Wesley as an itinerant preacher. At the time of his decease in 1802, he was the oldest preacher on the list, having faithfully preached the Gospel for 57 years. From a part of his obituary below we learn something of his life and commitment to the advancement of Christ's Kingdom. The reader is also provided hereby with a sample of the Methodist preacher's daily life and experiences in the earliest days of the movement.

> At a time when the land was covered with gross darkness, and there was little or no genuine vital religion to be found, and when those eminent servants and messengers of God, [John and Charles Wesley] and George Whitefield, were opposed and persecuted with great rage and violence, [Christopher Hopper] stood forth as a determined witness for God and His truth against the combined powers of earth and hell. The insults and violence of avowed enemies, and the persuasion and entreaties of mistaken friends, he equally disregarded; and persisted to testify, and frequently at the hazard of his life, "repentance toward God, and faith in our Lord Jesus Christ," wherever a door was opened, and he could have access. In private houses, barns, stables, on mountains or plains, in streets and market-places, in cities, towns, and villages, wherever any could be found that were willing to hear, he was ready to testify the gospel of the grace of God; and this he did with peculiar ability and success. He was a Boanerges, a son of thunder: his word was with

power, and stout-hearted sinners trembled from time to time under the awful and alarming message his Lord gave him to deliver. He feared the face of no man; he declared the whole counsel of God with clearness and energy wherever he came, and the Lord crowned the labours of His servant with great success. Scores, yea hundreds, were convinced of the error of their ways, and converted to God, by his instrumentality in different parts of the British Empire, especially during the early days of his ministry. He laboured nowhere without more or less fruit; and the seals of his mission were many, and may be found at this day in most parts of the kingdom in which he laboured. As to his character as a man and a Christian, he was a person of peculiar integrity, and of most unblemished morals. He was prudent, steady, zealous, and active, especially during his younger days. (John Telford, ed., *Wesley's Veterans. Lives of Early Methodist Preachers Told by Themselves*, I [Salem: Schmul Publishers, 1976], 172-174)

One by the name of Mr. Atmore, a close friend, last visited Christopher Hopper shortly before his death. His account is as follows:

When I entered the room, he was in a doze; but as soon as he awoke, he gave me his hand, and, with great affection, said, "O, my dear friend, how glad I am to see you! Providence has sent you. You and I have often met; and this will be our last meeting on earth. But we shall meet in our Father's house above .... I [have] preached on the only foundation God has laid in Zion for poor sinners to build their hopes of salvation upon.

On this foundation all my hopes are founded now; and it does support me! I have not a doubt—no, not the shadow of a doubt; and as for the enemy, I know not what is become of him. I have neither seen him nor heard of him for some time. I think he has quitted the field …."

The last day or two he lay quite composed; he spoke very little, but was frequently engaged in earnest, fervent prayer, often saying, "Come, Lord Jesus, come quickly." On Friday evening, March, 5, 1802, he entered into his Master's joy, in the eightieth year of his age. ("ibid., 161,162")

Mr. Wardrobe:
Beautiful Departure Of A Scottish Clergyman
(d. May, 1756)

Mr. Wardrobe was a Minister of Bathgate in Scotland. Although he may have been a Scottish Calvinist in his theological persuasions, he seems not to have been an enemy to the work of the Methodists in Scotland as some of the clergy proved to be. Mr. Wesley mentions him once as having "preached at the Orphan-House [on a particular] evening, to the no small amazement and displeasure of some of his zealous countrymen." It is quite likely that the Orphan-House mentioned in this *Journal* entry was begun and operated by the Methodists, thus causing Mr. Wardrobe's "zealous [Calvinist] countrymen" to be displeased with his preaching there.

"Sun. 30, May 1756. —I returned to Cork [writes Mr. Wesley in his *Journal*]. About that time I received a letter from Mr. Gillies, part of which follows:--

> "The Lord hath been pleased to inflict a heavy stroke upon us, by calling home his faithful servant, Mr. Wardrobe. Concerning his death, a Christian friend writes thus:--
>
> "'May 7. Four in the morning. I am just come

from witnessing the last sighs of one dear to you, to me, and to all that knew him. Mr. Wardrobe died last night. He was seized on Sabbath last, just as he was going to the kirk, with a most violent colic, which terminated in a mortification of his bowels. The circumstances of his death are worthy to be recorded. With what pleasure he received the message, and went off in all the triumph of a conqueror; crying out, *My warfare is accomplished: I have fought the good fight:* My victory is completed. Crowns of grace shall adorn this head, (taking off his cap,) and palms be put into these hands. Yet a little while, and I shall sing for ever. *I know that my Redeemer liveth.*—When he was within a few moments of his last, he gave me his hand, and a little after said, *Now lettest thou thy servant depart in peace; for mine eyes have seen thy salvation.* Were I to repeat half what he spoke, I should write you three hours. It shall suffice at this time to say, that as he lived the life, so he died the death, of a Christian. We weep not for him; we weep for ourselves. I wish we may know how to improve this awful judgment, so as to be also ready, not knowing when our Lord cometh.'"

A minister friend by the name of Mr. Adams writes as follows:

"On Friday night, about ten, I witnessed Mr. Wardrobe's (of Bathgate) entrance into the joy of his Lord. But ah! who can help mourning the loss to the Church of Christ? His amiable character gave him a distinguished weight and influence; which his Lord had given him to value, only for its subserviency to His honour and glory. He was suddenly taken ill on the last Lord's day, and from the first moment believed it was for death. I went to see him on Thursday evening, and heard some of the liveliest expressions of triumphant faith, zeal for the glory of Christ and the salvation of souls, mixed with the most amiable humility and modesty. 'Yet a little while,' said he, 'and this mortal shall put on immortality. Mortality shall be swallowed up of life; this vile body fashioned like to his glorious body. O for the victory! I shall get the victory. I know in whom I have believed.' Then, with a remarkably audible voice, lifting up his hands, he cried out, 'O for a draught of the well of the water of life, that I may begin the song before I go off to the Church triumphant! I go forth in thy name, making mention of thy righteousness, even thine only. I die at the feet of mercy.' Then, stretching out his arms, he put his hand upon his head, and with the most serene and steady, majestic eye I ever saw, looking upward, he said, 'Crowns of grace, crowns of grace, and palms in their hands! O Lord God of truth, into thy hands I commend my spirit!' After an unexpected revival, he said, 'O, I fear his tarrying, lest the prospect become more dark. I sometimes fear he may spare me to live, and be less faithful than he has helped me to be hitherto.' He says to me, 'You that are Ministers, bear a proper testimony against the professors of this age, who have a form of godliness without the power.' Observing some of his people about his bed, he said, 'May I have some seals among you! O where will the ungodly and sinners of Bathgate appear? Labour all to be in Christ.' Then he stretched out his hand to several, and said, 'Farewell, farewell, farewell! And now, O Lord, what wait I for? My hope is in thee!' Once or twice he said, 'Let me be laid across the bed to expire, where I have sometimes prayed, and sometimes meditated with pleasure.' He expressed his grateful sense of the assiduous care which Mr. Wardrobe, of Cult, had taken of him; and on his replying, 'Too much could not be done for so valuable a life,' he said, 'O speak not so, or you will provoke God! Glory be to God, that I have ever had any regard paid me for Christ's sake!' I am greatly sunk under the event. O help me by your prayers, to get the proper submission and improvement!" (John Wesley, *The Works of John Wesley*, II [Grand Rapids: Zondervan Publishing House, 1958], 367-368)

Richard Varley:
A Repentant Convict Dies With Cheerfulness
(d. December, 1756)

onvicted of the crime of highway robbery, Richard Varley was condemned to die by hanging. What is interesting is the fact that a whole week of time went by between his hearing the gospel preached in his cell and his beginning earnestly to seek his salvation. The reader is asked to take notice of the length of time involved prior to his receiving assurance that his sins had been truly forgiven.

The following is shared in a letter to Mr. Wesley by the father of the condemned. It is then followed by a letter written by the condemned man to his wife.

> "Blessed be God, who desireth not the death of a sinner! It pleased him not to cut off my son in his sins. He gave him time to repent; and not only so, but a heart to repent. He showed him his lost estate by nature, and that unless he was reconciled to God by his Son, and washed in his blood from all his sins, he could never be saved. After he was condemned at York for a robbery on the highway, I attended him in the condemned room; and, blessed be God, he enabled me to preach the

117

everlasting Gospel to him. It was on Saturday he was condemned. It was on the Saturday following the Lord touched his heart. He then began to wrestle with God in prayer, and left not off till Sunday in the afternoon, when God, who is rich in mercy, applied the blood of his Son, and convinced him, he had forgiven him all his sins. He felt his soul at peace with God, and longed to depart and to be with Christ. The following week his peace increased daily, till on Saturday, the day he was to die, he came out of the condemned room clothed in his shroud, and went into the cart. As he went on, the cheerfulness and composure of his countenance were amazing to all the spectators. At the place of execution, after he had spent some time in prayer, he rose up, took a cheerful leave of his friends, and said, 'Glory be to God for free grace!' His last words were, 'Lord Jesus, receive my soul.'"

Part of the other letter, he himself wrote to his wife, was as follows:

"My Dear,

"Righteous is the Lord, and just are his judgments! His hand of justice cuts my life short, but his hand of mercy saves my soul. You, for one, are a witness of the course of life I led. Were it in my power, I would gladly make amends to you and every one else that I have wronged. But, seeing it is not, I hope that God and you, and every one else, will accept of my willing mind. In a few hours I shall be delivered out of this miserable world. But, glory be to God, he has given repentance and remission of sins to me, the worst of sinners: He has taken away the sting of death, and I am prepared to meet my God. Let my example encourage every sinner to forsake sin, and come unto God through Jesus Christ. As a dying man I give you this advice:--Give yourself wholly up to God. Pray to Him, and never rest till you have secured an interest in the blood of Christ. Live in his fear, and you (as well as I) shall die in his favour. So no more from

"Your dying husband,
Richard Varley."

(John Wesley, *The Works of John Wesley,* II, [Grand Rapids: Zondervan Publishing House, 1958], 389-390)

Joseph Yarner:
His Countenance In Death Gave A Testimony Of Peace
(d. January, 1757)

"I buried," writes Mr. Wesley, "the remains of Joseph Yarner, an Israelite indeed. The peace which filled his heart during his last hours, gave such a bloom to his very countenance, as remained after death, to the surprise of all who remembered the cloud that used to hang upon it" (John Wesley, *The Works of John Wesley*, II [Grand Rapids: Zondervan Publishing House, 1958], 391).

We see that numerous accounts are shared by Mr. Wesley of those who, in the hour of death, are able to give audible testimony to the heaven they feel within. We all know, however, that not all are physically able to glorify their gracious Saviour and Redeemer with their latest breath. This may have been the case with the good man referred to above. He was nevertheless known as a righteous and blood washed man or Mr. Wesley would not have referred to him as "an Israelite indeed." In any case it is interesting to note that the "bloom" of "his very countenance" in death gave testimony of "the peace which filled his heart during his last hours" ("ibid., 391").

Mary Naylor:
From Soul Distress To Comfort
(d. April, 1757)

"**I** buried Mary Naylor," writes Mr. Wesley, "who for several years was a most eminent pattern of truly Christian courage, plainness of speech, and plainness of apparel. A week before," he continues, "I had an opportunity of telling her all that was in my heart concerning her change (not for the better) in all these particulars. In the beginning of her illness, she was in great darkness, and distress of soul; but while prayer was made for her, her bodily pain ceased, and her soul received comfort; and [a day later] she quietly fell asleep" (John Wesley, *The Works of John Wesley,* II [Grand Rapids: Zondervan Publishing House, 1958], 396).

In this case the "great darkness and distress of soul" was doubtlessly an indication of condemnation and spiritual problems yet unanswered. Many have come to the hour of death in just such distress. It is well if those around them do not endeavor to "heal" their spiritual sore "slightly, saying, Peace, peace; when there is no peace" (Jeremiah 8:11). Prayer should rather be made together with appropriate counsel as befits the case.

Elsewhere, Mr. Wesley writes: "From the words of our blessed Lord, 'He that followeth me shall not walk in darkness,' I largely showed that God never deserts any man, unless he first deserts God; and that, abstracting from the bodily disorders on the one hand, and violent temptation on the other, every believer may be happy as well as holy, and walk in the light all the days of his life" (John Wesley, *The Works of John Wesley*, III [Grand Rapids: Zondervan Publishing House, 1958], 271).

Miss Beeresford:

Testifies Brilliantly Of Christian Perfection
In Her Glorious Departure
(d. May, 1757)

In his *Journal* dated May 5, 1757, Mr. Wesley writes that upon request, he received from John Johnson the following information concerning a Miss Beersford.

She was described as one who lived an innocent life: a young woman who, even before she was justified, was serious and maintained the "form of godliness." It is said that "notwithstanding her fortune and her sickliness, she was never unemployed; she had no other work, working for the poor. And the whole tenor of her conversation was such, that it is still a common saying, 'If Miss Beersford is not gone to heaven, nobody ever will.'"

Her love for the word of God was fervent, missing no opportunity to hear it. It is said that "frequently she would not go to bed all night, lest she should miss the [five o'clock] morning preaching." She likewise missed no opportunity of attending the services in fellowship and worship with those in "whom her heart was closely united. Nor was she afraid or ashamed to own the poorest of them, wherever she met them, and whatever company she was in. The very sight of them occasioned a joy in her soul, which she neither could nor desired to hide."

The time came when the ill state of her health "confined her to her room." It is said that the prospect of departing this life caused her to rejoice "with joy unspeakable: More especially when she was delivered from all her doubts concerning Christian perfection." Those who knew her best testified that no one was ever "more athirst for this, for the whole mind that was in Christ. And she earnestly exhorted all her brethren vehemently to press after it."

While her bodily strength steadily weakened, she was the more strengthened in her soul. She requested of all who were with her, "Help me to rejoice; help me to praise God."

John Johnson then says that when he arrived at Ashbourn, she sent for him. Below is a detailed account of his conversations with her and her testimonies leading up to her soul's departure. Upon his appearance at her bedside she exclaimed,

> "'I am just at my journey's end. What a mercy, that I who have done so little for God, should be so soon taken up to him! O, I am full of love of God! I dare not exercise my faith fully upon God: The glory of the Lord is so great, that I cannot bear it: I am overwhelmed: My natural life is almost gone, with the brightness of his presence. Sometimes I am even forced to 'cry out, *Lord, stay thy hand till I come into glory.*' I asked, 'Have you lately felt any remains of sin in you?' She said, 'I felt pride some weeks ago.' And it seems this was the last time. She added, 'I have now no will; the will of God is mine. I can bring my dearest friends before the Lord; and while I am praying for them, the glory of the Lord so overpowers me that I am lost, and adore in silence the God of heaven.' She cried out, 'Tell all

from me, that perfection is attainable; and exhort all to press after it. What a blessing is it, that I have no weary hours; though I am confined to my bed night and day, and can take scarce any thing but water to refresh me, yet I am like a giant refreshed with wine.'

"Afterward she broke out, 'If I had lived in what the world calls pleasure, what a miserable creature should I have been now! What should I be if I had no God on my side? When the fire has made me bright, then I shall go to my God.' She prayed largely for all states of mankind: But particularly for the prosperity of the church; and for the society at Ashbourn, that God would continue and increase his work among them.

"When she altered for death, she called for her mother and brothers, to each of whom she gave an earnest exhortation. Then she said, 'Now I have no more to do here; I am ready to die. Send to Mr. W., and tell him I am sorry I did not sooner believe the doctrine of perfect holiness.' Blessed be God I now know it to be the truth!' After greatly rejoicing in God, for two days more, she said one morning, 'I dreamed last night I heard a voice, *Christ will come to-day for his bride.* It is for me. He will come for me to-day.' And a few hours after, without one struggle, or sigh, or groan, she sweetly fell asleep."

Another close acquaintance writes as follows:--

"Glory be to God for the blessed privilege I enjoyed, of being with her, night and day, for a month before she died! When I went to her first, she had kept her bed some days, and was extremely weak. And yet she spoke considerably plainer, than ever I heard her in my life. She called as soon as I entered the room, 'My dear friend, give me your hand. Let us rejoice that my time is so near approaching. Do not mourn; you know it is what we expected.' I was soon brought to wish her safe on the happy shore. She said, 'This is true friendship. But how is it that I do not feel greater transports of love, now I am so near the time of seeing my Lord face to face? Indeed I am ashamed to approach Him, before whom the angels veil their faces!' She often said, 'I take it as a fresh token of his love, that he sent you to me at this time.' Her pains were great; but she bore all with invincible patience and resignation, and often said, 'I find it good for me to be afflicted; in his time I shall come out thoroughly purified.' Afterward she said, 'I experience more upon this bed of my own nothingness, and the free grace of God in Christ, than ever I did in all my life. The best of my performances would be damnable without Christ.'

"Several days before her death, her love was so great, that she cried, 'I am overcome, I am overcome, I am overcome!' And when she had scarce strength to speak, she praised God in a wonderful manner. Even when she was light-headed, her talk was wholly concerning the things of God. She called to Mr. Wesley, as if he had been by her, and said, 'O Sir, how hard it is for the rich to enter into the kingdom of heaven! I am saved; but I am but just saved.' When her fever abated, she told me she had dreamed that she was with him. And sometimes I could scarce persuade her but he had been there.

"She after asked if I saw no more appearance of death in her face yet. When I told her there was, she begged I would indulge her with a looking-glass; and looking earnestly into it, she said with transport, 'I never saw myself with so much pleasure in my life.'

"On Saturday morning at six she said, 'My Saviour will come to-day and fetch his bride.' Yet about eight she said, 'If you had felt what I have done this morning, it would have killed you. I had lost sight of God.' (Perhaps in the last conflict 'with principalities and powers.') From this time she was filled with joy, but spoke little. Her eyes were still lifted up to heaven, till her soul was released, with so much ease, that I did not know when she drew her last breath." (John Wesley, *The Works of John Wesley*, II [Grand Rapids: Zondervan Publishing House, 1958], 400-403)

The account above includes a number of references to Christian perfection. It is a term often used to mean the same as entire sanctification. The latter term is referenced only once in the New Testament, where in his letter to the Thessalonians, Paul prays that God would "sanctify you wholly" (1 Thessalonians 5:23). In contrast, the terms perfect, perfection, and perfecting are used over and over again many times in both the Old and the New Testaments. Mr. Wesley, who habitually used biblical language makes use of this term often found in Holy writ. He defined Christian perfection as "loving God with all our heart, and our neighbor as ourselves." He taught that it consisted also in "all the mind that was in Christ, enabling us to walk as Christ walked," as well as "a circumcision of the heart from all filthiness, all inward as well as outward pollution" (John Wesley, *The Works of John Wesley,* XI [Grand Rapids: Zondervan Publishing House, 1958], 367-446).

Hannah Richardson:
Died Victoriously Who Once Vowed To
Help Stone A Preacher To Death
(d. December, 1757)

In the letter shared below, persecution of the Methodists is mentioned. The record clearly shows that those who were followers of the Wesleys often met with abuse. Not only did wicked mobs harass them with cruel jeering and mocking, but resorted also to pelting them with stones, bricks, and mud. Some of their homes and places of business were damaged or destroyed. Numbers of them suffered bodily harm and serious injury. John Nelson who initially shared this story of Hannah Richardson with Mr. Wesley by letter was himself the object of mistreatment simply because he was a Methodist preacher. He was by trade a stone mason but was mightily transformed in heart and called to proclaim the good news of the Gospel. He proved to be one of Mr. Wesley's most effective preachers. To Methodism's founder he writes:

"We have had four triumphant deaths lately, of three men and one woman. The woman was Hannah Richardson, of Brestfield. When Enoch Williams preached there, she was the bitterest persecutor in the town, and vowed, if ever he preached there again,

131

she would help to stone him to death. But he never went to try. The only one of 'this way' in the town was Ruth Blacker. Against her she was violently enraged, till Ruth went to her house, reasoned the case, and at length persuaded her to go to Dewsbury to hear Mr. Charles Wesley. That day God begot her by his word, so that she could never rest till she found Christ in her heart: And for two years she has been a steady follower of him. By her zeal and circumspect walking many have been since stirred up to seek the Lord. As soon as she was taken ill, she began to praise God more than ever, for the work he had wrought in her soul. She said, 'At first I thought I had no will, and that God's love was all that was in my heart: But when my little child gave a sudden shriek, I found my heart was not free; and it damped the love of God in my soul for two hours. But the Lord is come again, and now I am fully assured he does take up all the room in my heart. He has sanctified me throughout, body, soul, and spirit. I am a witness for Jesus Christ, that he is a greater Saviour than Adam was a sinner. O watch and pray, and ye shall not be overcome in the hour of temptation! Keep close to your meetings, and the Lord will meet you. If you neglect these, or private prayer, you will become barren in your own souls, and the god of this world will get an advantage over you. But if you keep close to God and one another, you will find Jesus a Saviour to the uttermost, as I, the most unworthy of mankind, do.' For some time before she died, her prayer was turned into praise. All her prayer then was,

'Thy will be done.' We have one by us that we think will hardly live till to-morrow, who is above seventy, and is as a shock of corn full ripe, crying out, 'Come, Lord Jesus!'" (John Wesley, *The Works of John Wesley*, II [Grand Rapids: Zondervan Publishing House, 1958), 432-433

The story of Hannah Richardson is but one of a number who once ferociously persecuted the Methodists only to experience later a supernatural change of heart so as to become themselves a member of that despised people.

Thomas Walsh:
"He Is Come! I Am His forever!"
(d. April, 1759)

Mr. Wesley says in one of his printed sermons: "I knew a young man who was so thoroughly acquainted with the Bible, that if he was questioned concerning any Hebrew word in the Old, or any Greek word in the New Testament, he would tell, after a little pause, not only how often the one or the other occurred in the Bible, but also what it meant in every place. His name was Thomas Walsh. Such a master of biblical knowledge I never saw before, and never expect to see again" (John Wesley, *The Works of John Wesley*, VII [Grand Rapids: Zondervan Publishing House, 1958], 54).

Thomas Walsh, a native of Ireland, was saved out of the ignorance and superstition of Roman Catholicism by the preaching and influence of the Methodists. The story of his conversion portrays intense struggle and final victory over former prejudices fixed in his mind by home and church. He ultimately became one of Mr. Wesley's most devoted and saintly traveling preachers

A description of Thomas Walsh as a preacher is recorded in Mr. Wesley's *Journal* dated Sunday, June 24, 1753:

135

Sun. 24.--Mr. Walsh preached at Short's Gardens, in Irish. Abundance of his countrymen flocked to hear, and some were cut to the heart. How many means does God use to bring poor wanderers back to Himself!

Sun. July 1.--He preached in Irish, in Moorfields. The congregation was exceeding large, and behaved seriously; though probably many of them came purely to hear what manner of language it was. For the sake of these he preached afterwards in English, if by any means he might win some. (John Wesley, *The Works of John Wesley,* II [Grand Rapids: Zondervan Publishing House, 1958], 295)

In "A Short History of the People called Methodists," Mr. Wesley adds the following description of Mr. Walsh's preaching:

Wherever he preached, whether in English or Irish, the word was sharper than a two-edged sword: so that I do not remember ever to have known any preacher who, in so few years as he remained upon earth, was an instrument of converting so many sinners from the error of their ways. (John Wesley, *The Works of John Wesley,* XIII [Grand Rapids: Zondervan Publishing House, 1958], 336)

The life of this unusual man was so short that we have but a comparatively small collection of his writings left us. However, it is well worth the reader's time and effort to look at length into his diary, where deep spiritual insight is shared, personal struggles against the powers of darkness are recorded, and luminous victory witnessed through the power of Christ. Few men have cultivated the art of seeking close fellowship with God as did Thomas Walsh.

One finds in his diary many instances of heartfelt enjoyment of God. The following is shared as a specimen:

> I sensibly felt the Lord impressing His image on my soul. O perfect love! It is all in all in religion. I want it above everything, even this fullness of God in Christ.
>
> > O shed it in my heart abroad,
> > Fullness of love, of heaven, of God!
>
> The Lord gives me to drink of His love, as out of a river. All things work together for my good. May every one that is godly praise Him for this, and trust in His name for ever! (John Telford, ed., *Wesley's Veterans. Lives of Early Methodist Preachers Told by Themselves*, V [Salem: Schmul Publishers, 1976], 164)

While the initial conversion of Mr. Walsh was indeed glorious and his victorious walk with God such as made him rejoice much in the enjoyment of divine love; and though he had by his preaching been made an effective instrument in the conversion of many, he nevertheless expressed often a desire that God would perfect His work in him. After a number of years he received that for which he had long sought. The reader is asked to take particular notice of the place. In his diary he wrote of this occasion as follows:

> At the Lord's Table I had not only a clear witness that all was forgiven me, but likewise strong assurance that God had purified my heart by faith. My soul was deeply affected with His love. The blessed Jesus is present with

and precious to me. Oh let my soul adore the Lord, and tell of His works with gladness. Let this be written for the generations to come.

I love, rejoice, and give thanks. I can truly say that Thou, O Lord, art my God for ever and ever. ("ibid., 164")

So arduous were the labours of this godly man in the business and calling of his Master that he seems to have hastened his own death through a kind of exhaustion, having died in the twenty-eighth year of his age. Mr. Wesley writes in his *Journal*, June 17, 1758:

I met Thomas Walsh once more in Limerick, alive, and but just alive. Three of the best physicians in these parts have attended him, and all agree that it is a lost case; that by violent straining of his voice, added to frequent colds, he has contracted a pulmonary consumption, which is now in the last stage, and consequently beyond the reach of any human help. Oh what a man, to be snatched away in the strength of his years! Surely Thy judgments are a great deep! (John Wesley, *The Works of John Wesley*, II [Grand Rapids: Zondervan Publishing House, 1958], 451)

We do not find in Mr. Walsh's diary anything recorded concerning the state of his soul during the last few months before his death. "But from the accounts of persons of undoubted veracity, who attended him during that time, we learn that his state was not indeed joyous, but grievous." According to these witnesses "He drank of his Lord's cup of sorrow, and was, in truth, deeply baptized with His baptism. He was

immerged in affliction's furnace, and plunged in the deepest waters."
According to another who knew him well,

> He was tempted, and sorely buffeted of the devil.
> The nature of his disorder exposed him to a degree of
> precipitancy and discomposure, which he was more
> than superior to while in better health. In short, so did
> the wisdom of God permit, that through the malice of
> Satan, the extreme violence of the disorder of his body,
> and the concurrence of several other circumstances, this
> servant of God was brought to the utmost extremity of
> spiritual distress and anguish of soul, consistent with
> keeping the faith at all; insomuch that it was but few
> degrees removed from despair of salvation.
>
> His great soul lay thus, as it were, in ruins, for some
> considerable time; and poured out many a heavy groan,
> and speechless tear, from an oppressed heart and dying
> body. He sadly bewailed the absence of Him whose
> wonted presence had so often given him the victory
> over the manifold contradictions and troubles which
> he endured for His name's sake. The intervals which he
> had of cessation from the conflict, and of comparatively
> quiet confidence in God, are not perhaps so well
> known; but that he had such, may well be supposed;
> for otherwise his soul and flesh must needs have failed
> before God.
>
> It was, however, not until a short time before his
> complete and eternal deliverance that his Lord appeared
> to his help; and by making Himself known as Jesus, his
> well-known Saviour, entirely eased the anguish of his

oppressed soul. The beams of His brightness dispersed the clouds; and the smiles of His countenance more than compensated for all his night of sorrow. He spoke, and said unto him, 'The winter is past; arise, my love, and come away!'

The manner of his deliverance was as follows: A few friends being at prayer with him, on Sunday evening, as soon as they concluded, he desired to be left alone, in order, as he said, "to meditate a little." They withdrew; and he remained deeply recollected for some time: just then, God dropping into his soul, no doubt, some lively foretaste of the joys to come, and spreading the day of eternity through the regions of his inward man, he at length burst out in transport, and pronounced, in a dying voice indeed, but with joy of angels, "He is come! He is come! My Beloved is mine, and I am His! His for ever!" and, uttering these words, he sweetly breathed out his soul into the arms of his Beloved, on April 8, 1759, and in the twenty-eighth year of his age. (John Telford, ed., *Wesley's Veterans. Lives of Early Methodist Preachers Told by Themselves*, V [Salem: Schmul Publishers, 1976],188-190)

General George Charles Dykern:
Saved From Infidelity So As To Die Gloriously
(d. April, 1759)

From Mr. Wesley's *Journal,* dated April 13, 1759, we read a most amazing account of a thorough conversion and victorious death. Just how Mr. Wesley came into possession of it is not told us, for unlike the other accounts, this one is not about a conversion among the Methodists. We can only assume that the following was originally conveyed by the German clergyman who attended the wounded and dying army general. The reader is asked to observe closely the scriptural methods by which this clergyman led an infidel to a living faith in Christ.

After the battle of Bergen, in Germany, many who sustained wounds were brought into Frankfort-on-the-Maine. Among them was the –

> "Right Honourable George Charles Dykern, Baron, Lieutenant-General of the Saxon troops, in the service of the King of France. He was born of an ancient and noble family in Silesia, on April 10, 1710, so that it was just on his birth-day he received his wound. He was of equal abilities as a Minister in the closet, and a General in the field. In his younger years he had gone through a

regular course of study in the University, and made great proficiency in Philosophy, especially in Mathematics. Afterwards he studied polemic divinity, till he reasoned himself into an infidel. During his illness he showed not the least desire of pious company or serious discourse, till the Surgeon let his *valet de chamber* know that he could not live long. The man then asked his master, whether he did not choose to be visited by a Clergyman. He answered with warmth, 'I shall not trouble those gentlemen: I know well myself what to believe and do.' His man, not discouraged, continued thus, 'My Lord, have you ever found me wanting in my duty all the time I have been in your service?' He answered, 'No.' 'Then,' replied he, 'I will not be wanting now. The Surgeons count you past hopes of recovery; but every one is afraid to tell you so. You stand upon the brink of eternity. Pray, Sir, order a Clergyman to be called.' He paused a little, but soon gave his hand to his servant, thanked him for his honesty, and ordered him to send for me [Dr. Fresenius, Senior of the Clergy at Frankfort]."

From this point in the account, the clergyman himself shares in detail the manner in which he dealt with this dying General whose spiritual condition was exceedingly desperate. The reader is asked to take particular notice of the pointed and most personal questions fearlessly asked by this clergyman. Time was not wasted as he, like an experienced and knowledgeable physician and surgeon, probed the very depths of his patient's heart, ultimately showing him a true and accurate diagnosis of his spiritual dilemma.

"When I came, the man told me plainly, the General

was a professed infidel. I went in, and, after a short compliment, said, 'I am told my Lord, your life is near an end; therefore I presume, without any ceremony, to ask you one plain question: Is the state of your soul such, that you can entertain a solid hope of salvation?' He answered, 'Yes.' 'On what do you ground this hope?' He replied, 'I never committed any willful sin. I have been liable to frailties; but I trust in God's mercy, and the merits of his Son, that he will have mercy upon me.' These words he uttered very slowly, especially, 'the merits of his Son.' I made the following reply: 'I am apt to believe you are not tainted with the grossest vices; but I fear you a little too presumptuously boast of never having committed willful sin. If you would be saved, you must acknowledge your being utterly corrupted by sin, and consequently deserving the curse of God and eternal damnation. As for your hoping for God's mercy, *through the merits of his Son*, I beg leave to ask, Do you believe God has a Son; that, in the execution of his office, he was humbled unto death, even the death of the cross; and that hereby he has given an ample satisfaction for us, and recovered our title to heaven?' He answered, 'I cannot now avoid a more minute description of the true state of my soul. Let me tell you, Doctor, I have some knowledge of philosophy, by which I have chosen for myself a way of salvation. I have always endeavoured to live a sober life to the uttermost of my power, not doubting but the Being of all beings would then graciously accept me. In this way I stood in no need of Christ, and therefore did not believe on him. But if I take the Scriptures to be a divine revelation, this way of mine, I perceive, is not the right one; I must believe in Christ, and through him come to God.' I replied, 'You say, if you take the Scriptures to be a divine revelation!' He fetched a deep sigh, and said, 'O God, thou wilt make me say, Because I take the Scriptures to be thy word.' I said, 'There are grounds and reasons enough to demonstrate the divine origin of Christianity, as I could show from its most essential principles, were not the period of your life so short; but we need not now that diffusive method, faith being the gift of God. A poor sinner, tottering on the brink of eternity, has not time to inquire about grounds and reasons: Rather betake yourself to earnest prayer for faith, which if you do, I doubt not but God will give it you.'"

The manner in which this clergyman dealt with the General can be considered an excellent model of personal evangelism. After first determining the basis upon which the General's hopes of salvation first rested, this clergyman destroys his confidence in past morality and hope of salvation through his philosophical learning. He fearlessly shows him that he "must acknowledge" his "being utterly corrupted by sin, and consequently deserving of the curse of God and damnation." He follows this, however, by mercifully showing the dying man the true object of saving faith and his need of exercising earnest prayer for such faith. We cannot but admire this clergyman's application of a theology so truly orthodox and scripturally based. It is not only sound but effective, as the rest of the account proves. After pleading with the

General to "betake [himself] to earnest prayer for faith," the clergyman continues:

> "I had no sooner spoken these words, but pulling off his cap, and lifting up his eyes and hands, he cried out, 'O Almighty God, I am a poor cursed sinner, worthy of damnation; but, Lord Jesus eternal Son of God, thou diedst for my sins also. It is through thee alone I can be saved. O give me faith, and strengthen that faith!' Being extremely weak, he was obliged to stop here. A little after he asked, 'Is faith enough for salvation?' 'Yes, Sir,' said I, 'if it be living faith.' 'Methinks,' said he, 'it is so already; and it will be more so by and by: Let us pray for it.' Perceiving he was very weak, to give him some rest I retired into the next room, but he soon sent to call me. I found him praying, and Jesus was all he prayed for. I reminded him of some scriptures, treating of faith in Christ, and he was much delighted with them. Indeed, he was quite swallowed up by the grace of Jesus, and would hear of nothing but 'Jesus Christ, and him crucified.' He cried out, 'I do not know how it is with me. I never in my life felt such a change. I have power to love Jesus, and to believe in him whom I so long rejected. O my Jesus, how merciful art thou to me!'"

Thus we see the General's prayers beginning to be answered. He feels a change he never in his life experienced before. He has power to love Jesus and believe in Him. Truly, 'Old things [had now] passed away and behold all things are become new." Mr. Wesley reminds us that "The faith that brings a soul to a state of salvation is a 'work of omnipotence.' It requires," says he, "no less power thus to quicken a dead soul, than to raise a body that lies in the grave. It is a new creation; and none can create a soul anew, but He who at first created the heavens and the earth" (John Wesley, *The Works of John Wesley*, VIII [Grand Rapids: Zondervan Publishing House, 1958], 5).

The faithful clergyman continues his account:

"About noon I stepped home; but he sent for me directly, so that I could scarce eat my dinner. We were both filled with joy, as partakers of the same grace which is in Jesus Christ; and that in such a manner as if we had been acquainted together for many years. Many Officers of the army came to see him continually, to all of whom he talked freely of Jesus, of the grace of the Father in him, and of the power of the Holy Ghost through him, wondering without ceasing at his having found Jesus, and at the happy change by which all things on this side eternity were become indifferent to him.

"In the afternoon he desired to partake of the Lord's Supper, which he received with a melting, praising, rejoicing heart. All the rest of the day he continued in the same state of soul. Toward evening he desired, that if his end should approach, I would come to him, which I promised; but he did not send for me till the next morning. I was told by his valet, that he slept well for some hours, and then, awaking, prayed for a considerable time, continually mentioning the name of our Lord, and his precious blood; and that he had desired several of the Officers to make his conversion known to his Court (That of the King of Poland.)

After some discourse, I asked, 'Has your view of Christ and his redemption been neither altered nor obscured since yesterday?' He answered, 'Neither altered, nor obscured. I have no doubt, not even a remote one. It is just the same with me, as if I had always thus believed and never doubted: So gracious is the Lord Jesus to me a sinner.'

"This second day he was unwearied in prayer and exercises of faith. Toward evening he sent for me in haste. When I came, I found him dying, and in a kind of delirium; so I could do no more than give him now and then a word of comfort. I prayed afterwards for him and those that were present, some of whom were of high birth and rank. I then, by imposition of hands as usual, gave him a blessing; which being done, he expired immediately. A Royal Prince who was there (Prince Xavier, of Saxony) could not forbear weeping. The rest of the Officers bewailed the loss of their General, yet praised God for having shown such mercy toward him.

"I wrote an account of it without delay to his mother, and had an immediate answer. She was a lady of seventy-two, of exemplary piety. She praised God for his mercy; adding, that He had now answered the prayers which she had never ceased to offer on his behalf for eleven years." (John Wesley, *The Works of John Wesley*, II [Grand Rapids: Zondervan Publishing House, 1958], 473-476)

In his "Plain Account of Christian Perfection," Mr. Wesley writes concerning the absolute necessity of prayer if salvation is ever attained. "God," says he, "does nothing [towards the salvation of any soul] but in answer to prayer; and even they who have been converted to God, without praying for it themselves (which is exceeding rare), were not without the prayers of others. Every new victory which a soul gains is the effect of a new prayer" (John Wesley, *The Works of John Wesley*, XI [Grand Rapids: Zondervan Publishing House, 1958], 437).

In the account shared above we can see this truth well illustrated. God first answered the prayers of the General's mother, those of the clergyman and finally the prayers of the General for himself.

Mr. Mason:

In His Last Illness, "God Broke In Upon His Soul"
(d. February, 1760)

"After preaching in Deptford," writes Mr. Wesley in his *Journal,* "I rode on to Welling, where I received (what few expected) an exceeding comfortable account of the death of Mr. Mason of Bexley." There was reason enough to be surprised at the "comfortable account" of Mr. Mason's death. In Mr. Wesley's own words this man "For many years ... seemed to be utterly senseless; neither justified, nor even convinced of sin. But in his last sickness, the God that heareth prayer broke in upon his soul: And," continues Mr. Wesley, "the nearer death came, the more did he rejoice, to the astonishment of all that saw him" (John Wesley, *The Works of John Wesley,* II [Grand Rapids: Zondervan Publishing House, 1958], 523).

In another part of his *Journal,* Mr. Wesley writes: "How long shall we forget that God can raise the [spiritually] dead? Were not we dead till he quickened us?" (John Wesley, *The Works of John Wesley,* III [Grand Rapids: Zondervan Publishing House, 1958], 55).

The Wife Of Joseph Fry:
"Fine Sport, My Dear Joe! The Devil Is Cast."
(d. July, 1760)

How often are believers found in a final battle with the enemy of their souls while approaching death's door? It is not as unusual as some might think for witnesses to find a friend or loved one struggling in a deplorable state of doubt and fear in their final hour. What is one to do if he or she should happen to be a witness of such a desperate scene? There is no better answer to this question than that found demonstrated in that which we read below.

Mr. Wesley informs his readers that he "received from Joseph Fry, a particular account of his late wife," who was said to be "an Israelite indeed." Mr. Fry describes his wife and her final struggle as follows:

> "She was a strict attendant on all the means of grace, and a sincere lover of the people of God. She had a remarkably good understanding, and much knowledge of the things of God. Though she was of an exceeding bashful temper, yet she was valiant for the truth; not sparing to speak very plain in defence of it, before persons of all conditions. Two years ago she began to

lose her health, and grew worse and worse, till September 29th. On that day she was very restless. Observing her to have an unusual colour, I judged she could not continue long. She was sensible of it, and said, 'Do not go from me; for my time is short. O it is an hard thing to die!' After a while, she said, 'Dear Jesus, shall it be so with me as with the wicked?' I was deeply affected at seeing her in such a state; yet something told me, 'All will be well.' I exhorted her, with all my might, to lean on Jesus; and found myself unusually blessed in so doing; but still she did not seem to receive it, till I observed her jaw was fallen. I was then concerned more than ever, lest she should die without hope. I spoke with more vehemence, while she lay speechless, with her eyes up to heaven; but on a sudden, she got her lips together again, and said, with a loud voice, 'Now, my love, I experience what you have said. After all, my Jesus is mine. The devil is conquered; there, there you may see him going with shame.' She then praised God so loud, that one might hear her in the street; and added, 'Fine sport, my dear Joe! The devil is cast.' After rejoicing in God some time, she closed her eyes; but in a little while she said, 'O was it not very pretty when the wise virgins went out in white to meet their Lord? Yet what would their robes have signified, without his righteousness?' and died." (John Wesley, *Works of John Wesley*, III [Grand Rapids: Zondervan Publishing House, 1958], 371-372)

Miss E----:
Wrestles With God For The New Birth And Dies With Joy
(d. December, 1760)

In December of 1760, Mr. Wesley wrote, that it was "About the close of this year, I received a remarkable account from Ireland." We are not told the full name of this young lady but her story below does give us some indication of Methodist success in Ireland, notwithstanding the persecution they sorely suffered there.

As a fifteen year old girl Miss E-- often "heard the preaching of the Methodists, so called." Although those occasions did not seem to make a "deep impression" on her, it is said that "she retained a love for them ever after."

At the age of nineteen "she was seized with a lingering illness." Realizing her need to ready her soul for eternity, "she began to wrestle with God in prayer, that his love might be shed abroad in her heart. 'Then,' said she, 'how freely could I give up all that is dear to me in this world!' And from this very time she did not expect, nor indeed desire, to recover; but only to be cleansed from sin, and to go to Christ."

There were those who while visiting her, endeavored to convince her that she "need not fear" that her "innocence would bring her to heaven." But her earnest reply was that "Unless the merits of Christ plead for me,

153

and his nature be imparted to me, I can never enter there." She was ceaselessly "breaking out into these and the like expressions, 'O that I knew my sins were forgiven! O that I was born again! My one wish is, to know God, and be with him eternally.'

"She frequently sung or repeated that verse,

O that he would himself impart,
And fix his Eden in my heart,--
The sense of sin forgiven!
How would I then throw off my load,
And walk delightfully with God,
And follow Christ to heaven!

"She had an earnest desire to see some of the Methodists, and spoke to several, to ask some of those in Tullamore to visit her. At length her importunity prevailed, and James Kelly was sent for." Mr. Kelly continues the account below. When he appeared at her bedside, she said,

"'I am exceeding glad to see you. I have had a longing desire of it this month past. I believe the power of God is with you. If I had health and strength, there should not be a sermon preached, or a prayer put up, in your preaching house, but I would be there.'

"I told her, 'I hope the Spirit of the Lord will be your present and eternal Comforter.' She answered, 'I can find no comfort in any thing but in God alone.' While she spoke, her soul was melted down. The love of God was shed abroad in her heart, the tears ran down her cheeks, and she began to rejoice in God exceedingly. Her mother, seeing this, was fully convinced that there was more in religion than she had herself experienced;

and began to pray, with many tears, that God would show her his salvation. This so affected me, that I could not refrain from tears myself; so we all wept, and prayed, and sang praise together.

"On my going to her a second time, I found her truly alive to God. 'O,' she said, 'how I have longed to see you, that we may be happy in God together! Come let us sing an hymn.' I gave out,

> Of him that did salvation bring,
> I could for ever think and sing.

She sung all the time with exceeding joy. Afterwards she said, 'This is a weary world; but I have almost done with it. O how I long to be gone! Some people tell me I may recover; but I do not thank them; I do not count them my friends.' On my saying occasionally, 'There is no satisfaction for sin, but that which Christ has made by his precious blood;' she answered, 'That is all the satisfaction I want; and I believe he both lived and died for me.'

"After this, she gave a strict charge that none should be admitted to see her but such as could speak for God; saying, 'I do not love to have a word spoken, which is not to edification. O how unsuitable to me, are all things which do not tend to the glory of my God!' On her spitting a large quantity of blood, one said, 'You are in great pain.' She answered, 'I think little of it. My blessed Redeemer suffered greater pain for me.'

"When I stood up to go away, she said, 'I now take my leave of you. Perhaps we may not meet again in this world; but I trust we shall meet in heaven. I am going to God. O may it be soon! I now feel an heaven in my soul.'

"The last time I came was on Sunday, December 14. Hearing she was extremely ill and wanted rest, we did not go up, but after a while began singing below. She immediately heard, sat up in bed, and insisted on our being brought into the room and singing there. Many times she repeated these words, 'Come, Lord Jesus, come quickly!' And this she continued to do till, on Wednesday, 17, she resigned her soul into the hands of her dear Redeemer." (John Wesley, *The Works of John Wesley*, III [Grand Rapids: Zondervan Publishing House, 1958], 31-33)

Patrick Ward:

*A Condemned Prisoner Faces Death, First With Doubts
And Finally With Assurance*
(d. November, 1761)

From his early days at Oxford and participation in the Holy Club
with its various works of mercy, Mr. Wesley often visited those in
prison. In several instances, he saw those who were facing the death
sentence radically changed in heart and made ready for their departure
to a better world. Mr. Wesley shares below just one such account.

> I was desired by the condemned prisoners to give them
> one sermon more. And on *Thursday*, Patrick Ward,
> who was to die on that day, sent to request I would
> administer the sacrament to him. He was one-and-
> twenty years of age, and had scarce ever had a serious
> thought, till he shot the man who went to take away his
> gun. From that instant he felt a turn within, and never
> swore an oath more. His whole behaviour in prison
> was serious and composed: He read, prayed, and wept
> much; especially after one of his fellow prisoners had
> found peace with God. His hope gradually increased
> till this day, and was much strengthened at the Lord's

Supper; but still he complained, "I am not afraid, but I am not desirous, to die. I do not find that warmth in my heart. I am not sure my sins are forgiven." He went into the cart, about twelve, in calmness, but mixed with sadness. But in a quarter of an hour, while he was wrestling with God in prayer, (not seeming to know that any one was near him,) "The Holy Ghost," said he, "came upon me, and I knew that Christ was mine." From that moment his whole deportment breathed a peace and joy beyond all utterance, till, after having spent about ten minutes in private prayer, he gave the sign. (John Wesley, *The Works of John Wesley*, III [Grand Rapids: Zondervan Publishing House, 1958], 74)

It is worthy of our notice that this young man was not willing to assume himself fully ready for death without an inward assurance that Christ was his. This was attained only after a time of wrestling with God in prayer. How beautiful is his eventual testimony! Would to God, all who claim to have been born again could say, "The Holy Ghost came upon me, and I knew that Christ was mine."

Thomas Salmon:
"Cheerfully Went To God."
(d. February, 1762)

"**I** buried the remains of Thomas Salmon," writes Mr. Wesley "a good and useful man. What was peculiar in his experience was, he did not know when he was justified; but he did know when he was renewed in love, that work being wrought in a most distinct manner. After this he continued about a year in constant love, joy, and peace; then, after an illness of a few days, he cheerfully went to God" (John Wesley, *The Works of John Wesley*, III [Grand Rapids: Zondervan Publishing House, 1958], 80-81).

Because Mr. Salmon "did not know when he was justified," we must not suppose that he was without the experience of justification prior to being "renewed in love."

Mr. Wesley is found using various terminology when referring to a second work of God in the human heart. Being "renewed in love" is but one of them. "Christian perfection" or the being "perfected in love" were other ways he was known to refer to what is most often spoken of as "sanctification" in our day. Concerning the use of this term Mr. Wesley offers the following counsel:

He shows that the "term sanctified, is continually applied by St. Paul, to all that were justified. That by this term alone, he rarely, if ever, means, 'saved from all sin.' For this reason, "it is not proper to use it in that sense, without adding the word *wholly, entirely,* or the like" (John Wesley, *The Works of John Wesley,* XI [Grand Rapids: Zondervan Publishing House, 1958], 388).

Mary Ramsey:
"A True Daughter Of Affliction" Dies Well
(d. March, 1762)

"I buried the remains of Mary Ramsey," writes Mr. Wesley, "a true daughter of affliction, worn out by a cancer in her breast, with a variety of other diseases. To these was added, for a time, great darkness of mind; the body pressing down the soul. Yet she did not murmur or repine, much less charge God foolishly. It was not long before he restored the light of his countenance; and shortly after she fell asleep" (John Wesley, *The Works of John Wesley*, III [Grand Rapids: Zondervan Publishing House, 1958], 81).

Mr. Wesley often makes mention of intensive pain and discomfort of the physical frame causing "great darkness [or depression] of mind; the body," as he explains it, "pressing down the soul." Happy is the soul that through prayer and faith ultimately surmounts such physical sufferings without murmuring, repining or charging God foolishly and thus finds Jesus truly near after all. To have the light of God's countenance revealed through all of one's sufferings makes the ultimate difference.

Mr. Grimshaw:
A Faithful Anglican Clergyman, Followed To His Grave By The Tears Of His Parishioners
(d. April, 1762)

Mr. Grimshaw was an Anglican clergyman who, after an evangelical conversion, became a friend to the Wesleys and the Methodist cause. Mr. Wesley shares below, not only the account of his approach to death, but a summary also of his life, including years of useful ministry. Truly, this faithful shepherd of souls can be looked upon as a pattern for all who are engaged in pastoral ministry. The reader is asked to take particular notice of the Lord's dealings with him, including various awakenings and the unexpected answer to his prayers for inward peace and joy.

It was at this time that Mr. Grimshaw fell asleep. He was born September 3. 1708, at Brindle, six miles south of Preston, in Lancashire, and educated at the schools of Blackburn and Heskin, in the same county. Even then the thoughts of death and judgment made some impression upon him. At eighteen he was admitted at Christ's College, in Cambridge. Here bad example so carried him away, that for more than two years he seemed utterly to have lost all sense of seriousness; which did not revive till the day he was ordained Deacon, in the year 1731. On that day he was much affected with the sense of the importance of the ministerial office; and this was increased by his conversing with some at Rochdale, who met once a week to read, and sing, and pray. But on his removal to Todmorden soon after, he quite dropped his pious acquaintance, conformed to the world, followed all its diversions, and contented himself with "doing his duty," on Sundays.

But about the year 1734, he began to think seriously again. He left off all diversions; he began to catechize the young people, to preach the absolute necessity of a devout life, and to visit his people, not in order to be merry with them, as before, but to press them to seek the salvation of their souls.

At this period also he began himself to pray in secret four times a day; and the God of all grace, who prepared his heart to pray, soon gave the answer to his prayer; not, indeed, as he expected: Not in joy or peace; but by bringing upon him very strong and painful convictions of his own guilt, and helplessness, and misery; by discovering to him what he did not suspect before, that his heart was deceitful and desperately wicked; and, what was more afflicting still, that all his duties and labours could not procure him pardon, or gain him a title to eternal life. In this trouble he continued more than three years, not acquainting any one with the distress he suffered, till one day, (in 1742,)

being in the utmost agony of mind, there was clearly
represented to him, Jesus Christ pleading for him with
God the Father, and gaining a free pardon for him. In
that moment all his fears vanished away, and he was
filled with joy unspeakable. "I was now," says he,
"willing to renounce myself, and to embrace Christ for
my all and all. O what light and comfort did I enjoy
in my own soul, and what a taste of the pardoning love
of God!"

All this time he was an entire stranger to the people
called Methodists, whom afterwards he thought it his
duty to countenance, and to labour with them in his
neighbourhood. He was an entire stranger also to all
their writings, till he came to Haworth, May 26, of
this year. And the good effects of his preaching soon
became visible: Many of his flock were brought into
deep concern for salvation, were in a little time after
filled with peace and joy through believing; and (as in
ancient times) the whole congregation have been often
seen in tears on account of their provocations against
God, and under a sense of his goodness in yet sparing
them.

His lively manner of representing the truths of God
could not fail of being much talked of, and bringing
many hundreds out of curiosity to Haworth church;
who received so much benefit by what they heard, that,
when the novelty was long over, the church continued
to be full of people, many of whom came from far, and
this for twenty years together.

Mr. Grimshaw was now too happy himself, in

the knowledge of Christ, to rest satisfied without taking every method he thought likely to spread the knowledge of his God and Saviour. And as the very indigent constantly made their want of better clothes to appear in, an excuse for not going to church in the day-time, he contrived, for them chiefly, a lecture on Sunday evenings; though he had preached twice in the day before. God was pleased to give great success to these attempts, which animated him still more to spend and be spent for Christ. So the next year he began a method, which was continued by him for ever after, of preaching in each of the four hamlets he had under his care three times every month. By this means the old and infirm, who could not attend the church, had the truth of God brought to their houses; and many, who were so profane as to make the distance from the house of God a reason for scarce ever coming to it, were allured to hear. By this time the great labour with which he instructed his own people, the holiness of his conversation, and the benefit which very many from the neighbouring parishes had obtained by attending his ministry, concurred to bring upon him many earnest entreaties to come to their houses, who lived in neighbouring parishes, and expound the word of God to souls as ignorant as they had been themselves. This request he did not dare to refuse: So that while he provided abundantly for his own flock, he annually found opportunity of preaching near three hundred times to congregations in other parts.

And for a course of fifteen years, or upwards,

he used to preach every week, fifteen, twenty, and
sometimes thirty times, beside visiting the sick, and
other occasional duties of his function. It is not easy
to ascribe such unwearied diligence, chiefly among
the poor, to any motive but the real one. He thought
he would never keep silence, while he could speak
to the honour of that God who had done so much
for his soul. And while he saw sinners perishing for
lack of knowledge, and no one breaking to them the
bread of life, he was constrained, notwithstanding the
reluctance he felt within, to give up his name to still
greater reproach, as well as all his time and strength, to
the work of the ministry.

During this intense application to what was the
delight of his heart, God was exceeding favourable to
him. In sixteen years he was only once suspended from
his labour by sickness; though he dared all weathers,
upon the bleak mountains, and used his body with less
compassion than a merciful man would use his beast.
His soul at various times enjoyed large manifestations
of God's love; and he drank deep into his Spirit. His
cup ran over; and at some seasons his faith was so
strong, and his hope so abundant, that higher degrees
of spiritual delight would have overpowered his mortal
frame.

In this manner Mr. Grimshaw employed all his
powers and talents, even to his last illness; and his
labours were not in vain in the Lord. He saw an
effectual change take place in many of his flock; and a
restraint from the commission of sin brought upon the

parish in general. He saw the name of Jesus exalted, and many souls happy in the knowledge of him, and walking as became the Gospel. Happy he was himself, in being kept by the power of God, unblamable in his conversation; Happy in being beloved, in several of the last years of his life, by every one in his parish; who, whether they would be persuaded by him to forsake the evil of their ways, or no, had no doubt that Mr. Grimshaw was their cordial friend. Hence, at his departure a general concern was visible through his parish. Hence his body was interred with what is more ennobling than all the pomp of a royal funeral: For he was followed to the grave by a great multitude, with affectionate sighs, and many tears; who cannot still hear his much-loved name, without weeping for the guide of their souls, to whom each of them was dear as children to their father.

His behaviour, throughout his last sickness, was of a piece with the last twenty years of his life: From the very first attack of his fever, he welcomed its approach. His intimate knowledge of Christ abolished all the reluctance nature feels to a dissolution; and, triumphing in Him, who is the resurrection and the life, he departed, April the 7th, in the fifty-fifth year of his age, and the twenty-first of his eminent usefulness. (John Wesley, *The Works of John Wesley*, III [Grand Rapids: Zondervan Publishing House, 1958], 83-86)

Thomas Jones:
His Fears Of Death Were Scattered.
(d. July, 1762)

The founder of Methodism was known to practice medicine after a fashion. To him it was a necessary expediency, seeing that many of the poor all around him could not afford to pay for the help of professional physicians. So it was that he personally studied and received instruction from various ones in the profession. He then allotted time for the receiving of patients, giving them both counsel and various medications of a primitive nature. We read below of an occasion, however, in which his medical counsel was not appreciated by the physicians attending a Mr. Jones who along with many others at the time were suffering from an "epidemic disorder."

> On Monday and Tuesday the congregation at the House was far larger than on any week-day before. And there was much life among the people, which perhaps was increased by the epidemic disorder. This generally attacked first the head; afterward the throat and the breast. Mr. Jones, who had been drooping for some time, was seized with this three weeks since.

While I was at Youghall, he sent for a Physician, who applied a blister to his head. In two or three days a second Physician was called in; who told his relations he was better and better. Returning from Bandon, and observing what was prescribed, I could not help saying, 'When a fever neither intermits, nor remits, the bark is no better than poison.' At hearing this, the Doctors were much displeased, and declared again he was a great deal better. On Wednesday morning, a little before two, his spirit returned to God.

So died honest Thomas Jones, *secundum artem*! A man whom God raised from nothing, by a blessing on his unwearied diligence, to a plentiful fortune. Yet when riches increased on every side, he did not set his heart upon them. Some years since he retired from business, but was still full employed in building and in doing good. His natural temper was rough, and so was his speech, which occasioned him many trials. But notwithstanding this, he was generous and compassionate, and never weary of well-doing. From the beginning of his illness he was continually in prayer; for some time with much fear and distress. But I saw no signs of this after I came from Bandon: I believe his fears were then all scattered; and he waited with calm, though earnest, desire for the salvation of God. (John Wesley, *The Works of John Wesley*, III [Grand Rapids: Zondervan Publishing House, 1958], 98)

It is observed that many face death with "much fear and distress." Some will say this is only natural and a part of being human. However, we are assured in God's word that such fear—the fear of death and judgment may be altogether dispelled. 1 John 4:18 tells us that "perfect love casteth out fear [that fear that hath torment]." One may notice that deliverance from such fear was achieved by "continual prayer" in the case of Thomas Jones.

Ann Steed:

Voices Praise With Her Dying Breath
(d. October, 1762)

By the time the Wesleyan revival had continued in its expansion for a couple decades, there appeared a noticeable increase in the number of converts giving testimony to the experience of entire sanctification. In his *Journal*, Mr. Wesley takes particular notice of this fact. He writes that they were hearing of "persons [entirely] sanctified in London, and most other parts of England, and in Dublin, and many other parts of Ireland, as frequently as of persons justified; although instances of the latter were far more frequent than they had been for twenty years before."

In this same *Journal* entry, he admits that "many of these did not retain the gift of God." To him, however, this was "no proof that it was not [once] given them. That many retain it to this day is matter of praise and thanksgiving. And many of them," he continues, "are gone to Him whom they loved, praising him with their latest breath." As an example of these he mentions the name of Ann Steed whom he says was "the first witness in Bristol of the great salvation."

This saintly woman was, as he says, "worn out with sickness and pain." As she approached that final moment, however, she "commended to God all that were around her, lifted her eyes, cried aloud, 'Glory! Hallelujah!' and died" (John Wesley, *The Works of John Wesley*, III [Grand Rapids: Zondervan Publishing House, 1958],116).

Joseph Norbury:
"On The Wing For Paradise"
(d. November 1763)

I visited," writes Mr. Wesley in his *Journal*, "Joseph Norbury, a good old soldier of Jesus Christ. I found him just on the wing for paradise, having rattled in the throat for some time. But his speech was restored when I came in, and he mightily praised God for all his mercies. This was his last testimony for a good Master. Soon after he fell asleep" (John Wesley, *The Works of John Wesley*, III [Grand Rapids: Zondervan Publishing House, 1958], 156).

How precious it is to hear from the dying lips of one who is praising "God for all his mercies." Who would not wish to leave their final "testimony for a good Master" and be thus a blessing to others in the hour of death as well as in life?

Several days later, Mr. Wesley writes: "I buried the remains of Joseph Norbury, a faithful witness of Jesus Christ. For about three years he has humbly and boldly testified, that God had saved him from all sin: And his whole spirit and behaviour in life and death made his testimony beyond exception" ("ibid., 157").

Whenever Mr. Wesley mentions being "saved from all sin," he is referring to the experience of entire sanctification or Christian perfection. On one occasion, he described this experience as follows:

"Many persons ... have experienced so deep and universal a change, as it had not before entered into their hearts to conceive. After a deep conviction of inbred sin, of their total fall from God, they have been so filled with faith and love, (and generally in a moment,) that sin vanished, and they found from that time, no pride, anger, desire, or unbelief. They could rejoice evermore, pray without ceasing, and in everything give thanks" ("ibid., 156").

William Hurd:
"His End Was Peace"
(d. February, 1764)

"**I** buried the remains of William Hurd," writes Mr. Wesley, "a son of affliction for many years continually struggling with inward and outward trials. But his end was peace" (John Wesley, *The Works of John Wesley*, III [Grand Rapids: Zondervan Publishing House, 1958], 159).

In his sermon "On the Death of Mr. Fletcher," Mr. Wesley explains the meaning of that peace referred to above.

> I do not conceive this immediately to refer to that glorious peace which is prepared for him in the presence of God to all eternity; but rather to that which he will enjoy in the present world, before his spirit returns to God that gave it. Neither does it seem directly to refer to outward peace, or deliverance from outward trouble; although it is true, many good men, who had been long buffeted by adversity, and troubled on every side, have experienced an entire deliverance from it, and enjoyed a remarkable calm before they went hence. But this seems chiefly to refer to inward peace; even that "peace of God which passeth all understanding."

Therefore it is no wonder that it cannot be fully and adequately expressed in human language. We can only say, it is an unspeakable calmness and serenity of spirit, a tranquility in the blood of Christ, which keeps the souls of believers, in their latest hour, even as a garrison keeps a city; which keeps not only their hearts, all their passions and affections, but also their minds, all the motions of their understanding and imagination, and all the workings of their reason, in Christ Jesus. This peace they experienced in a higher or lower degree, (suppose they continued in the faith,) from the time they first found redemption in the blood of Jesus, even the forgiveness of sins. But when they have nearly finished their course, it generally flows as a river, even in such a degree as it had not before entered into their hearts to conceive. A remarkable instance of this, out of a thousand, occurred many years ago:--Enoch Williams, one of the first of our Preachers that was stationed at Cork, (who had received this peace when he was eleven years old, and never lost it for an hour,) after he had rejoiced in God with joy unspeakable, during the whole course of his illness, was too much exhausted to speak many words, but just said, "Peace! peace!" and died. (John Wesley, *The Works of John Wesley*, VII [Grand Rapids: Zondervan Publishing House, 1958], 433)

George Nixon:
Frustrated In His Desire To Die
(d. June, 1765)

In his *Journal*, dated June 16, 1765, Mr. Wesley writes of having received a letter from Prudence Nixon in which she related the strange account of her husband who had died a short time before.

> In November last, on a Sunday evening, he was uncommonly fervent in prayer, and found such a desire as he never had before, "to depart, and to be with Christ." In the night she awaked, and found him quite stiff, and without either sense or motion. Supposing him to be either dying or dead, she broke out into a vehement agony of prayer, and cried for half an hour together, "Lord Jesus! give me George! Take him not away." Soon after he opened his eyes, and said earnestly, "You had better have let me go." Presently he was raving mad, and began to curse and blaspheme in the most horrid manner. This he continued to do for several days, appearing to be under the full power of an unclean spirit. At the latter end of the week she

cried out, "Lord, I am willing! I am willing he should go to thee." Quickly his understanding returned, and he again rejoiced with joy unspeakable. He tenderly thanked her for giving him up to God, kissed her, lay down and died. (John Wesley, *The Works of John Wesley,* III [Grand Rapids: Zondervan Publishing House, 1958], 225)

Many questions arise in response to such a story. How can we account for this husband's turning to madness upon his return and especially in answer to his wife's prayers? How can we account for his turning to cursing and blaspheming or his "appearing to be under the full power of an unclean spirit" following prayer for his return? That God in His wise Providence takes His children to Himself in a day of His own choosing is fairly well understood. Can we suppose that the account above might illustrate the possibility of frustrating God's plan and timing so as to cause adverse results? Mr. Wesley himself leaves us without attempting to provide answers. This may mean that he was just as baffled as we.

Henry Perronet:
"Cheerfully Gave up His Spirit to God"
(d. December 1765)

We are reminded by the Apostle John *that "There is no fear in love: but perfect love casteth out fear; because fear hath torment. He that feareth is not made perfect in love"* (1 John 4:18). What a blessing it is to be delivered from the fear of death and the coming Judgment. We find that such deliverance was given to the dying man described in the account below as a result of his earnest and importunate praying.

"I buried," writes Mr. Wesley, "the remains of Henry Perronet, who had been a child of sorrow from his infancy. But from the time he was taken ill, his mind was more and more composed. The day and night before his death, he was praying continually; till, all fear being taken away, he cheerfully gave up his spirit to God" (John Wesley, *The Works of John Wesley*, III [Grand Rapids: Zondervan Publishing House, 1958], 239).

We see that spirit of cheerfulness was added to this deliverance from fear. Gracious is the Lord who gives an answer of peace and joy to those who truly seek Him.

·

Henry Jackson:
"Now My Soul Is Prepared."
(d. February, 1766)

On or near the date of February 23, 1766, Mr. Wesley was given a letter written by the daughter of a saintly man, who died strong in faith and with a beautiful testimony upon his lips. A full week's time had passed from the beginning of his illness till his soul's happy departure. During that week he proved to be a great blessing to his family and all who came to see him. Should it not be the wish of all who love God and the souls of mankind to be a blessing in death as well as in life? The daughter's account is shared in her own words as follows:

> "On Thursday, the 13th of this month, my honoured father looked so beautiful and comely that we all wondered. At night, in his first sleep, he was taken very ill. On Friday morning I asked him what he could take. He answered, 'I am to eat no more.' His illness increased; but he was still calm and composed, and resigned to the will of God. Indeed I always beheld in him such faith, love, and divine resignation as I never saw in any other. On Sunday he said, 'Now my soul is prepared, and made ready to meet the Lord.' From

this time he was filled with longing desires to depart and to be with Christ; crying out, 'I cannot stay: I must go to my Beloved, to be with him for ever.' Monday, 17. He said, 'I have fought a good fight; I have finished my course; I have kept the faith. Henceforth there is laid up for me a crown of glory, which the righteous Judge shall give me at that day.' Tuesday, 18. After receiving the blessed sacrament, he declared to the Minister, 'My anchor is cast within the veil, both sure and immovable.' And as long as he had his speech, he preached Christ to every one that came to see him. Indeed his whole life, for many years, was but one dedication of his body and soul to God; praying continually, and being lost in praise and thanksgiving to his adorable Saviour. In all the various dispensations of God's providence towards him and his family, he was still magnifying and praising his holy name; always thankful, humble, loving, and obedient. Nothing was able to move him one moment, or put him out of temper; but he received every thing from the hand of God, with faith, patience, and resignation. Before his speech failed, he blessed all his children, grandchildren, and great-grandchildren; and on Thursday morning, February 20, yielded up his soul to God, being ninety-nine years and five months old." (John Wesley, *The Works of John Wesley,* III [Grand Rapids: Zondervan Publishing House, 1958], 242-243)

What a beautiful way to finish one's passage here below! One is constrained in his heart to say, "Let me die the death of the righteous, and let my last end be like his" (Numbers 23:10).

Margaret Lewen:
Sees Jesus As She Departs This Life
(d. November, 1766)

In his old age, my grandfather (Forrest S. McPherson) was heard to say that when he died, his desire was that he might first see Jesus and then his mother. Having been witness to his saintly mother's death in 1894 when he was but a thirteen year old lad and she a young mother of thirty-six, he sorely felt this loss to the end of life. She was a pious Methodist who truly loved God and was heard to sing before she died, "I am dying to die no more." Grandfather, himself, passed away in the spring of 1971 assuring us that he would see us in heaven. O, what must it be like to land on heaven's shore and see Jesus together with saintly loved ones?

One who rendered an exciting and glorious testimony of seeing Jesus *immediately prior to death* is shared below by Mr. Wesley from his *Journal*.

At my return to London, I found it needful to hasten to Leytonstone; but I came too late. Miss Lewen died the day before, after an illness of five days. Some hours before, she witnessed that good confession,--

185

> Nature's last agony is o'er,
> And cruel sin subsists no more.

Awhile after, she cried out earnestly, "Do you not see him? There he is! Glory! glory! glory! I shall be with him for ever,--for ever,--for ever!" (John Wesley, *The Works of John Wesley*, III [Grand Rapids: Zondervan Publishing House, 1958], 268)

So died Margaret Lewen! A pattern to all young women of fortune in England: A real Bible Christian. So she "rests from her labours, and her works do follow her."

Immediately following this *Journal* account above, Mr. Wesley comments on a service held in the West-Street Chapel in London. It seems to have been an All Saints Day observance. Notice the significance placed upon the communion of saints both in heaven and here below.

Sat. November 1.—"God, who hath knit together his elect in one communion and fellowship," gave us a solemn season at West-Street (as usual) in praising him for all his Saints. On this day in particular, I commonly find the truth of these words:--

> The Church triumphant in his love,
> Their mighty joys we know;
> They praise the Lamb in hymns above,
> And we in hymns below.
> ("ibid., 268")

Miss Hatton:

"Grieve Not At My Happiness."
(d. January, 1767)

While shepherding his flock in the parish of Madeley, England, the saintly John Fletcher often took time to give counsel and comfort by written correspondence to those who sought it. One of those to whom he gave such assistance was a Miss Hatton. It is evident that at the time he was writing the letter shared below, she was suffering from an illness that was soon to take her life. Mr. Fletcher, in a masterful and most tender manner, points her to the scriptural way which insures victory and triumph in death.

> "My Dear Friend,--The dream of life will soon be over; the morning of eternity will soon succeed. Away then with all the shadows of time! Away from them to *the Eternal Substance—to Jesus, the First and the Last, by whom, and for whom, all things consist.* If you take Jesus to be your head, by the mystery of faith, you will be united to the resurrection and the life. The bitterness of death is past, my dear friend. *Only* look to Jesus. He died for you—died in your place—died

under the frowns of heaven, that we might die under its smiles. Regard neither unbelief nor doubt. Fear neither sin nor hell. Choose neither life nor death. All these are swallowed up in the immensity of Christ, and are triumphed over in His cross. Fight the good fight of faith. Hold fast your confidence in the atoning, sanctifying blood of the Lamb of God. Confer no more with flesh and blood. Go, meet the bridegroom. Behold He cometh! Trim your lamp. Quit yourself like a soldier of Jesus. I *entreat* you, as a companion in tribulation; I *charge* you, as a minister, go, at every breath you draw, to Him, who says, 'Him that cometh unto me, I will in no wise cast out;' and 'He that believeth in Me, though he were dead, yet shall he live.' Joyfully sing the believer's song. 'O death, where is thy sting? O grave, where is thy victory? Thanks be to God, who giveth us the victory, through our Lord Jesus Christ!' Let your surviving friends triumph over you, as one faithful unto death,--as one triumphing in death itself."

Three weeks beyond the writing of this letter, the young lady thus addressed had passed safely through the valley of death. In a letter written to Mr. Ireland, Fletcher describes her departure from this life as follows:

"Miss Hatton died full of serenity, faith, and love. The four last hours of her life were better than all her sickness. When the pangs of death were upon her, the comforts of the Almighty bore her triumphantly through, and some of her last words were: 'Grieve not at my happiness. This world is no more to me than a bit of burnt paper. Grace! Grace! A sinner saved! I wish I could tell you half of what I feel and see. I am going to keep an everlasting Sabbath. O death, where is thy sting? O grave, where is thy victory? Thanks be to God, who giveth me the victory, through my Lord Jesus Christ!' It is very remarkable that she had hardly any joy in her illness; but God made her ample amends in her extremity. He keeps His strongest cordial for the time of need. Blessed, for ever blessed, be His holy name!" (L. Tyerman, *Wesley's Designated Successor: The Life, Letters, and Literary Labours of the Rev. John William Fletcher* [Stoke-on-Trent: Tentmaker Publications, 2001], 136-137)

Mary Clarke:

Thoroughly Restored So As To Rejoice In Death
(d. January, 1767)

In a *Journal* entry, Mr. Wesley writes: "I buried, the remains of Mary Clarke, (formerly Gardiner,) who, having been much hurt in the late contests, was during a lingering illness, first thoroughly convinced of her fall from God, and afterward thoroughly restored. She then vehemently exhorted all not to stray from the fold; and died rejoicing in the full salvation of God" (John Wesley, *The Works of John Wesley*, III [Grand Rapids: Zondervan Publishing House, 1958], 270).

Mention of the "hurt" Mary received "in the late contests" seems to be a reference to the trouble caused by two men whose names were George Bell and Thomas Maxfield. Through erroneous teaching and fanaticism they caused divisiveness among members, leading some away from the fellowship and sound teaching within Methodist societies ("ibid., 242").

Her vehement exhortation to all not to stray from the fold seems to have come as a warning derived from her own personal experience. Nevertheless, God in His mercy seems to have used "a lingering illness" to bring her to a restoration of spiritual health. It is well that in her death she was able to rejoice "in the full salvation of God."

Richard Morris:
Unconvinced Of Sin Until Approach Of Death
(d. February, 1767)

"I buried the remains of Richard Morris," writes Mr. Wesley, "who had been in the society twenty years, and was a right honest man, but never convinced of sin till death began to look him in the face: And then he rather *saw* than *felt* his need of Christ. Yet when he called upon him, even in his dull way, he was soon assured of his love, and continued praising and rejoicing till his spirit returned to God" (John Wesley, *The Works of John Wesley*, III [Grand Rapids: Zondervan Publishing House, 1958], 272-273).

From his "A Plain Account of Christian Perfection," Mr. Wesley shows how being convinced of sin is a necessary part of finding redemption in the Savior's blood.

> "Indeed, how God may work, we cannot tell; but the general manner wherein He does work, is this: those who once trusted in themselves that they were righteous, that they were rich, and increased in goods, and had need of nothing, are, by the Spirit of God applying His word, convinced that they are poor and naked. All the

things that they have done are brought before them, so that they see the wrath of God hanging over their heads, and feel that they deserve the damnation of hell. In their trouble they cry unto the Lord, and He shows them that He hath taken away their sins, and opens the kingdom of Heaven in their hearts,--'righteousness, and peace, and joy in the Holy Ghost.' Sorrow and pain are fled away, and 'sin has no more dominion over' them. Knowing they are justified freely through faith in His blood, they 'have peace with God through Jesus Christ'; they 'rejoice in hope of the glory of God,' and 'the love of God is shed abroad in their hearts.'"

(John Wesley, *The Works of John Wesley*, XI [Grand Rapids: Zondervan Publishing House, 1958], 380-81)

Ellen Stanyers:
Found Her Balm In Gilead
(d. June 1767)

After publicly reading a passage from the prophet Esaias, Jesus gave notice to the residents of his home town the true nature of His mission in the following words: *"The Spirit of the Lord is upon me, because he hath anointed me to preach the gospel to the poor; he hath sent me to heal the brokenhearted, to preach deliverance to the captives, and recovering of sight to the blind, to set at liberty them that are bruised" (Luke 4:18).*

From his *Journal* Mr. Wesley shares an account of a young lady who, because of a most serious and mortal threat, became fully distracted with fear and terror. With help from the Methodists, however, she found that Jesus was able to heal her broken and distracted heart, provide deliverance from all her fears and set her bruised mind and soul at liberty with peace and joy. Her story is told as follows:

> It was about this time that a remarkable passage happened at Macclesfield, in Cheshire. One Ellen Stanyers, a young woman of that town, very religious in her own way, but quite a stranger to the Scripture-way of salvation, had her work from one of the shops in the town. A young man belonging to the same shop fell

in love with her. Fearing lest her refusing him would disoblige her master, she gave him encouragement, and afterwards, though she never intended it, promised to marry him. One day, as she was sitting at her work, this sin was brought to her remembrance, and lay so exceeding heavy upon her mind that she was utterly distressed. She took her work, and carried it to her master, telling him, she had destroyed her soul with it. At the same time she told the young man, she was resolved never to have him. He came to her and said, "If you do not keep your word, I will hang myself at your door; and then I will come and take you away with me to the devil." She was so frighted she fell into black despair. Her father carried her to a Clergyman, and afterwards to another, who seemed to pity her case, but knew not how to comfort her. Willing to try every way, he ordered one to read to her Burkitt upon the New Testament, till she cried, "Take it away; I cannot bear it!" and attempted to run away: But her father held her; and, when she struggled, beat her, and told her she should hear it, whether she would or no. She grew worse and worse; could neither eat, drink, nor sleep; and pined away to a mere skeleton. She wandered about, as one distracted, in the fields and lanes, seeking rest, but finding none. She was exceedingly tempted to destroy herself; but that thought came into her mind, "If I do, I shall leap into hell immediately. I must go thither; but I will keep out of it as long as I can." She was wandering about one day, when a person met her, and advised her to hear the Methodists. Although she hated them, yet she was willing to do anything for ease, and so one evening came to the preaching. After the service was over, she desired to speak to the Preacher, Mr. Pawson; but she talked quite wildly. However, he encouraged her to come to the Saviour of sinners, and cry to him for deliverance. "The next day" (so Mr. P. continues the account) "about twelve of us met together, and prayed with her. I found great freedom, and a full confidence that God would deliver her. After prayer, she said, 'I never felt my heart pray before. I felt my heart go along with the Preacher's words; they have done me good at my heart. My despair is all gone, I have a hope that I shall be saved.' The next morning two or three prayed with her again. She spent all the day with one or another of the Methodists, and did not go home till night. Her father then asked, 'Nelly, where have you been all this time?' She answered, 'I have been among the Methodists.' 'The Methodists!' said he, 'have you got any good there?' She replied, 'Yes, I bless God I have. I now hope I shall be saved.' 'Well,' said he, 'I care not where you go, if you only get relief.' She then went to bed, but could not sleep. While she was meditating on what she had heard, those words were brought to her mind, 'Is there no balm in Gilead? Is there no Physician there?' With the words of the Lord spoke peace to her soul; and in one and the same moment all pain and sorrow fled away, and she was entirely healed, both body and mind. Early in the morning she came to the house of one of our friends, and, clapping her hands together, cried out in an ecstasy of joy, 'O my Jesus, my Jesus, my Jesus! What is it that he has done for me? I feel he has forgiven all my sins.' Taking up an hymnbook, she opened it on those words:--

> I the chief of sinners am,
> But Jesus died for me!

She was quite transported, being overwhelmed with peace and joy unspeakable. At the same time she was restored to the full use of her reason, and in a little while was strong and healthy as ever. She immediately desired to be admitted into the society, and for about a year enjoyed unspeakable happiness. She then received a call from her Beloved, and died full of faith and love." (John Wesley, *The Works of John Wesley*, III [Grand Rapids: Zondervan Publishing House, 1958], 283-285)

Katherine Murray:
A Woman Who Prevailed In Both Life And Death
(d. July, 1767)

The case of Katherine Murray is very instructive. The reader follows the struggles and experiences of this young lady from her days of prejudice against the Methodists, conviction of sin, and darkness of soul to the day of her joyous conversion and ultimate cleansing from all sin. The reader is asked to take particular notice of the fact that she was never at rest without a continual consciousness of the Spirit's witness and of her Savior's smile and approbation shining upon her. If her case at times was found to be otherwise, she would cease not to wrestle with God in prayer until her joy returned. Last of all, the reader is asked to notice the marvelous experiences and testimonies of this woman as she entered into the valley of the shadow of death, culminating in a glorious and victorious departure.

> "Katherine Murray was born February 2, 1729, at Carrick-on-Suir. She feared God from a child, and abstained from lying and speaking bad words. When about thirteen, she stole some twigs of gooseberry-bushes from a neighbour, and planted them in her father's garden. Immediately she felt she had sinned,

knew she deserved hell, and feared it would be her portion. She began praying three times a day; but, notwithstanding, her sin followed her every where. Day and night it was before her, till after some time, that conviction gradually wore off.

"In the year 1749, her sister heard the Methodists, so called. She was soon convinced of sin, joined the society, and advised her to do so too. But hearing one named that was in it, she was filled with disdain: 'What! Meet with such a man as that!' Yet not long after, she was convinced that the sins of her own heart, pride and passion in particular, were as abominable in the sight of God, as the sins of that man or any other. This conviction was exceeding sharp. She could no longer despise any, but only cry out, day and night, 'God be merciful to me a sinner!'

"In February she went to hear Mr. Reeves. He preached on part of the hundred-and-third Psalm. She was now more deeply than ever convinced of heart-sin, of unbelief in particular; and had such a sight of the excellency of faith, that she determined to seek it with all her heart.

"In the May following, she was sitting in her room, lamenting her state, and crying to God for mercy, when suddenly she had a sight of our Lord, from the manger to the cross. But it did not bring comfort; on the contrary, it so heightened her distress, that she cried aloud, and alarmed the family; nor could she refrain till her strength failed, and she fainted away. Often her sleep departed from her; her food was tasteless, and she mingled her drink with weeping; being resolved never to rest, till she found rest in Him whom alone her soul desired.

"It was not long before the Lord looked upon her. As she was in prayer, she had a clear representation of our blessed Lord as crowned with thorns, clothed with the purple robe. In a moment her soul rested on him, and she knew he had taken away her sins. Distress was gone; the love of God flowed into her heart, and she could rejoice in God her Saviour. Her soul was so ravished with his love, that she could not hold her peace, but cried out to all she knew, 'You may know your sins forgiven, if you will come unto Jesus.'

"Yet a while after, she dressed herself as fine as ever she could, and went to worship God, as she expressed it, 'proud as a devil.' Upon the spot God convinced her of her folly, of her pride and vanity. She was stripped of all her comfort, yea, and brought to doubt the reality of all she had before experienced. The devil then laboured to persuade her that she had sinned the sin against the Holy Ghost; and pushed it so, that she thought her life would fail, and she should instantly drop into the pit. But the Lord did not leave her long in the snare; he appeared again, to the joy of her soul. Her confidence was more strong than ever, and the fear of God more deeply rooted in her heart. She abhorred all sin, that in particular which had occasioned her distress; of which, indeed, she had a peculiar detestation to her last hours.

"God now made her heart strong; she walked

seven years in the clear light of his countenance, never feeling a moment's doubt of his favour, but having the uninterrupted witness of his Spirit. It was her meat and drink to do his will: His word, read or preached, was her delight, and all his ways were pleasant to her. She said, she never came from a sermon unimproved; often so refreshed as to forget weariness or pain. And she was truly diligent 'in business,' as well as 'fervent in spirit.'

"And now she thought she should never be removed, God had made her hill so strong. But soon after this, she was present when her sister was ill-used by her husband. She gave way to the temptation, fell into a passion, and again lost all her happiness. Yet not long; she continued instant in prayer, till God again healed her backsliding.

"But from this time, as her temptations were more violent, so she had a keener sense of the remains of sin. Though she enjoyed a constant sense of the favour of God, yet she had also much fear, lest inbred sin should prevail over her, and make her bring a scandal upon the Gospel. She spent whole days in prayer, that God would not suffer her to be tempted above that she was able, and that with every temptation he would make a way for her to escape. And she was heard, so that her whole conversation adorned the doctrine of God her Saviour.

"Yet she suffered much reproach, not only from the children of the world, but also from the children of God. These wounds sunk deep into her soul, and often made her weep before the Lord. Sometimes she felt resentment for a short time, of which darkness was the sure consequence; but if at any time she lost the consciousness of pardon, it almost took away her life; nor could she rest satisfied a moment, till she regained the light of his countenance. She always judged it was the privilege of every believer, constantly to 'walk in the light;' and that nothing but sin could rob any, who had true faith, of their confidence in a pardoning God.

"She was tried from within and without for about five years, yet kept from all known sin. In the year 1761, it pleased God to show her more clearly than ever, under a sermon preached by John Johnson, the absolute necessity of being saved from all sin, and perfected in love. And now her constant cry was, 'Lord, take full possession of my heart, and reign there without a rival!' Nor was this at all hindered by her disorders, the gravel and colic, which about this time began to be very violent.

"In the year 1762, she believed God did hear her prayer; that her soul was entirely filled with love, and all unholy tempers destroyed; and for several months she rejoiced evermore, prayed without ceasing, and in everything gave thanks. Her happiness had no intermission, day or night; yea, and increased while her disorder increased exceedingly.

"But in the beginning of the year 1763, when some unkind things were whispered about concerning her, she gave way to the temptation, and felt again a degree of anger in her heart. This soon occasioned a doubt, whether she was not deceived before in thinking she was saved from sin. But she said, 'Whether I *was* or no, I am sure I *may be*; and I am determined *now* to seek it from the Lord.'

"From this time her disorders gradually increased. Whenever I [Mr. Johnson] was in town, I visited her from time to time, and always found her, whatever her pains were, resigned to the will of God; having a clear sense of his favour, and a strong confidence that he would finish his work in her soul.

"So soon as I came to town, January, 1767, she sent for me. I found her confined to her bed, and frequently in such racking pain, that it was thought she could not live many minutes; but she said, 'My pain is nothing; the presence of the Lord bears me up above it all. I have not a murmuring thought; neither the shadow of a doubt. My way to glory is plain before me.' I asked if she was not afraid of having great sufferings before the soul and body were parted. She said, 'Not in the least. I expect to have sharp pain just before I depart;' (which was so;) 'but I do not concern myself about what I shall suffer. It is all at the disposal of the Lord.'

"Two days after, I went again to see her. She said, 'My happiness is much increased. For a day and a night my pains have been exquisite; yet in the midst of all, my heart did dance and sing. The Lord so smiles upon me, I cannot express it in words.' February 6. She sent for me again. I found her in a rapture of love, singing and praising God; so that I was constrained to say, 'O Lord, thou hast highly favoured me, in permitting me to see such a Christian!' I cannot attempt to describe how she then appeared; it was with such a smile as I never saw before. Most of the preceding day she had spent in singing praise to God, and telling of his goodness to all that came near her; her soul, she said, being so happy, that she could not be silent.

"When I spoke to her of death, she said, 'It is not death to me; it is only sleep; death is my friend! Death is welcome: Its sting is gone! I shall soon be with my Lord! O that I could sing on to all eternity! My work of praise is begun, and shall never end.' I asked, 'Do you find the greatest inclination to prayer or praise?' She said, 'O praise! Praise! I am full of love; and I cannot doubt but I shall love and praise him to all eternity.' I then asked her concerning her former profession, of being saved from sin. She said, 'Sir, I have it *now!* I have it *now!* and more abundantly. My soul is so full of love, that my body is almost overpowered. It will be but a little while, and we shall meet in glory.'

"Mon. 9. I visited her again, and found her singing as well as her weak body would permit. I asked, 'Are you as happy now, as when I saw you last?' She said, 'I am; I have not the shadow of a doubt. I had many conflicts with a wicked heart; but those are all over now; the Lord has finished his work.' She conversed now like one on Pisgah's top, in sight of the new Jerusalem; often saying, 'My work is begun, which shall never end; I shall praise him to all eternity.'

"She was asked, 'Can you wait the Lord's leisure to release you?' She said, 'Yes, yes; so long as he pleases.

My pain is gone; this also he had done for me; and why should I not wait patiently?' But it was not long before her pains returned with redoubled violence; and sometimes a groan was extorted from her; but not the least complaint. Yes, she often broke out in a rapture of love, crying, 'I cannot express the happiness I feel.'

"Fri. 13. After dozing a little, she awaked in a transport, saying, 'O! you cannot conceive the joy I feel. You know but in part; but when that which is perfect is come, you shall know even as you are known.' She spoke with regard to some glorious views which she then had of her dear Redeemer.

"During her last pains, which were the sharpest, of all, the devil made his last effort. She was in a violent struggle about half an hour. Then she stretched out her hands, and said, 'Glory to Jesus! O love Jesus! love Jesus! He is a glorious Jesus! He has now made me fit for himself! When the harvest is ripe, the sickle is put in.' She asked for a little wine-and-water; but she could not swallow it. She said, 'I have long been drinking wine-and-water here; now I shall drink wine in my Father's kingdom.' She lay still about a quarter of an hour, and then breathed her soul into the hands of her Redeemer." (John Wesley, *The Works of John Wesley*, III [Grand Rapids: Zondervan Publishing House, 1958], 288-292)

A Poor Backslider
Is Made To See Jesus
(d. July, 1767)

The account shared below from Mr. Wesley's *Journal* illustrates well this great man's interest in recovery of the spiritually wayward and those who have made shipwreck of faith. We can assume that he had a personal part in the recovery of this dying one from the "black despair" he initially suffered to that great and glorious prospect he later enjoyed.

> A poor backslider, whom I found ten days ago dying in black despair, told me, "Now I am not afraid to die. I see Jesus just before me, and his face is all glory." Instances of this kind do by no means prove that a saint cannot fall, even for ever; but only that God is "pitiful, and of tender mercy, not willing any should perish." (John Wesley, *The Works of John Wesley*, III [Grand Rapids: Zondervan Publishing House, 1958], 287)

In his sermon entitled, "A Call to Backsliders," Mr. Wesley "inquires what the chief of those reasons are, some or other of which induce so many backsliders to cast away hope; to suppose that God hath forgotten to be gracious." He then gives in that sermon "a clear and full answer to each of those reasons" (John Wesley, *The Works of John Wesley*, VI [Grand Rapids: Zondervan Publishing House, 1958], 514-527).

A Scottish Sexton's
Supernatural Vision

Although the following account is not one that describes an actual death scene, it does have, as the reader will see, a meaningful reference thereto in the words "Be ready for my second coming."

"Before I left Glasgow," writes Mr. Wesley, "I heard so strange an account, that I desired to hear it from the person himself. He was a sexton, and yet for many years had little troubled himself about religion. I set down his words, and leave every man to form his own judgment upon them:--

> "Sixteen weeks ago, I was walking, an hour before sunset, behind the high-kirk; and, looking on one side, I saw one close to me, who looked in my face, and asked me how I did. I answered, 'Pretty well.' He said, 'You have had many troubles; but how have you improved them?' He then told me all that ever I did; yea, and the thoughts that had been in my heart; adding, 'Be ready for my second coming:' And he was gone I knew not how. I trembled all over, and had no strength in

me; but sunk down to the ground. From that time, I groaned continually under the load of sin, till at the Lord's Supper it was all taken away." (John Wesley, *The Works of John Wesley,* III [Grand Rapids: Zondervan Publishing House, 1958], 293)

Having testified to an initial and supernatural visitation from the Master, this sexton seems to have understood His words as a warning to be ready for a second appearance or coming for his soul at the close of life. His testimony gives us much reason to believe that he was truly endeavoring to fulfill that admonition. This great Wesleyan revival having taken place years before the practice of making altar calls and use of mourner's benches, many early Methodists found answers to their spiritual needs while participating in the Lord's Supper—a truly scriptural means of grace.

William New:

"The Chariot! The Chariot Of Israel!"
(d. September, 1767)

In his *Journal* dated September 25, 1767, we read that Mr. Wesley "preached at Bristol in the evening, on those words: *'For our light affliction, which is but for a moment, worketh for us a far more exceeding and eternal weight of glory'*" (2 Cor. 4:17). This text "had been chosen by William New, a little before God called him hence." For several years he had suffered from a severe case of asthma. He was confined to his bed the last seven or eight months of his life but was visited from time to time by a friend, who provided the following account.--

> "He was one of the first Methodists in Bristol, and always walked as became the Gospel. By the sweat of his brow he maintained a large family, leaving six children behind him. When he was no longer able to walk, he did not discontinue his labour; and, after he kept his room, he used to cut out glass, (being a glazier,) to enable his eldest son, a child about fourteen, to do something toward the support of his family. Yea, when he kept his bed, he was not idle; but still gave him what assistance he could.

"He was formerly fond of company and diversions; but, as soon as God called him, left them all, having a nobler diversion,--visiting the sick and afflicted, in which he spent all his leisure hours. He was diligent in the use of all the means of grace; very rarely, during his health, missing the morning preaching at five, though he lived above a mile from the Room.

"About a year ago, he took his leave of the society; telling them, that it was with great pleasure he had joined and continued with them; and it was in this despised place the Lord first manifested himself to his soul; that no tongue could tell what he had since enjoyed under that roof; that the same Jesus had enabled him to hold on thus far, and he hoped to be with him soon; adding, 'I do not expect to see you any more here, but have no doubt of meeting you in glory.'

"During the last twenty days of his life, he took no other sustenance than, now and then, a tea-spoon full of wine, or of balm-tea. About fourteen days before his death, his tongue turned black, with large chops in it, through the heat of his stomach; and his lips were drawn two or three inches apart, so that it was difficult for him to speak. In this condition he lay waiting for his discharge, saying, sometimes, 'I am as it were, two persons: The body is in torturing pain; the soul is in sweet peace.' He frequently said, 'I long to be gone! Come, Lord Jesus; come quickly!' He said, 'I desire to see none but Jesus. To him I leave my dear wife and children: I have no care about them.'

"The next day Satan violently assaulted his faith;

but instantly our Lord appeared in all his glory, and he was filled with love and joy unspeakable, and said, 'Call my friend, and let him see a dying Christian. O what do I feel! I see my Lord has overcome for me. I am his: Praise the Lord! Praise the Lord! Hallelujah! Hallelujah!' He desired them that were present to sing; and began,

Jesu, lover of my soul!

He then desired the text for his funeral sermon might be 2 Cor. Iv. 17.

"The next time I saw him, having desired him to make signs rather than speak, which was painful to him, he said, 'Here is a sign' (pushing out his feet, and holding up his hands,) 'a dying Christian, full of love and joy! A crown, a never-fading crown awaits me; I am going to everlasting habitations.' He then desired us to sing, and quickly added, 'He is come! He is come! I want to be gone: Farewell to you all!' When he could no longer speak, he continued smiling, clapping his hands, and discovering an ecstasy of joy in every motion.

"After a while his speech returned, and he said, 'To-day is Friday: To-morrow I expect to go.' One said, 'Poor Mr. New!' He said, 'It is rich New: Though poor in myself, I am rich in Christ.'

"I saw him on Saturday in the same spirit, praising God with every breath. He appeared quite transported, pointing upwards, and turning his fingers round his head, alluding to the crown prepared for him. I said,

'Your Lord has kept the best wine unto the last.' 'Yes, yes,' said he; 'it is in my soul.' When I took my leave he pressed my hand, pointed upward, and again clapped his hands. Afterward he spoke little, till he cried out, 'The chariot, the chariot of Israel!' and died." (John Wesley, *The Works of John Wesley*, III [Grand Rapids: Zondervan Publishing House, 1958], 298-300)

Benjamin Colley:
Reclaimed Backslider Dies Without Doubt Or Fear
(d. November, 1767)

While following in his *Journal* the life and ministry of Mr. Wesley, one becomes conscious of the many he says he "buried." They are observed over and over again to be from his widely scattered and growing Methodist flock. Many were converted under his preaching and nourished by his care and that of his preachers.

In the following account Mr. Wesley describes the deceased as one who "did 'rejoice evermore,' and 'pray without ceasing.'" To be able to "rejoice evermore, pray without ceasing and in everything give thanks," was one of the scriptural descriptions of Christian perfection often cited by Mr. Wesley. In a *Journal* entry he writes:

> I buried, the remains of that excellent young man, Benjamin Colley. He did "rejoice evermore," and "pray without ceasing;" and I believe his backsliding cost him his life. From the time he missed his way, by means of Mr. Maxfield, he went heavily all his days. God, indeed, restored his peace, but left him to be buffeted of Satan in an uncommon manner: And his trials did not end but with his life. However, some of his last

words were, "Tell all the society, tell all the world, I die without doubt or fear." (John Wesley, *The Works of John Wesley,* III [Grand Rapids: Zondervan Publishing House, 1958] 303)

The reader may be somewhat puzzled by the words: "I believe his backsliding cost him his life." In his sermon entitled, "A Call to Backsliders," Mr. Wesley refers to the "sin unto death" mentioned in the First Epistle of St. John as possibly meaning a sin that God has determined to punish with physical death while saving the soul. As he explained it, "The body is destroyed, that the soul may escape destruction." He wrote, "I see no absurdity at all in this interpretation of the word. It seems to be one meaning (at least) of the expression, 'a sin unto death.'"

It is interesting that the name of Mr. Maxfield should be mentioned here as the "means" by which this young convert "missed his way," causing "his backsliding." Mr. Maxfield had originally been one of the first lay preachers sent out by Mr. Wesley in the early years of the Methodist movement. As time went on, however, he proved himself to be more and more fanatical and divisive. Those who followed his leadership placed undue value on dreams and visions, and in several respects contradicted sound teaching. Concerning the excesses of this man and others like George Bell, Mr. Wesley once said, "The reproach of Christ I am willing to bear; but not the reproach of enthusiasm (fanaticism), if I can help it" ("ibid., 303").

Rebecca Mills:
Uniformly Praised God In Life And Death
(d. November, 1767)

"**I** buried the remains of Rebecca Mills," writes Mr. Wesley. "She found peace with God many years since, and about five years ago was entirely changed, and enabled to give her whole soul to God.

> From that hour she never found any decay, but loved and served him with her whole heart. Pain and sickness, and various trials, succeeded almost without any intermission: But she was always the same, firm and unmoved, as the rock on which she was built; in life and in death uniformly praising the God of her salvation. The attainableness of this great salvation is put beyond all reasonable doubt by the testimony of one such (were there but one) living and dying witness." (John Wesley, *The Works of John Wesley*, III [Grand Rapids: Zondervan Publishing House, 1958], 303)

Mr. Wesley speaks of this lady as one who, five years before "was entirely changed, and enabled to give her whole soul to God." He furthermore speaks of her as attaining "this great salvation." Such terminology is used by Mr. Wesley to describe a second work of grace, often known as entire sanctification or Christian perfection. From his "A Plain Account of Christian Perfection," we share a paragraph in which he defines more particularly this "great salvation," or Christian perfection as he understood and taught it.

> In one view, it is purity of intention, dedicating all the life to God. It is the giving God all our heart; it is one desire and design ruling all our tempers. It is the devoting, not a part, but all, our soul, body and substance, to God. In another view, it is all the mind which was in Christ, enabling us to walk as Christ walked. It is the circumcision of the heart from all filthiness, all inward as well as outward pollution. It is a renewal of the heart in the whole image of God, the full likeness of Him that created it. In yet another, it is the loving God with all our heart, and our neighbor as ourselves. Now, take it in which of these views you please (for there is no material difference), and this is the whole and sole perfection, as a train of writings prove to a demonstration, which I have believed and taught for these forty years, from 1725 to the year 1765. (John Wesley, *The Works of John Wesley*, XI [Grand Rapids: Zondervan Publishing House, 1958], 444)

Elizabeth Vandome:
A Living And Dying Witness Of Perfect Love
(d. January, 1769)

A month or two before Elizabeth Vandome was taken ill, she dictated the following letter to Mr. Wesley.—

"Dear and Rev. Sir,

"When I first heard the Gospel from you, I was convinced of sin, and nothing could satisfy me but a sense of pardoning love. For a month the garment of weeping was put upon me night and day; till one day, as I was repeating those words,

> I trust in Him that stands between
> The Father's wrath and me;
> Jesus, thou great eternal mean,
> I look for all from thee!

I was struck down to the ground, and felt the arm of the Lord revealed in me: I knew that God was reconciled; I felt sanctification begun. The fight of faith ensued; and for three quarters of a year I was struggling with my own will. Sometimes I was in an agony; I was ready to weep my life away, fearing the sin I felt in my heart would never be done away. Yet I believed there was a rest for the people of God; a rest from all sin. One day, conversing with one about the things of God, he said, 'You would have all things become new, before you believe. But that is not the way. You must believe first.' When he went away, the Spirit of prayer and supplication rested upon me. Yet I felt 'bound down with twice ten thousand ties.' However, I wrestled on, till the Lord broke in upon my soul like the sun in his glory. He loosed me at once from all my bonds, and I knew I loved him with all my heart. Jesus appeared with hair as white as wool, and garments down to his feet, and gave me to sit with him in heavenly places. And from that time (which is seven or eight and twenty years ago) I have felt no temper contrary to love. I have no desire contrary to the will of God. On this bed of sickness I have communion with the church triumphant. I know that

> Jesus is my brother now,
> And God is all my own.

When the tempter comes, my soul cleaves to Jesus, and I am kept in perfect peace.

"I thought it my duty to leave this short account of the gracious dealings of God with my soul, as you was the instrument he was pleased to make use of, for the beginning and furthering of his work. O may the Lord strengthen you and your brother, and increase in you every fruit of his Spirit; and when you fail on earth, may we meet in heaven, and praise the great Three-One to all eternity!"

The following paragraph was added by one "Lydia Vandome." Who this person was we are not informed. Having with Elizabeth the same last name suggests she may have been a sister. In any case, she was a witness to the glorious experiences and final scenes surrounding the departure of this saint of early Methodism and shares a part of it below.

"This account was written some time past, when she was sick in bed. But since then God raised her up, and enabled her still to be useful to others, though in great weakness of body. When she took to her bed again, about three weeks ago, she had a remarkable dream:--She thought she saw Mr. W., labouring with his might, to keep the people from falling into a deep pit, which very few of them perceived. The concern she was in awaked her in great emotion. On Tuesday evening last, she desired us to set her up in bed, to meet her class. Her voice faltered much. She earnestly exhorted them all to live near to God, and to keep close together; adding, 'I shall soon join the church above.' She spoke no more; all was silent rapture, till, on Friday morning, without sigh or groan, she resigned her spirit to God.

Lydia Vandome."

In a closing comment, Mr. Wesley writes: "Such a living and dying witness of the perfect love of God, which she enjoyed for eight-and-twenty years, one would think sufficient to silence all the doubts and objections of reasonable and candid men" (John Wesley, *The Works of John Wesley*, III [Grand Rapids: Zondervan Publishing House, 1958], 350-352).

Michael Hayes:
"As He Lived, So He Died, Praising God"
(d. March, 1769)

"I buried the remains of Michael Hayes," writes Mr. Wesley, "a good old soldier of Jesus Christ. He had lived above an hundred and four years, mostly in vigorous health. His speech and understanding continued to the last; and as he lived, so he died, praising God" (John Wesley, *The Works of John Wesley,* III [Grand Rapids: Zondervan Publishing House, 1958], 354).

Long life is good when it is enriched by the inward life of God and when the praise of the Savior emanates from a soul that is cleansed through the blood of Christ. From Mr. Wesley's *"A Plain Account of Christian Perfection,"* we share a lively description of that great salvation which inspires true praise to God.

> "This great gift of God, the salvation of our souls, is no other than the image of God fresh stamped on our hearts. It is a 'renewal of believers in the spirit of their minds, after the likeness of Him that created them.' God hath now laid 'the axe unto the root of the tree, purifying their hearts by faith,' and 'cleansing all the thoughts of their hearts by the inspiration of His Holy

Spirit.' Having this hope, that they shall see God as He is, they 'purify themselves even as He is pure,' and are 'holy, as He that hath called them is holy, in all manner of conversation [or life style].' Not that they have already attained all that they shall attain, either are already in this sense perfect. But they daily 'go on from strength to strength, beholding' now, 'as in a glass, the glory of the Lord, they are changed into the same image, from glory to glory, by the Spirit of the Lord.'" (John Wesley, *The Works of John Wesley,* XI [Grand Rapids: Zondervan Publishing House, 1958], 378-79)

Such is one description of the great salvation that made the heart of Michael Hayes praise His God both during his long life as well as in the hour of death.

Elizabeth Oldham:

A Witness To Three Glorious Departures
(d. March, 1769)

The following accounts, recorded in his *Journal*, March, 1769, were told to Mr. Wesley by Elizabeth Oldham, who was a widow of one of his preachers.

She first spoke of her mother, who, when realizing her life was coming to an end, requested that her son be called that he might see her die. Upon his arrival, he asked his mother if she had "any fear of death? She said, 'O no! That is gone long since. Perfect love casts out fear.'" She then asked him, "'Do not you see him? There he is, waiting to receive my soul!' She then sang with a clear voice,

'Praise God from whom all blessings flow.'

And ended her song and her life together."

Mrs. Oldham then spoke of her husband who, not being well. was in doubt each "time he took horse whether he should not drop by the way" before completing his round of preaching appointments. For this reason, "he carried a paper in his pocket, telling who he was, and [where] he was going." Five weeks before, he felt very weak, and "feared he should not be able to preach." She, however, said to her husband, "'My dear, go into the pulpit, and the Lord will strengthen thee.'" Accordingly, the Lord did strengthen him after he had spoken but a few words. "'Neither,'" said she, "'did he speak in vain: Many were comforted; several justified.'" One of the ladies who had received help said, "'He is going to rest soon, and I shall go with him.'" As it turned out, he did die "in full triumph the next Lord's Day; and she two hours after."

Mrs. Oldham, however, confessed that "a day or two before" the death of her husband, she "felt a kind of unwillingness to give him up." She said that she "was mourning before the Lord concerning this, when he said to my inmost soul, 'Wilt thou not give him back to me, whom I have fitted for myself?' She said, 'Lord, I do, I do give him up.' And immediately he changed for death."

Finally, it was but the following Sunday that she was speaking to her "little maid," whom she described as being "always a serious and dutiful child, three years and a half old." She asked the child, "'Hannah, dost thou love God?' She eagerly answered, 'Yes, mammy, I do.' She added, 'I will go to God; I will go to God;' leaned down, and died" (John Wesley, *The Works of John Wesley*, III [Grand Rapids: Zondervan Publishing House, 1958], 355-356).

The Memorable Illness And Deaths Of Two Remarkable Children

(d. March, 1770)

In his *Journal* dated, Wednesday, March 21, 1770, Mr. Wesley informs his readers that he "… procured an account of two remarkable children, which," writes he, "I think ought not to be buried in oblivion."

The reader is asked to take notice of two areas of emphasis in this account: (1) the reality of heart religion, and (2) the doctrine of assurance.

Nine-year-old William Cooper and his eleven-year-old sister Lucy lived with their mother at Walsal, in Staffordshire. In the later part of 1768, Billy "was convinced of sin,…"; while in this state of deep conviction, he "would frequently say he should go to hell, and the devil would fetch him." There were times when "he cried out, 'I hate him.'" When asked whom it was he hated so, he "with great vehemence," would answer, 'God.'" Such an answer so terrified his mother, "who not knowing what was the matter with the child, [did her best] to keep it secret."

It was, however, but a few days later that a great change took place in Billy. He was happily given a deep sense of God's pardoning love.

It is said that, "His mouth was then filled with praise, declaring to all what God had done for his soul."

Not many days after Billy was awakened and made to enjoy the salvation of his soul, "God was pleased to convince his sister" of sin also. She was constrained to seek pardoning grace and her Redeemer "soon put a song of praise into her mouth also, so that they mightily rejoiced together in God their Saviour." During this same time, it is said that "they were both heavily afflicted in their bodies. But so much the more was the power of God manifested, causing them to continue in the triumph of faith, throughout their sharpest pains."

On an occasion when one of their sisters came in to them for a visit, "Billy told her he had been very ill. 'But,' said he, 'I do not mean in my body, but in my soul: I felt my sins so heavy, that I thought I should go to hell; and I saw the devil ready to drag me away. Nay, for a week, I thought myself just in the flames of hell.' He continued to speak, saying that "'The sins that troubled me most were, telling lies, and quarrelling with my sister. I saw, if God did not forgive me, I was lost: And I knew quarrelling was a great sin in Lucy as in me; and if she did not get a pardon and feel the love of Jesus, she could not go to heaven.'"

Lucy then spoke up and referred to a sermon she had lately heard in which two kinds of people were described. The one was "washed in the blood of Christ and the other not." She said, "I found I was not, and therefore, if I died so, must go to hell." She was then asked, what sin it was that lay most on her conscience. She replied, "Taking His name in vain, by repeating my prayers when I did not think of God."

Billy, on one occasion, was making the confession that he had loved money. Lucy immediately responded with, "And so did I." She went so far in her confession as to admit that she "was angry if [she] had not as much as Billy. I loved money more than God," said she, "and he might justly have sent me to hell for it."

Most interestingly, one asked Billy how he knew his sins were forgiven. His answer was quite simple. "Christ told me so," said he. "I had a great struggle in my heart with the devil and sin, till it pleased Jesus to come into my soul. I now feel his love in my heart, and he tells me he has forgiven my sins."

On another occasion, Billy was asked, how he did. His reply was that he was "Happy in Jesus: Jesus," said he, "is sweet to my soul." He was then asked, "Do you choose to live or die? He answered, "Neither. I hope, if I live, I shall praise God; and if I die, I am sure I shall go to him; for he has forgiven my sins, and given me his love."

Lucy was then asked "how long she had been in the triumph of faith. She answered, 'Only this week. Before I had much to do with Satan, but now Jesus has conquered him for me.'" During this exchange, Lucy gave evidence of "feeling great pain of body," but she considered such pain to be a help in bringing her "nearer to Jesus."

When one brought up the thought and mystery of "knowing the voice of Christ," Lucy said, "The voice of Christ is a strange voice to them who do not know their sins forgiven; but I know it, for he has pardoned all my sins, and given me his love. And O what a mercy that such a hell-deserving wretch as me, as *me*, should be made to taste of his love!"

One of the pitiful symptoms of Billy's illness was "frequent fits." These he endured with patience, and upon recovering from each occurrence would express himself to be "happy in the love of Christ," noting that "he bore more for my sins."

> "One night, a gentleman and his wife came to see them; and the gentlewoman, looking on Lucy, said, 'She looks as if nothing was the matter with her; she is so pleasant with her eyes.' She replied, 'I have enough

to make me look so; for I am full of the love of God.'
While she spoke, her eyes sparkled exceedingly, and the
tears flowed down her cheeks. At this Billy smiled, but
could not speak; having been speechless for more than
an hour. It seemed he was just going into eternity; but
the Lord revived him a little; and as soon as he could
speak, he desired to be held up in bed, and looked
at the gentleman, who asked him how he did. He
answered, 'I am happy in Christ, and I hope you are.'
He said, 'I hope I can say I am.' Billy replied, 'Has
Christ pardoned your sins?' He said, 'I hope he has.'
'Sir,' said Billy, 'hope will not do; for I had this hope,
and yet if I had died then, I should surely have gone to
hell. But he has forgiven me all my sins, and given me
a taste of his love. If you have this love, you will know
it, and be sure of it; but you cannot know it without
the power of God. You may read as many books about
Christ as you please;' (he was a great reader;) 'but if you
read all your life, this will only be in your head, and
that head will perish: So that, if you have not the love
of God in your heart, you will go to hell. But I hope
you will not: I will pray to God for you, that he may
give you his love.'"

When another came to visit the two children, they were again
asked of their welfare. "Billy said, 'Happier and happier in Christ.'"
He then asked the visitor if he were not also enjoying such happiness.
The response was, "'No: I am not so happy as you.'" Billy then said,
"'I am afraid you do not pray to Christ; for I am sure he is willing to
make you happy.'"

There was one who sat nearby and seemed unusually impressed "with the discourse, but did not speak. Billy, observing her, said, 'And you do not pray as you ought: For if you had the love of Christ in your heart, you would not look down so. I wish you and every one had it.'" Another spoke up and said, "'My dear, would you not give it them, if you might?'" His answer was, "'No; for that would be to take Christ's work out of his hands.'"

Among the many who had heard "what great things God had done" for these two children, there were skeptics who suggested that it would not always be the same with them. "'If you,' said they, 'should live to come into the world again, he would leave you in the dark.'" To which they said, "'We do not think so, for our Jesus has promised that he will never leave us.'"

One young woman, continued to give argument in this same manner. Billy then responded by asking her, "'Miss, are you assured of your interest in Christ?' She answered, 'I hope I am in Christ, but assurance is no way essential.' He replied, 'But if you have his love, you will be sure you have it: You will know it in your heart. I am afraid your hope is only in your head.'" He then asked again. "'Do you never quarrel with anybody?' She said, 'No.' 'But,' says he, 'you quarrel with God's word: For he has promised me, none shall pluck me out of his hand; and you say, the world will: So you make God a story-teller.' At this she went away displeased."

Among all those who came to see these children while one or the other could speak, few left without being questioned concerning the spiritual state of their souls. Without fear they were warned of "the danger of dying without an assurance of the love of God."

> "One coming to see them, was talked to very closely by Billy, till she could bear no more. She turned to Lucy, and said, 'You were always good children, and never told stories.' 'Yes, Madam,' said Lucy, 'but I did, when

231

I was afraid of being beat; and when I said my prayers; for I did not think of God; and I called him, My Father, when I was a child of wrath: And as to praying, I could not pray till it pleased him by his Spirit to show me my sins. And he showed me, we might say as many prayers as we would, and go to church or meeting; yet all this, if we had not Christ for our foundation, would not do.'

"When they were asked, if they were afraid to die, they always answered, 'No; for what can death do? He can only lay his cold hand upon our bodies.'

"One told Lucy, now she can live as you please, since you are sure of going to heaven.' She replied, 'No, I would not sin against my dear Saviour if you would give me this room full of gold.'

"On the Monday before he died, Billy repeated that hymn with the most triumphant joy,--

> Come, let us join our cheerful songs
> With angels round the throne!

"Afterwards he repeated the Lord's Prayer. The last words he spoke intelligibly were, 'How pleasant is it to be with Christ, for ever and ever,--for ever and ever! Amen! Amen! Amen!'"

As he lay in a speechless condition, he became conscious of those coming into the room, some of whom he feared knew not God. Those who were witnesses to this scene observed that "he seemed much affected, wept and moaned much, waved his hand, and put it on his sister's mouth; intimating, as she supposed, that she should speak to them."

A day later "his happy spirit returned to God." His sister, Lucy, died soon after (John Wesley, *The Works of John Wesley*, III [Grand Rapids: Zondervan Publishing House, 1958], 389-393).

A Gay Young Woman Hears A Timely Message
(d. February, 1772)

The following story shared with Mr. Wesley impressed him as being "very remarkable."

"A gay young woman" was said to have come up to London and was motivated by curiosity to hear the preaching of a sermon. The message resulted in her being "cut to the heart." One who happened to be standing nearby observed that she was deeply affected and took the opportunity to talk to her. She expressed great disappointment that she should have no further opportunity to hear more sermons since she would be going into the country the next day. Nevertheless, she "begged her new acquaintance to write to her there, which she promised to do."

While in the country, her convictions greatly increased. So severe were they "that she resolved to put an end to her own life." With this purpose in mind, "she was going up stairs, when her father called her, and gave her a letter from London." Upon opening it she found gracious words of hope "from her new acquaintance." Therein she was assured that, "Christ is just ready to receive you: Now is the day of salvation." Her response was both immediate and full of faith.

She cried out, "it is, it is! Christ is mine!" and was filled with joy unspeakable. She begged her father to give her pen, ink, and paper, that she might answer her friend immediately. She told her what God had done for her soul, and added, "We have no time to lose! The Lord is at hand! Now, even now, we are stepping into eternity." She directed her letter, dropped down, and died. (John Wesley, *The Works of John Wesley*, III [Grand Rapids: Zondervan Publishing House, 1958], 453-454)

This account does not tell us who was preaching nor does it inform us where in London this young lady happened to hear the preaching that so inwardly affected her. From the context it seems most likely it was in the open air and may well have been one of the many occasions when Mr. John Wesley himself was calling sinners to repentance in the open area of Moorfields.

John Downes:

Both A Preacher And Genius Who Died In The Pulpit After A Life Of Enjoying Heavenly Fellowship with God.
(d. November, 1774)

In a *Journal* entry dated November 4, 1774, Mr. Wesley refers to a remarkable man by the name of John Downes who was not only one of his preachers but a genius in various ways. One Friday afternoon, he "was saying, 'I feel such a love to the people at West-Street (a Methodist preaching site in London), that I could be content to die with them. I do not find myself very well; but I must be with them this evening.' He went thither and began preaching, on, 'Come unto me, ye that are weary and heavy-laden.' After speaking ten or twelve minutes, he sunk down, and spake no more, till his spirit returned to God." The *Journal* entry then continues with a marvelous description of this man:

> I suppose he was by nature full as great a genius as Sir Isaac Newton. I will mention but two or three instances of it:--When he was at school, learning Algebra, he came one day to his master, and said, "Sir, I can prove this proposition a better way than it is proved in the book." His master thought it could not be; but upon trial, acknowledged it to be so. Some time after, his

father sent him to Newcastle with a clock, which was to be mended. He observed the clockmaker's tools, and the manner how he took it in pieces, and put it together again; and when he came home, first made himself tools, and then made a clock, which went as true as any in the town. I suppose such strength of genius as this, has scarce been known in Europe before.

Another proof of it was this:--Thirty years ago, while I was shaving, he was whittling the top of a stick: I asked, "What are you doing?" He answered, "I am taking your face, which I intend to engrave on a copper-plate." Accordingly, without any instruction, he first made himself tools, and then engraved the plate. The second picture which he engraved, was that which was prefixed to the "Notes upon the New Testament." Such another instance, I suppose, not all England, or perhaps Europe, can produce.

During the last several months of his life, it is said that "he had far deeper communion with God, than ever he had had in his life; and for some days he had been frequently saying, 'I am so happy, that I scarce know how to live.'" Moreover, he was heard also to say, "I enjoy such fellowship with God, as I thought could not be had on this side of heaven." Mr. Wesley then expressed these final and affectionate words of his friend: "And having now finished his course of fifty-two years, after a long conflict with pain, sickness, and poverty, he gloriously rested from his labours, and entered into the joy of his Lord" (John Wesley, *The Works of John Wesley,* IV [Grand Rapids: Zondervan Publishing House, 1958], 34-35).

Thomas Vokins:
From Despair To Glory
(d. February, 1775)

"I saw," writes Mr. Wesley, "a glorious instance of the power of faith. Thomas Vokins, a man of a sorrowful spirit, used always to hang down his head like a bulrush. But a few days since, as he was dying without hope, God broke in upon his soul; and from that time he has been triumphing over pain and death, and rejoicing with joy full of glory" (John Wesley, *The Works of John Wesley*, IV [Grand Rapids: Zondervan Publishing House, 1958], 39).

To be of "a sorrowful spirit" so as to lead to "dying without hope" is surely a most miserable and distressing condition for any soul. In Proverbs 14:10 we read that "The heart knoweth his own bitterness; and a stranger doth not intermeddle with his joy." Commenting upon this verse, Dr. Adam Clarke writes:

> Under spiritual sorrow, the *heart* feels, the *soul* feels; all the *animal* nature feels, and suffers. But when the peace of God is spoken to the troubled soul, the joy is indescribable; the *whole man* partakes of it. And a stranger to these religious feelings, to the travail of

the soul, and to the witness of the Spirit, does not *intermeddle* with them; he does not understand them: indeed they may be even foolishness to him, because they are spiritually discerned. (Adam Clarke, *Clarke's Commentary* III, [New York & Nashville: Abingdon Press, nd.], 741)

Martha Wood:
Sees The Heavens Opened
(d. August, 1775)

It is an extraordinary blessing to hear dying saints testify of the peace, joy and glorious expectations of heaven they are enjoying before they depart. Most, however, who are in their passage from this life, do so without declaring that they actually see heaven opening up before them. Nevertheless, there are at times marvelous exceptions reported. Mr. Wesley provides us with one of those exceptions in the following account forwarded to him from one of his preachers.

"About three weeks since, a person came and told me, Martha Wood, of Darleston, was dying, and had a great desire to see me. When I came into the house, which, with all that was in it, was scarce worth five pounds, I found, in that [poor and lowly] cottage, such a jewel as my eyes never beheld before. Her eyes even sparkled with joy, and her heart danced like David before the ark: In truth, she seemed to be in the suburbs of heaven, upon the confines of glory.

"She took hold of my hand, and said, 'I am glad to see you; you are my father in Christ: It is twenty years since I heard you first. It was on that text, *Now ye have sorrow. But I will see you again, and your heart shall rejoice, and your joy no man taketh from you.* In that hour God broke into my soul, delivered me from all sorrow, and filled my heart with joy; and, blessed be his name, I never have lost it, from that hour to this.'

"For the first ten years, she was sometimes in transports of joy, carried almost beyond herself; but for these last ten years, she has had the constant witness that God has taken up all her heart. 'He has filled me,' said she, 'with perfect love; and perfect love casts out fear. Jesus is mine; God, and heaven, and eternal glory, are mine. My heart, my very soul is lost, yea, swallowed up, in God.'

"There were many of our friends standing by her bedside. She exhorted them all, as one in perfect health, to keep close to God. 'You can never,' said she, 'do too much for God: When you have done all you can, you have done too little. O, who that knows Him, can love, or do, or suffer too much for Him!'

"Some worldly people came in. She called them by name, and exhorted them to repent and turn to Jesus. She looked at me, and desired I would preach her funeral sermon on those words, 'I have fought the good fight; I have finished my course; I have kept the faith. Henceforth there is laid up for me a crown of righteousness, which the Lord, the righteous Judge, will give me at that day.'

"She talked to all round about her in as scriptural and rational a manner as if she had been in her full strength, (only now and then catching a little for breath,) with all the smiles of heaven in her countenance. Indeed several times she seemed to be quite gone; but in a little while the taper lit up again, and she began to preach, with divine power, to all that stood near her. She knew every person, and if any came into the room whom she knew to be careless about religion, she directly called them by name, and charged them to seek the Lord while he might be found. At last she cried out, 'I see the heavens opened; I see Abraham, Isaac, and Jacob, with numbers of the glorified throng, coming nearer and nearer. They are just come!' At that word, her soul took its flight, to mingle with the heavenly host. We looked after her, as Elisha after Elijah; and I trust some of us have catched her mantle." (John Wesley, *The Works of John Wesley*, IV [Grand Rapids: Zondervan Publishing House, 1958], 52-53)

It is most interesting to notice that the conversion of this dear lady took place during the sermon of a Methodist preacher. This was not uncommon in the days of the Wesleyan revival. It is also worth noting that she never lost her joy from the moment of conversion till the day of her death. Finally, would we not all, like the saintly Martha Wood, wish to be a blessing to others in the hour of death as well as in life?

Jane Binknell And Ann Davis:

Final Overcomers Of Pain, Heaviness
And Spousal Mistreatment
(d. December, 1775)

Throughout the history of early Methodism there were numerous ones who faced much that would discourage any Christian believer. Nevertheless, in spite of pain, discomforts, persecution and losses, we read of their happy and victorious departures from this life. In the two accounts shared below from his *Journal*, Mr. Wesley describes the one dying in "sweet peace;" the other in "triumphant joy." It is to be remembered that if we wish to die well, we must live well in righteousness and true holiness while sojourning in this vale of tears.

> In the evening I preached a kind of funeral sermon at Snowfields, for that upright woman, Jane Binknell. For many years she was a pattern of all holiness; and for the latter part of her life, of patience. Yet as she laboured under an incurable and painful disorder, which allowed her little rest, day or night, the corruptible body pressed down the soul, and frequently occasioned much heaviness. But before she went, the

clouds dispersed, and she died in sweet peace; but not in such triumphant joy as did Ann Davis, two or three weeks before. She died of the same disorder; but had withal, for some years, racking pains in her head day and night, which in a while rendered her stone-blind. Add to this, that she had a *kind* husband; who was continually reproaching her for living so long, and cursing her for not dying out of the way. Yet in all this she did not "charge God foolishly;" but meekly waited till her change should come. (John Wesley, *The Works of John Wesley*, IV [Grand Rapids: Zondervan Publishing House, 1958], 63-64)

Reading of such suffering saints as these cannot but remind us of a line Mr. Wesley shares in another part of his *Journal*. "Heaven," says he, "its choicest gold by torture tried!" ("ibid., 68"). Surely, though they be tried as was Job, God, in the end, is sure to reward them accordingly.

Mr. Hall:

A Brother-in-law To Mr. Wesley
Who Was Given Deep Repentance Before Death
(d. January, 1776)

"**I** came just time enough," writes Mr. Wesley, "not to see, but to bury, poor Mr. Hall, my brother-in-law, who died on Wednesday morning; I trust, in peace; for God had given him deep repentance." In words filled with loving hope, he expresses a persuasion that, "Such another monument of divine mercy, considering how low he had fallen, and from what height of holiness, I have not seen, no, not in seventy years! I had designed to visit him in the morning; but he did not stay for my coming." Unusually bad roads had delayed Mr. Wesley's travels on that occasion. "It is enough," he concludes, "if after all his wanderings, we meet again in Abraham's bosom" (John Wesley, *The Works of John Wesley*, IV [Grand Rapids: Zondervan Publishing House, 1958], 64).

It is true that the life of Mr. Hall was marred by sin and backsliding, proving to be a great disappointment and concern to the Wesley family. There is, however, another reference to Mr. Hall that is worthy of our notice. Susanna Wesley, the mother of John and Charles Wesley, sometimes referred to as "the mother of Methodism," received the witness of the Spirit that her sins were forgiven in a way that was common during the rise of the Wesleyan revival of the eighteenth century. While at the communion table she received the cup at the hands of her son-in-law (Mr. Hall) and upon hearing him pronounce those words, "The blood of our Lord Jesus Christ which was given for thee," she testified that "the words struck through [her] heart and [she] knew God had for Christ's sake forgiven [her] of [her] sins" (John Wesley, *The Works of John Wesley,* I [Grand Rapids: Zondervan Publishing House, 1958], 222-23).

Henry Terry:
Passed From Terror To Hope And Finally Joy
(d. January, 1777)

Often times God reaches wayward hearts by taking in death someone dear. Such was the case with Henry Terry, whose mother gave Mr. Wesley the following story which he then shared in his *Journal*. Notice Henry's expressions of terror at the prospect of "going to hell." Notice how, while in deep despair, he settles not for a superficial peace and healing of his soul, but prays on until his heart is fully set free and he is able to "rejoice with joy unspeakable."

> Mon. 20.—Mrs. T. gave us a remarkable account:--
> On Saturday, the 11th instant, her little boy, a child of eminent piety, between five and six years old, gave up his spirit to God. She was saying to one in the house, "My son is gone to glory." A youth standing by, cried out, "But I am going to hell." He continued praying all Sunday and Monday; but in utter despair. On Tuesday he found a hope of mercy, which gradually increased. The next morning he rejoiced with joy unspeakable, knowing his sins were blotted out; and

soon after Henry Terry (the son of many tears to his poor mother) slept in peace.

Happy are the seekers who are permitted to continue their seeking without being interrupted by "altar nurses" who endeavor to talk them into a profession before the Spirit witnesses that the work is done (John Wesley, *The Works of John Wesley*, IV [Grand Rapids: Zondervan Publishing House, 1958], 92).

Elizabeth Duchesne:
Her End Was Peace
(d. January, 1777)

In the midst of John Wesley's various labors he is often found preaching the funeral services of Methodists who have died in the Lord. Many of them had been formerly converted and spiritually nourished under his ministry or that of his preachers. In his *Journal* dated January 22, 1777, he records having "buried the remains of Elizabeth Duchesne."

He describes her as "a person eminently upright of heart, yet for many years a child of labour and sorrow. For near forty years she was zealous of good works, and at length shortened her days by labouring for the poor beyond her strength. But her end was peace. She now rests from her labours, and her works follow her" (John Wesley, *The Works of John Wesley*, IV [Grand Rapids: Zondervan Publishing House, 1958], 91).

What is the full meaning of Mr. Wesley's statement when he declares that "her end was peace?" One of the dictionary definitions of peace describes it as "an undisturbed state of mind" or an "absence of mental conflict." However, the peace of God as understood by Mr. Wesley is more than just the absence of various kinds of conflict and mental anxiety. It is not just an absence of undesirable impressions within mind and heart that would leave us like a blank page, feeling nothing. When God comes to the soul He actually adds something. He gives a heavenly felicity and tranquility that is consciously enjoyed. He gives to the soul that peace which is a part of the fruit of the Spirit—"a peace of God which passeth all understanding" (Philippians 4:7). So when one is filled with the Spirit of Christ, he or she has peace because Christ is there and peace is one of the characteristics of the Almighty.

William Green:
Lived And Died In "Full Assurance Of Faith"
(d. June, 1777)

"**I** went on to Rotherdam," wrote Mr. Wesley in his *Journal*, "and was glad to find, that the society is not discouraged by the death of that good man, William Green, who had been as a father to them from the beginning. He never started [or was found to be overcome with anxiety and frustration] either at labour or suffering; but went on calm and steady, trusting God with himself and his eight children, even while all the waves and storms went over him. He died, as he lived in the full assurance of faith, praising God with his latest breath" (John Wesley, *The Works of John Wesley*, IV [Grand Rapids: Zondervan Publishing House, 1958], 102).

Some will question the meaning of what Mr. Wesley refers to as the "full assurance of faith." He often makes reference to this subject in his writings, one of which is found in a letter written to the Rev. Mr. Church. Therein he shows that those who are newly justified do receive "an assurance [of sins] forgiven, clear at first, but soon clouded [too often] with doubt or fear." In contrast, he assures us that "full assurance of faith" involves an assurance that one's sins are forgiven, with "so clear a perception that Christ abideth in [the heart of the believer] as utterly

251

excludes all doubt and fear, and leaves them no place, no, not for an hour" (John Wesley, *The Works of John Wesley*, VIII [Grand Rapids: Zondervan Publishing House, 1958], 393).

This assurance Mr. Wesley taught was one of present pardon and not an assurance of final perseverance. In other words, it was not to be confused with a Calvinistic "eternal security" or an unconditional assurance that guaranteed final salvation on the basis of past experience in grace (John Wesley, *The Works of John Wesley*, I [Grand Rapids: Zondervan Publishing House, 1958], 160).

Mr. Wesley once wrote, "Does not talking, without proper caution, of a justified or sanctified state, tend to mislead men; almost naturally leading them to trust in what was done in one moment? Whereas we are every moment pleasing or displeasing to God, according to our works; according to the whole of our present inward tempers and outward behaviour" ("Wesley, *The Works of John Wesley*, VIII, 338").

Happy are they who, like William Green, can praise God with their latest breath because of a full assurance of faith in that defining moment.

Dr. Dodd:

Executed For Forgery But Died In Peace

(d. June, 1777)

The subject of this account was undoubtedly a clergyman of the Church of England who held the degree of Doctor of Divinity. In earlier years he carried on a theological debate with Mr. Wesley by correspondence. Herein, he took exception to the latter's views of Christian perfection as found in several printed sermons (John Wesley, *The Works of John Wesley*, XI [Grand Rapids: Zondervan Publishing House, 1958], 450-454). The justice system in 18th century England was exceedingly severe and so it was that Dr. Dodd was executed for forgery on June 27th, 1777 ("ibid., 454").

Previous to his execution, Dr. Dodd prevailed upon Mr. Wesley to visit him while in confinement. His several visits proved to be of spiritual assistance.

"I have," writes Mr. Wesley, "been frequently desired to give some account of the conversations I had with Dr. Dodd." By submitting to this request he expressed the hope that it might "enable many who love to think for themselves to form an impartial judgment of one that has been so variously represented" ("ibid., 454"). The personal account of his correspondence and visits with this man is as follows:

I had no knowledge of Dr. Dodd till he told that excellent woman, Mrs. Lefevre, that he was going to publish something against Mr. Wesley. She advised him to send it to me first. He did so, and was so far at least satisfied with my answer, that his treatise against Christian perfection never saw the light. This was about thirty years ago. And here our intercourse ended; which indeed was very slight, as I had never seen him, either in private or public.

When he was imprisoned, he sent to me, desiring to see me. But I was not willing to go, supposing he only wanted me to intercede for him with great men; which I judged would be lost labour. He sent a second time, but I did not go. The gentleman who brought the third message told me plainly, "Sir, I will not go without you." I then went with him to Wood-Street Compter, where the Doctor then was. The Keeper (an extremely well-behaved man) told me, "Sir, of all the prisoners that have been in this place, I have not seen such a one as Dr. Dodd. I could trust him in any part of the house. Nay, he has gained the affection of even these wretches, my turnkeys." When I came into his room, and sat down by his bed-side, (for he had then a fever,) we were both of us silent for some time; till he began, "Sir, I have long desired to see you; but I little thought our first interview would be in such a place as this." I replied, "Sir, I am persuaded God saw this was the best, if not the only, way of bringing you to himself; and I trust it will have that happy effect." He said earnestly, "God grant it may! God grant it may!"

We conversed about an hour; but I was agreeably disappointed. He spoke of nothing but his own soul, and appeared to regard nothing in comparison of it. So that I went away far better satisfied than I came.

A few days after, I saw him again: the day before he was removed to Newgate, in order to his trial, which was to be the day following. I then stayed but about half an hour. I found him in the same temper as before, affected as one in such circumstances ought to be; but withal, calm and composed. I asked, "Sir, do not you find it difficult to preserve your recollection, amidst all these lawyers and witnesses?" He answered, "It is difficult; but I have one sure hold,--'Lord, not as I will, but as thou wilt.'"

Being obliged to take a long journey, I did not see him again till after he had lost the hope of life; the sentence which had been referred to the twelve Judges having been confirmed by them. He was now in Newgate. Entering into that house of woe, I was utterly surprised: It was as quiet and still as a College in the University. It seemed as if even the felons were unwilling to disturb him. We conversed about an hour; but had not one word about any but spiritual things. I found his mind still quiet and composed; sorrowing, but not without hope. And I could not but observe, that all these times he never blamed any one but himself. He did not appear to have the least touch of resentment to any man, receiving everything as at the hand of God.

On Wednesday (two days before his death) I paid

him one visit more. As we were talking, Mrs. Dodd came in; but when she came near him, she sunk down. He catched her in his arms and carried her to a chair; but had such a command over himself, that his eyes only spoke, though without tears, being afraid of adding to her distress. I now told him, "Sir, I think you do not ask enough, or expect enough, from God, your Saviour. The present blessing you may expect from him is, to be filled with all joy, as well as peace in believing." "O Sir," said he, "it is not for such a sinner as me to expect any joy in this world. The utmost I can desire is peace; and, through the mercy of God, that I have." We then spent a little time in prayer, and I solemnly commended him to God.

On Friday morning all the prisoners were gathered together, when he came down into the court. He seemed entirely composed. But when he observed most of them lifting up their hands, praying for him, blessing him, and weeping aloud, he was melted down, burst into tears too, and prayed God to bless them all. When he came out of the gate, an innumerable multitude were waiting, many of whom seemed ready to insult him. But the moment they saw him, their hearts were changed, and they began to bless him and pray for him too. A Clergyman, (Mr. P.,) being desirous to see the last of him, pressed on, though with difficulty and danger, and kept near him quite to the place of execution. One of his fellow-prisoners seemed to be in utter despair. Dr. Dodd, forgetting himself, laboured to comfort him; and strongly applied the promises. After some time spent in prayer, he pulled his cap over his eyes; and sinking down, seemed to die in a moment. I make no doubt, but in that moment the angels were ready to carry him into Abraham's bosom. (John Wesley, *The Works of John Wesley*, XI [Grand Rapids: Zondervan Publishing House, 1958], 454-456)

We might well be startled and even amazed at Mr. Wesley's suggesting to Dr. Dodd that by simply asking the Almighty, he could expect "to be filled with all joy, as well as peace in believing." Considering the circumstances of the case most would naturally conclude that ecstasies of joy could never be experienced at such a time. Nevertheless, the words of Mr. Wesley illustrate well his belief in that religion of the heart, described by the Apostle Paul as "the kingdom of heaven" which is "righteousness and peace and joy in the Holy Ghost" (Romans 14:17). As noticed in the above account, however, Mr. Wesley was ultimately satisfied with Dr. Dodd's testimony of inner peace and display of godly composure. By his final statement he seems to have had no doubt that the Doctor's final salvation was assured.

James Gerrish:
Cries Out To God At The Approach Of Death
(d. October, 1779)

One emphasis Mr. Wesley is often found to make in his sermonizing is the real danger and deceitfulness of riches. One of those sermons was based upon the text, "They that will be rich fall into temptation and a snare, and into many foolish and hurtful desires, which drown men in destruction and perdition" (1 Timothy 6:9). According to Mr. Wesley, the previous verse tends to fix the meaning of riches. "Having food and raiment [literally coverings; 'for the word,' says Wesley, 'includes lodging as well as clothes'], let us be therewith content" (1 Timothy 6:8). Accordingly, he understands the Apostle's definition of riches to be, "whatever is above the plain necessities and conveniences of life" (John Wesley, *The Works of John Wesley*, VII [Grand Rapids: Zondervan Publishing House, 1958], 1-3). Such truth with warning is seldom sounded from today's pulpits. Nevertheless, the danger of pursuing riches is just as real as it ever was.

The account shared below is but one example and illustration of the truth referred to above. Mr. Wesley, of course, could not but have rejoiced in the ultimate reclamation of James Gerrish. Not all who are ensnared by the deceitfulness of riches have ended life as fortunately.

Fri. 24.—James Gerrish, jun., of Roade, near Frome, was for several years zealous for God: But he too grew rich, and grew lukewarm, till he was seized with a consumption. At the approach of death he was "horribly afraid;" he was "in the lowest darkness, and in the deep." But "he cried unto God in his trouble," and was "delivered out of his distress." He was filled with peace and joy unspeakable, and so continued till he went to God. His father desired I would preach his funeral sermon; which I accordingly did this day, at Roade. (John Wesley, *The Works of John Wesley,* IV [Grand Rapids: Zondervan Publishing House, 1958], 167)

What a contrast there is between the horrible fear of death with spiritual darkness of soul and the being "filled with peace and joy unspeakable."

Mr. Ritchie:
"I Am Happy, Happy, Happy In His Love."
(d. April, 1780)

According to his *Journal* dated, Wednesday, April 19, 1780, Mr. Wesley had hurried to Otley, hoping to see Mr. Ritchie while yet alive. Upon his arrival, however, he found that death had swifter wings. "But," writes Mr. Wesley, "he had first witnessed a good confession." One had said to him just before he died, "You will be better soon." His reply was, "I cannot be better, for I have God in my heart. I am happy, happy, happy in his love."

"Mr. Wilson, the Vicar, after a little hesitation, consented," says Mr. Wesley, "that I should preach [Mr. Ritchie's] funeral sermon: This I did to-day. The text he had chosen was, 'Unto you therefore which believe, he is precious' (1 Peter 2:7). Perhaps," writes Mr. Wesley, "such a congregation had hardly been in Otley church before. Surely the right hand of the Lord bringeth mighty things to pass!" (John Wesley, *The Works of John Wesley*, IV [Grand Rapids: Zondervan Publishing House, 1958], 178).

Some may wonder why the above mentioned Vicar would be at all hesitant to allow Mr. Wesley to preach Mr. Ritchie's funeral sermon. First of all, very few of the Anglican clergy were sympathetic to the Methodist movement and its widely spreading revival, even though John and Charles Wesley were Anglican priests themselves. Methodist preaching that insisted on the experience of heart religion was fanaticism to many of the established clergy. Secondly, traveling Methodist preachers disregarded parish boundaries. There was often the feeling that Methodists were making inroads upon their territories. Envy was stirred when crowds appeared to hear them preach in the fields and market places.

The reader will notice that the last testimony of Mr. Ritchie was happiness in the love of God. It is popular in our day for those in the pulpit to relegate "happiness" to the humanistic realm. "Happiness," they tell us "is dependent upon daily circumstances or daily occurrences and would infer that it has nothing to do with consciousness of "God in [the] heart," as was testified by Mr. Ritchie before his soul's departure.

In contrast, Mr. Wesley and early Methodists described "happiness" as the "soul's delighting in God. "

"There is but one God in heaven," writes Mr. Wesley, "above and in the earth beneath; so there is only one happiness for created spirits, either in heaven or earth. This one God made our heart for himself; and it cannot rest till it resteth in him" (John Wesley, *The Works of John Wesley*, VI [Grand Rapids: Zondervan Publishing House, 1958], 431).

To Mr. Wesley there is an inseparable connection between holiness and happiness ("ibid., 360"). This holiness and happiness is dependent upon the inward kingdom of heaven—"righteousness, and peace, and joy in the Holy Ghost," together with the inward witness that sins are forgiven and that one is pleasing God.

Mrs. Cole:
"Died In Full, Joyous Peace"
(d. November, 1780)

"I came to Luton," writes Mr. Wesley, "and found that child of sorrow and pain, Mrs. Cole, was gone to rest. For many years she had not known an hour's ease; but she died in full, joyous peace. And how little does she regret all that is past, now the days of her mourning are ended!" (John Wesley, *The Works of John Wesley*, IV [Grand Rapids: Zondervan Publishing House, 1958], 194).

In his sermon entitled, "The Trouble and Rest of Good Men," Mr. Wesley has some comments that apply to the departure of Mrs. Cole and all dying saints just entering the glory of eternal rest. We share a few of those comments below.

> Let us view ... the state of a Christian at his [or her] entrance into the other world. Suppose the "the silver cord" of life just "loosed," and "the wheel broken at the cistern;" the heart can now beat no more; the blood ceases to move; the last breath flies off from the quivering lips, and the soul springs forth into eternity. What are the thoughts of such a soul that has just

subdued her last enemy, death? that sees the body of sin lying beneath her, and is new born into the world of spirits? How does she sing, "'O death, where is thy sting? O grave, where is thy victory? Thanks be unto God,' who hath given me 'the victory, through our Lord Jesus Christ!' O happy day, wherein I shall begin to live! wherein I shall taste my native freedom! When I was 'born of a woman' I had 'but a short time to live,' and that time was 'full of misery;' that corruptible body pressed me down, and enslaved me to ... pain. But the snare is broken, and I am delivered. Henceforth I know [it] no more. That head is no more an aching head: Those eyes shall no more run down with tears: That heart shall no more pant with anguish and fear; be weighed down with sorrow or care: Those limbs shall no more be racked with pain .... I shall never cease, day or night, to love and praise the Lord my God with all my heart, and with all my strength. But what are ye? Are 'all these ministering spirits sent forth to minister to' one 'heir of salvation?' Then, dust and ashes, farewell! I hear the voice of heaven saying, 'Come away, and rest from thy labours. Thy warfare is accomplished; thy sin is pardoned; and the days of thy mourning are ended.'" (John Wesley, *The Works of John Wesley*, VII [Grand Rapids: Zondervan Publishing House, 1958], 371-72)

Robert Wilkinson:
"I Have Been In Heaven."
(d. December, 1780)

Robert Wilkinson was described as "an Israelite indeed; a man of faith and prayer; who [was] a pattern of all good works." His initial conversion was somewhat unique. He had previously experienced much difficulty believing that God had pardoned his sins.

On Sunday, July, 12, Joseph Watson preached in the chapel in Weardale. He gave out that hymn—

> All ye that pass by,
> To Jesus draw nigh.
> To you is it nothing that Jesus should die?

Then, all within me cried out,

> That sinner am I,
> Who on Jesus rely,
> And come for the pardon God cannot deny.

I then believed that God for Christ's sake had forgiven my sins, and found that peace which arises from a sense of reconciliation.

Mr. Wilkinson, writes that "In the year 1768, I was sent to call sinners to repentance in and about the city of Carlisle." In this way he began years of ministry as one of Mr. Wesley's itinerant preachers. Like many of his fellow laborers, he suffered his share of persecution, hardship and suffering; "but," says he, "blessed be God, He delivered me out of the hands of all my enemies and gave me several seals to my ministry."

In his final illness, it is reported that "He bore all his afflictions with great patience, frequently lifting up his heart to God, and repeating these words:

> But He knoweth the way that I take: when He hath tried me, I shall come forth as gold. My foot hath held His steps, His way have I kept, and not declined. Neither have I gone back from the commandment of His lips; I have esteemed the words of His mouth more than my necessary food (Job xxiii.). When he perceived that he should die, he exhorted his wife to cast all her care upon the Lord, and encouraged her to believe that His grace was sufficient for her.
>
> He then prayed for her and his two children; earnestly entreating the Lord to protect them in this troublesome world, and to supply all their wants.
>
> He next prayed fervently for Mr. Wesley, that the presence of the Lord might continue with him all the days, and crown him at last with eternal glory.
>
> He then remembered his three fellow laborers in the circuit, praying that the Redeemer would assist us in the great work; that He would go forthwith, and bless

the labours of all the preachers, and that the kingdom of the Redeemer might spread unto the ends of the earth, and preserve them until they join the church triumphant.

In the night season he had a severe conflict with Satan, and his spirit wrestled with God in prayer. Yea, he was in an agony, as he said afterwards. At last the tempter fled; and he seemed as if he was admitted into heaven, to converse with God, with angels and saints.

He suddenly awaked his wife (who was in the same room), and said, "Thou hast been sleeping, but I have been in heaven. Oh what has the Lord discovered to me this night! Oh the glory of God! the glory of God in heaven! The celestial city! The New Jerusalem! Oh the lovely beauty! the happiness of paradise! God is all love; He is nothing but love. Oh help me to praise Him! Oh help me to praise Him! I shall praise Him for ever! I shall praise Him for ever!"

In this glorious fashion Robert Wilkinson departed this life. Concerning the funeral held the following Sunday, it was said that the place of service "was well filled, and the Lord made it a solemn time." One who witnessed this occasion observed that "there was scarcely a dry eye in the congregation."

George Shadford, a colleague of Mr. Wilkinson, writes that he had "often taken notice how the Lord makes the triumphant death of good men a peculiar blessing to His children who are left behind." Such was the case at this time. "The people of God were remarkably blessed in hearing the dying testimony of our dear friend. The worldly people and the backsliders were cut to the heart."

When the sermon was concluded, Mr. Shadford uttered the following: "Earth has lost, and heaven has gained, a child of God. Let us pray the Lord to add another to the church militant." In answer to that prayer, a young man's soul was set "at liberty, so that he went from the solemn place as the shepherds from the heavenly vision, blessing, praising, and glorifying God."

There were clergy of the Church of England who did not show themselves friendly to the Methodists. However, the minister of this "parish behaved exceedingly kind: he came to the preaching-house, stayed awhile, and then walked slowly before the corpse," while the people sang a hymn of praise. Upon their arrival at the church, they sang, according to Mr. Shadford, "those awful words--

> Thee we adore, eternal Name,
> And humbly own to Thee,
> How feeble is our mortal frame,
> What dying worms we be!"

Mr. Shadford continued his description of the scene: "The people sang lustily and with a solemn spirit; for the divine presence was with us all the way through, and in such a manner as I never knew before at any funeral." He further shares the following:

> When the minister read these words, "Not to be sorry as men without hope," Mrs. Wilkinson, who hung upon my arm with her two little babes, was so overwhelmed with the presence of God that she could not refrain from crying out, "Sorry, no! Glory be to God! glory be to God! Glory, and praise, and blessing, be ascribed unto God, for ever and ever!" Her spirit seemed as if it was ready to launch into the eternal world, to be with Jesus and her happy husband. A remarkable power

fell on all that could hear her; so that the people were melted into tears; some of sorrow, others of joy.

So it was that Robert Wilkinson "died in the full triumph of faith." The death and burial services of this Methodist saint proved to be the beginning of a revived work of God in and around Grimsby. People throughout the countryside caught spiritual fire and carried it back to their little societies.

Mr. Shadford closes his account of his friend and colleague's passing with this prayerful wish: "Oh, what a blessing to live and die a Christian! May I also be a follower of those who 'through faith and patience inherit the promises'! In my life, and at my death, may I be like him!" (John Telford, ed., *Wesley's Veterans,* V [Salem: Schmul Publishers, 1976], 233-241).

Mary Charlton:
Never Lost Sight Of The Pardoning Love Of God
(d. May, 1781)

"I preached a funeral sermon," writes Mr. Wesley, "for Mary Charlton, an Israelite indeed. From the hour that she first knew the pardoning love of God, she never lost sight of it for a moment. Eleven years ago, she believed that God had cleansed her from all sin; and she showed that she had not believed in vain, by her holy and unblamable conversation" (John Wesley, *The Works of John Wesley*, IV [Grand Rapids: Zondervan Publishing House, 1958], 204).

In the minds of some, it would be inconceivable to suppose that a consciousness of the pardoning love of God could be maintained indefinitely from the moment of one's justification. And yet it is said that Mary Charlton "never lost sight of it for a moment."

Always accompanying this pardoning love of God is that "peace which passeth all understanding." Such a peace is experienced by all from the time they first find "redemption in the blood of Jesus. But," writes Mr. Wesley, "when they have nearly finished their course, it generally flows as a river, even in such a degree as it had not before entered into their hearts to conceive."

Mr. Wesley then shares a "remarkable instance of this in one of his sermons." He tells of one by the name of "Enoch Williams, one of the first of our Preachers," says he, "that was stationed at Cork, (who had received this peace when he was eleven years old, and never lost it for an hour,) after he had rejoiced in God with joy unspeakable, during the whole course of his illness, was too much exhausted to speak many words, but just said, 'Peace! peace!' and died" (John Wesley, *The Works of John Wesley*, VII [Grand Rapids: Zondervan Publishing House, 1958], 433).

Mr. Thompson:
A Dying Anglican Clergyman Wishes To See Mr. Wesley
(d. September, 1782)

Late in life Mr. Wesley had gained some respect and even esteem from various fellow Anglican clergymen. One here shows his confidence in Mr. Wesley's ability to give that most valuable and needed assistance when approaching the gates of death. Mr. Wesley, on his part, gives evidence of his love and compassion by speedily complying with the dying man's desire to see him.

> Being informed ... here, that my old friend, Mr. Thompson, Rector of St. Gennis, was near death, and had expressed a particular desire to see me, I judged no time was to be lost. So, borrowing the best horse I could find, I set out, and rode as fast as I could. On the way, I met with a white-headed old man, who caught me by the hand, and said, "Sir, do you not know me?" I answered, "No." He said, "My father, my father! I am poor John Trembath." I desired him to speak to me in the evening at Launceston; which he did. He was for some time reduced to extreme poverty, so as to hedge and ditch for bread; but in his distress he cried

to God, who sent him an answer of peace. He likewise enabled him to cure a gentleman that was desperately ill, and afterward several others; so that he grew into reputation, and gained a competent livelihood. "And now," said he, "I want for nothing; I am happier than ever I was in my life."

I found Mr. Thompson just alive, but quite sensible. It seemed to me as if none in the house but himself was very glad to see me. He had many doubts concerning his final state, and rather feared, than desired, to die; so that my whole business was to comfort him, and to increase and confirm his confidence in God. He desired me to administer the Lord's Supper, which I willingly did; and I left him much happier than I found him, calmly waiting till his change should come. (John Wesley, *The Works of John Wesley*, IV [Grand Rapids: Zondervan Publishing House, 1958], 235)

Charles Greenwood:

The Melancholy One Who Became "Unspeakably Happy"
(d. February, 1783)

Sadness, despondency and depression are symptoms too often found among the churched as well as the unchurched. Some, to be sure, suffer depression because of physical or psychological disorders. Others are heavy in soul and sick at heart because of unmet spiritual needs. This seems to have been the case with the man Mr. Wesley describes below.

> To-day Charles Greenwood went to rest. He had been a melancholy man all his days, full of doubts and fears, and continually writing bitter things against himself. When he was first taken ill, he said he should die, and was miserable through fear of death; but two days before he died, the clouds dispersed, and he was unspeakably happy, telling friends, "God has revealed to me things which it is impossible for man to utter." Just when he died, such glory filled the room, that it seemed to be a little heaven; none could grieve or shed a tear, but all present appeared to be partakers of his joy. (John Wesley, *The Works of John Wesley*, IV [Grand Rapids: Zondervan Publishing House, 1958], 243)

The Apostle Paul wrote of the inward "kingdom of God" as consisting of "righteousness and peace and joy in the Holy Ghost" (Romans 14:17). The Apostle John writes: "Herein is our love made perfect, that we may have boldness in the day of judgment: because as he is, so are we in this world. There is no fear in love; but perfect love casteth out fear" (1John 4:17, 18). John is referring to that fear that has torment, including the fear of death and judgment. We are assured by the account shared above that Charles Greenwood was not only saved from his doubts, fears and melancholy condition but was given before his departure a "taste of the powers of the world to come."

Mr. Vincent Perronet:
A Fellow Anglican Clergyman Who Died Full of Love
(d. May, 1785)

The Rev. Vincent Perronet was the parish clergyman at Shoreham. He was one of the very few fellow Anglican clergymen who gave his support and encouragement to John and Charles Wesley in the advancement of the Methodist revival. John Wesley considered him a gracious friend and often made visits to his home for periods of rest. He was welcomed often as a visiting minister to the pulpit at Shoreham.

Once in his *Journal*, Mr. Wesley records that, "When old Mr. Perronet heard that his favourite child, the stay of his old age, was dead, he broke into praise and thanksgiving to God who had 'taken another of his children out of this evil world!'"

Sometime later we read in the *Journal*, "I paid one more visit to Mr. Perronet, now in his ninetieth year. I do not know so venerable a man. His understanding is little, if at all impaired; and his heart seems to be all love. A little longer I hope he will remain here, to be a blessing to all that see and hear him." Then in December of 1784, we read: "Going on to Shoreham, we found that venerable man, Mr. Perronet, ninety-one years of age, calmly waiting for the conclusion of a good warfare. His bodily strength is gone, but his understanding is little impaired; and he appears to have more love than ever."

The following is the account of this saintly clergyman's departure to a better world.

> On this day [Saturday May 7, 1785] that venerable saint, Mr. Perronet, desired his granddaughter, Miss Briggs, who attended him day and night, to go out into the garden, and take a little air. He was reading, and hearing her read, the three last chapters of Isaiah. When she returned, he was in a kind of ecstasy; the tears running down his cheeks, from a deep sense of the glorious things which were shortly to come to pass. He continued unspeakably happy that day, and on Sunday was, if possible, happier still. And indeed heaven seemed to be as it were opened to all that were round about him. When he was in bed, she went into his room to see if anything was wanting; and as she stood at the feet of the bed, he smiled, and broke out, "God bless thee, my dear child, and all that belong to thee! Yea, He will bless thee!" Which he earnestly repeated many times, till she left the room. When she went in, the next morning, Monday, 9, his spirit was returned to God!
>
> So ended the holy and happy life of Mr. Vincent Perronet, in the ninety-second year of his age. I follow hard after him in years, being now in the eighty-second year of my age. O that I may follow him in holiness; and that my last end may be like his! (John Wesley, *The Works of John Wesley*, IV [Grand Rapids: Zondervan Publishing House, 1958], 294, 305-306)

Coal Miner Thomas:
"I Am Willing To Go To Him."
(d. No date)

In his sermon entitled, "A Call to Backsliders," Mr. Wesley provides an unusual account of one by the name of Thomas. He was a coal miner who lived in Kingswood, near Bristol and who was, in the words of Mr. Wesley, "an eminent sinner, and afterwards an eminent saint." However, as time went on, "he renewed his acquaintance with his old companions, who by degrees" influenced him in a return to his old ways so that "he dropped all his religion, and was two-fold more a child of hell than before."

> One day he was working in the pit (or coal mine) with a serious young man, who suddenly stopped and cried out, "O Tommy, what a man was you once! How did your words and example provoke many to love and to good works! And what are you now? What would become of you, if you were to die as you are?" "Nay, God forbid," said Thomas, "for then I should fall into hell headlong! O let us cry to God!" They did so for a considerable time, first the one, and then the other.

They called upon God with strong cries and tears, wrestling with him in mighty prayer. After some time, Thomas broke out, "Now I know God hath healed my backsliding. I know again, that my Redeemer liveth, and that he hath washed me from my sins with his own blood. I am willing to go to him." Instantly part of the pit caved in and crushed him to death in a moment. (John Wesley, *The Works of John Wesley,* VI [Grand Rapids: Zondervan Publishing House, 1958], 521)

Wesley's Heartfelt Farewell To An Irish Congregation

By the time the insertion below was written into Mr. Wesley's *Journal*, he was 82 years of age and only five years away from the end of life's course. He had often said that he wished to end his life and ministry together. He did not want to outlive his usefulness. Though he had suffered his share of persecution in the early days of the Methodist movement, he lived long enough to see public sentiment change in his favor. The warm hospitality shown him by Dr. Fall as described in the anecdote below is but one example of the honor eventually shown him in his old age. Even his enemies were compelled to respect him while multitudes of common people truly loved him.

> Sun. May 1.—At eight I preached in the Court-House [in Waterford, Ireland] to a larger congregation than before. At eleven I went to the cathedral, one of the most elegant churches in Ireland. The whole Service was performed with the utmost solemnity. After Service, the senior Prebend, Dr. Fall, invited me to dinner; and desired when I came again, I would take a bed at his

house. I doubt that will never be!

At four I preached at the head of the Mall, to a Moorfields congregation, all quiet and attentive. Monday, 2. The congregation at five in the morning was larger than that on Saturday evening; and all of them appeared to have (for the present at least) a real concern for their salvation. O that it may not pass away as the morning dew!

I took a solemn farewell of this affectionate people, concluding with those awful words:--

> Now on the brink of death we stand:
> And if I pass before,
> You all may safe escape to land,
> And hail me on the shore.

Death was never far from the thoughts of Mr. Wesley. The prospect of glory was always real to him as was the hope of meeting on the other side that host of converts he had had a part in preparing for a better world (John Wesley, *The Works of John Wesley*, IV [Grand Rapids: Zondervan Publishing House, 1958], 304).

Rev. John Fletcher:

The Legacy, Last Illness And Death
Of The Saintliest Man Wesley Ever Knew
(d. August, 1785)

Before the inspiring story is shared of the Rev. John Fletcher's departure from this life, it may be appropriate to give a short account of the man himself for those who may know little of him.

"One equal to him I have not known; one so inwardly and outwardly devoted to God." These were the words of John Wesley in sincere description and testimony of his saintly friend, John Fletcher. This man was not only a very close and affectionate friend of Mr. Wesley, but the celebrated apologist of early Methodist doctrine and theology. Until his untimely death, he was Wesley's designated successor as chief leader of the Methodists. True it is that some in late years have endeavored to magnify theological differences between them but such differences when inspected closely are minimal in their significance. One needs only to read his "Checks to Antinomianism" to see the masterful way in which he repeatedly and successfully vindicated Mr. Wesley's theological stance against the Calvinists and others who were openly opposing and attacking early Methodist teachings. In a personal letter to a friend, dated February, 1772, Mr. Wesley writes as follows:

I am glad [God] has given to others both the power

283

and the will to answer them that trouble me; so that I may not always be forced to hold my weapons in one hand, while I am building with the other. I rejoice, likewise, not only in the abilities, but in the temper, of Mr. Fletcher. He writes as he lives; I cannot say that I know such another Clergyman in England or Ireland. He is all fire; but it is the fire of love. His writings, like his constant conversation, breathe nothing else, to those who read him with an impartial eye. (John Wesley, *The Works of John Wesley,* XII [Grand Rapids: Zondervan Publishing House, 1958], 349)

A native of Switzerland, Mr. Fletcher took the usual course of study for the ministry at the University of Geneva. This being the very seat of Calvin's teachings, Mr. Fletcher was thoroughly schooled in Calvinistic theology. However, being disgusted by the necessity he should be under to subscribe to the doctrine of absolute election and predestination if ordained there, he gave up the idea of going into the ministry at that time.

It was not until he had been in England for a time that he came in contact with the Methodists. He readily joined a Methodist society when recognizing their teachings to be the most consistent with Scripture. Following his own evangelical conversion, Mr. Fletcher eventually answered God's call to pastoral labors in the Anglican parish of Madeley. Here he proved himself to be a godly and effective shepherd of souls for twenty-five years until his death in 1785. This writer, having personally visited his church on different occasions in late years, found it gratifying to observe spiritual fruit still arising from the seed sown many years before. Current members of the congregation testify to the great appreciation they have for their heritage. Mr. Fletcher's pulpit and writing desk can still be seen. Likewise, one may view his tomb just outside the church wall and the house, just a stone's throw away, in which he lived and completed most of his writings.

When referring to Mr. Fletcher as the principal defender of early Methodist teachings, Dr. Richard S. Taylor writes: "His kindly, often witty, refutation of antinomianism has never been answered, and his lucid, inspiring expositions of salvation never surpassed" (John Fletcher, *The Works of the Reverend John Fletcher* [Salem: Schmul Publishers, 1974], book jacket).

The late Dr. S. I. Emery reminds us that Mr. Fletcher was called "The Arminian of the Arminians." He says, "His writings are pungent and deeply spiritual. His reasoning is clear, scriptural and forceful .... Read his works to be enlightened, practice them and be holy" (ibid.).

The account of Mr. Fletcher's final days and death is shared below, taken from *The Life of The Rev. John Fletcher* by Joseph Benson.

> 1. "Some weeks before he was taken ill," says Mrs. Fletcher, "he mentioned to me a peculiar manifestation of love which he received in his own home, with the application of those words, 'Thou shalt walk with me in white.' He added, 'It is a little thing so to hang upon God by faith as to feel no departure from him, and no rising in the heart against him. This does not satisfy me. And I sometimes find such gleams of light and love, such wafts, as it were, of the heavenly air, so powerful, as if they would just then take my soul with them to glory! But *I am not filled*. I want to be filled with all the fullness of God.' In conformity to these sentiments, when he was in his last illness he expressed himself thus: '*I am filled*, most sweetly filled.' This

conveyed much to my mind, as I understood by it the accomplishment of his large desires.

2. "Some time before the beginning of his last sickness, he was peculiarly penetrated with a sense of the nearness of eternity. There was scarce an hour in which he was not calling upon us to drop every thought and every care, that we might attend to nothing but the drinking deeper into God. We spent much time in wrestling with God, and were led in a peculiar manner to abandon our whole selves, our souls and bodies, into the hands of God; ready to do and willing to suffer whatever was well-pleasing to him.

"And now the time drew near when his faith was to be called to its last grand exercises. A little before this, being on his knees in prayer for light, whether he should go to London or not, the answer to him seemed to be, 'Not to London, but to the grave.' When he acquainted me with this, he said, with a heavenly smile, 'Satan would represent it to me as something dreaded, enforcing those words, "The cold grave! The cold grave!"' On the Sunday following, (I think it was the next day,) that anthem was sung in church, 'The Lord is my shepherd, therefore can I lack nothing. He shall feed me in green pastures, and lead me forth beside the waters of comfort. He shall convert my soul, and bring me forth in the paths of righteousness for his name's sake. Yea, though, I walk through the valley of the shadow of death, I shall fear no evil; for thou art with me; thy rod and staff shall comfort me. Thou shalt prepare a table before me against them that trouble me.

Thou hast anointed my head with oil, and my cup shall be full.'

"In his return home he observed in how uncommon a degree these words had been blessed to his soul. And from that very time I do not remember to have seen in him any, the least marks of temptation. He showed an unusual cheerfulness and liveliness in every part of his work, and seemed to increase in strength of body as well as in strength of soul. Truly it was to him according to his faith. He feared no evil, and his cup was filled with righteousness, and peace, and joy in the Holy Ghost.

"On Thursday, August 4th, he was employed in the work of God from three in the afternoon till nine at night. When he came home he said, 'I have taken cold;' but seemed not to regard it. He was far from well on Friday and Saturday; but was uncommonly drawn out in prayer. On Saturday night he was abundantly worse, and his fever appeared very strong. I begged that he would by no means think of going to church in the morning. But he told me it was the will of the Lord, in which case I never dared to persuade.

3. "The Rev. Mr. Gilpin," as he has informed us, "called upon him in the morning, with an earnest request that he would permit him, if not to take the whole of his duty on that day, at least to share it with him. But this he would by no means be prevailed upon to suffer, assuring him, with an air of holy confidence, that God would sufficiently strengthen him to go through the duties of the day. This was his last appearance in public; and several who were present

upon this memorable occasion were affected beyond all description with the melancholy circumstances of the day. He opened the reading service with apparent strength; but before he had proceeded far in it, his countenance changed, his speech began to falter, and it was with the utmost difficulty that he could keep himself from fainting. Every eye was riveted upon him, deep solicitude was painted on every face, and confused murmurs of distress ran through the whole congregation. In the midst of this affecting scene, Mrs. Fletcher was seen pressing through the crowd, and earnestly entreating her dying husband no longer to attempt what appeared to be utterly impracticable. But he, as though conscious that he was engaged in his last public work, mildly refused to be entreated; and struggling against an almost insupportable languor constrained himself to continue the service. The windows being opened, he appeared to be a little refreshed, and began to preach with a strength and recollection that surprised all present. In the course of his sermon the idea of his weakness was almost lost in the freedom and energy with which he delivered himself. Mercy was the subject of his discourse; and while he expatiated on this glorious attribute of the Deity, its astonishing effects, he appeared to be carried above all the fears and feelings of mortality. There was something in his appearance and manner that gave his word an irresistible influence upon this solemn occasion. An awful concern was awakened through the whole assembly, and every one's heart was uncommonly moved. Upon the hearts of his friends, in particular, a most affecting impression was made at this season; and what deepened that impression was the sad presentiment, which they read in each other's countenance, of their pastor's approaching dissolution.

"After sermon he walked up to the communion-table, uttering these words: 'I am going to throw myself under the wings of the cherubim, before the mercy-seat.' Here the same distressing scene was renewed with additional solemnity. The people were deeply affected while they beheld him offering up the last languid remains of a life that had been lavishly spent in their service. Groans and tears were on every side. In going through the last part of his duty, he was exhausted again and again; but his spiritual vigor triumphed over his bodily weakness. After several times sinking on the sacramental-table, he still resumed his sacred work, and cheerfully distributed, with his dying hand, the love-memorials of his dying Lord. In the course of this concluding office, which he performed by means of the most astonishing exertions, he gave out several verses of hymns, and delivered many affectionate exhortations to his people, calling upon them, at intervals, to celebrate the mercy of God in short songs of adoration and praise. And now, having struggled through the service of near four hours' continuance, he was supported with blessings in his mouth, from the altar to his chamber, where he lay for some time in a swoon, and from whence he never walked into the world again.

"After this," proceeds Mrs. Fletcher, "he dropped into a sleep for some time, and on waking, cried out with a pleasant smile, 'Now, my dear, thou seest I am no worse for doing the Lord's work. He never fails me when I trust in him.' Having eaten a little dinner, he dozed most of the evening, now and then waking up with the praises of God in his mouth. At night his fever returned, but it was not violent; and yet his strength decreased amazingly. On Monday and Tuesday we had a little paradise together. He lay on a couch in the study; and, though often changing posture, was sweetly pleasant, and frequently slept a good while together. When he was awake, he delighted in hearing me read hymns and treatises on faith and love. His words were all animating, and his patience beyond expression. When he had a very nauseous medicine to take, he seemed to enjoy the cross, according to a word which he used often to repeat, 'We are to seek a perfect conformity to the will of God; and leave him to give us pleasure or pain, as it seemeth him good.'

"I asked him whether he had any directions to give me if he should be taken from me; since I desired to form my whole life thereby. He replied, 'No, not by *mine:* the Holy Ghost shall direct thee. I have nothing particular to say.' I said, 'Have you any conviction that God is about to take you?' He said, 'No: only I always see death so inexpressibly near, that we both seem to stand on the verge of eternity.' While he slept a little, I besought the Lord, if it were his good pleasure, to spare him to me a little longer. But my prayer seemed to have no wings: and I could not help mingling continually therewith, Lord, give me perfect resignation! This uncertainty made me tremble, lest God was going to put into my hands the bitter cup with which he threatened my husband. Some weeks before, I myself was ill of a fever, and not without danger. My husband then felt the whole parting scene, and struggled for a perfect resignation. He said, 'O Polly, shall I ever see the day when thou must be carried out to bury! How will the little things which thy tender care has prepared for me, in every part of the house, wound and distress me! How is it? I think I feel jealousy! I am jealous of the worms! I seem to shrink at the thought of giving my dear Polly to the worms.'

"Now all those reflections returned upon my heart with the weight of a millstone. I cried to the Lord, and these words were deeply impressed on my spirit. *Where I am, there shall my servants be, that they may behold my glory.* This promise was full of comfort to my soul. I saw that in Christ's immediate presence was our home, and that we should have our reunion in being deeply centered in him. I received it as a fresh marriage for eternity; as such I trust for ever to behold it. All that day, whenever I thought of the expression, *to behold my glory*. It seemed to wipe every tear, and was as the ring whereby we were joined anew.

"Awaking some time after, he said, 'Polly, I have been thinking it was Israel's fault that they asked for *signs*. We will not do so; but, abandoning our whole selves to the will of God, will lie patiently before him; assured that he will do all things well.'

"'My dear love, said I, 'if I have ever done or said

291

any thing to grieve thee, how will the remembrance wound my heart, if thou shouldest be taken from me!' He entreated me, with inexpressible tenderness, not to allow the thought, declaring his thankfulness for our union, in a variety of words written on my heart with the adamantine pen of friendship deeply dipped in blood.

"On Wednesday, he told me he had received such a manifestation of the full meaning of those words, 'God is love,' as he could never be able to express. 'It fills my heart,' said he, 'every moment: O Polly, my dear Polly, *God is love!* Shout! shout aloud! I want a gust of praise to go to the ends of the earth! But it seems as if I could not speak much longer. Let us fix on a sign between ourselves. Now,' said he, tapping me twice with his finger, 'I mean, God is love. And we will draw each other into God. Observe! By this we will draw each other into God.'

"Sally coming in, he cried out, 'O Sally, God is love! Shout, both of you! I want to hear you shout his praise!' All this time the medical friend, who attended him diligently, hoped he was in no danger: as he had no headache, but much sleep, without the least delirium, and an almost regular pulse. So was the disease, though commissioned to take his life, restrained by the power of God.

"On Thursday his speech began to fail. While he was able, he spoke to all that came in his way. Hearing that a stranger was in the house, he ordered her to be called up. But the uttering only two sentences made him ready to faint away. And, while he had any power of speech, he would not be silent to his friendly doctor. 'O, sir,' said he, 'you take much thought for my body: permit me to take thought for your soul!' When I could scarce understand anything he said, I spoke these words, '*God is love.* O for that gust of praise! I want to sound!'—Here his voice again failed. All this time he was much in pain, and suffered many ways: but those who were present can conceive. If I did but name his sufferings, he would smile and make the sign.

"On Friday, observing his body covered with spots, I felt a sword pierce through my soul. As I was kneeling by his side, with my hand in his, entreating the Lord to be with us in this tremendous hour, he strove to say many things, but could not articulate the words. All he could do was to press my hand, and frequently repeat the sign. At last he breathed out, 'Head of the Church, be head to my wife!'

"When I was forced to leave him for a few moments, Sally said to him, 'My dear master, do you know me?' He replied, 'God will put his right hand under you.' She added, 'O my dear master, should you be taken away, what a disconsolate creature will my poor, dear mistress be!' He replied, 'God will be her all in all.'

"He always took a peculiar pleasure in repeating or hearing those words,

> *'Jesus' blood through earth and skies,*
> *Mercy, free, boundless mercy cries.'*

Whenever I repeated them to him he would answer

'Boundless! Boundless! Boundless!' He now added though not without much difficulty,

> *'Mercy's full power I soon shall prove,*
> *Loved with everlasting love.'*

"On Saturday, in the afternoon, his fever seemed quite off, and a few friends standing near his bed, he reached his hand to each: and, looking on a minister, said, 'Are you ready to assist to-morrow?' His recollection surprised us, as the day of the week had not been named in the room. Many were of opinion he would recover; and one of them said to him, 'Do you think the Lord will raise you up?' He strove to answer, and could just pronounce, 'Raise me up in the resur'----meaning in the resurrection. To another, who asked the same question, he said, 'I leave it all to God.'

"In the evening the fever came again, and with greater violence than ever. The mucous then falling on his throat, almost strangled him. It was supposed the same painful symptom would grow more and more violent to the last. As I felt this exquisitely, I cried to the Lord to remove it. And, glory be to his name, he did! From that time it returned no more.

"As night drew on, I perceived him dying very fast. His fingers could hardly make the sign, which he scarce ever forgot: and his speech seemed quite gone. I said, 'My dear creature, I ask not for myself: I know thy soul: but, for the sake of others, if Jesus be very present with thee, lift up thy right hand.' Immediately he did. 'If the prospect of glory sweetly open before thee, repeat the sign.' He instantly raised it again, and in half a minute, a second time. He then threw it up, as if he would reach the top of the bed. After this, his hands moved no more. But on my saying, 'Art thou in pain?' He answered 'No.' From this time he lay in a kind of sleep, though with his eyes open and fixed. For the most part he sat upright against pillows, with his head a little inclining to one side. And so remarkable composed, yea, triumphant was his countenance, that the least trace of death was scarcely discernible in it. Eighteen hours he was in this situation, breathing like a person in common sleep. About thirty-five minutes past ten, on Sunday night, August 14, his precious soul entered into the joy of his Lord, without one struggle or groan, in the fifty-sixth year of his age.

"And here I break off my mournful story; but on my bleeding heart the fair picture of his heavenly excellence will be for ever drawn."

5. The reader will not think me tedious, if I subjoin here the account which the Rev. Mr. Gilpin has given of this last scene of the life of this incomparable man: "After having manifested so much resolution and constancy in fighting 'the good fight of faith,' it is no wonder that Mr. Fletcher was permitted to 'finish his course with joy,' and that the concluding scenes of his warfare were peculiarly triumphant and glorious. Equally prepared for every event, he met his last great trial with all that composure and steadiness which had invariably distinguished him upon every former occasion of suffering. He entered 'the valley of the shadow of

death,' as one who feared no evil. He considered it as the high-road to that incorruptible inheritance which is reserved for the saints; and, looking forward with a hope full of immortality, he saw, beyond its limited gloom, those everlasting hills of light and glory to which his soul aspired.

"A few days before his dissolution, he appeared to have reached that desirable point where the last rapturous discoveries are made to the souls of dying saints. Roused, as it were, with the shouts of glory, he broke into a song of holy triumph, which began and ended with the praises of God's unfathomable love. He labored to declare the secret manifestations he enjoyed; but his sensations were too powerful for utterance, and, after looking inexpressible things, he contended himself with calling upon all around him to celebrate and shout out that adorable love, which can never be fully comprehended or adequately expressed. This triumphant frame of mind was not a transient feeling, but a state that he continued to enjoy, with little or no discernible interruption, to the moment of his death. While he possessed the power of speech, he spake as one whose lips had been touched with 'a live coal from the altar;' and when deprived of that power, his countenance discovered that he was sweetly engaged in the contemplation of eternal things.

"On the day of his departure, as I was preparing to attend my own church, which was at the distance of nine miles from Madeley, I received a hasty message from Mrs. Fletcher, requesting my immediate attendance at the vicarage. I instantly followed the messenger, and found Mr. Fletcher with every symptom of approaching dissolution upon him. I had ever looked upon this man of God with an extraordinary degree of affection and reverence; and on this afflicting occasion my heart was uncommonly affected and depressed. It was now in vain to recollect that public duty required my presence in another place: unfitted for every duty except that of silently watching the bed of death, I found it impossible to withdraw from the solemn scene to which I had been summoned. I had received from this evangelical teacher, in days that were past, many excellent precepts with respect to holy living; and now I desired to receive from him the important lesson with respect to holy dying. And truly this concluding lesson was of inestimable worth, since so much patience and resignation, so much peace and composure, were scarcely ever discovered in the same circumstances before. 'Let me die the death of the righteous, and let my last end be like his!'

"While their pastor was breathing out his soul into the hands of 'a faithful Creator,' his people were offering up their joint supplications on his behalf in the house of God. Little, however, was seen among them on that trying occasion, but affliction and tears. Indeed, it was a day much to be remembered for the many affecting testimonies of distress which appeared on every side. The whole village wore an air of consternation, and sadness, and not one joyful song was heard among all its inhabitants. Hasty messengers were passing to and fro with anxious inquiries and confused reports; and the members of every family sat together in silence that day; awaiting with trembling expectation the issue of every hour. After the conclusion of the evening service, several of the poor, who came from distant parts, and who were usually entertained under Mr. Fletcher's roof, still lingered about the house, and seemed unable to tear themselves away from the place without a sight of their expiring pastor. Secretly informed of their desire, I obtained them the permission they wished. And the door of the chamber being set open, immediately, before which Mr. Fletcher was sitting upright in his bed, with the curtains undrawn, unaltered in his usual venerable appearance, they slowly moved one by one along the gallery, severally pausing as they passed by the door, and casting in a look of mingled supplication and anguish. It was, indeed, an affecting sight, to behold these unfeigned mourners successively presenting themselves before the bed of their dying benefactor, with an inexpressible eagerness in their looks, and then dragging themselves away from his presence with a distressing consciousness that 'they should see his face no more.'

"And now the hour speedily approached that was to put a solemn termination to our hopes and fears. His weakness very perceptibly increased, but his countenance continued unaltered to the last. If there was any visible change in his feelings, he appeared more at ease and more sweetly composed, as the moment of his dismission drew near. Our eyes were riveted upon him in awful expectation. But, whatever he had felt before, no murmuring thought was suffered, at this interesting period, to darken the glories of so illustrious a scene. All was silence, when the last angelic minister suddenly arrived, and performed his important commission with so much stillness and secrecy that it was impossible to determine the exact moment of its completion. Mrs. Fletcher was kneeling by the side of her departing husband, one who had attended him with uncommon assiduity during the last stages of his distemper sat at his head; while I sorrowfully waited near his feet. Uncertain whether or not he was totally separated from us, we pressed nearer, and hung over his bed in the attitude of listening attention. His lips had ceased to move, and his head was gently sinking upon his bosom: we stretched out our hands; but his warfare was accomplished, and the happy spirit had taken its everlasting flight.

"Such was the undisturbed and triumphant death of this eminently holy and laborious pastor, who entered into rest on the evening of Sunday, August 14, 1785. Blessed are the dead who die in the Lord! They rest from their painful labors, and are followed by those exemplary works which they considered as unworthy a place in their remembrance: they escape from the windy storm and tempest, and are brought to their desired haven: they have a right to the tree of life, they enter in through the gates into the city, and stand with everlasting acceptance in the presence of God.

"This afflicting providence is severely felt by the

survivor, who has lost, at this separating stroke, whatever she had counted most valuable on this side of eternity. But, while she feels all the anguish of an immediate separation from her dearest friend, she looks forward with a joyful hope of being one day united to his happy spirit, where the pangs of parting can be known no more. Mrs. Fletcher was surrounded upon this sad occasion by a multitude of sincere mourners, who, while they deplored the loss of their inestimable pastor, recollected, with peculiar satisfaction, that the last years of his life had been years of abundant consolation and peace; and who now rejoice that, in his removal from among them, he left behind him a lively representative of himself; one who enters into his labors and watches over his flock; a support to the needy, a guide to the ignorant, and 'a mother in Israel.'"

6. So far Mr. Gilpin. Mrs. Fletcher adds: "When I call to mind his ardent zeal, his laborious endeavors to seek and save the lost, his diligence in the employment of his time, his Christlike condescension toward me, and his uninterrupted converse with Heaven, I may well be allowed to add, My loss is beyond the power of words to paint. I have often gone through deep waters; but all my afflictions were nothing to this. Well: I want no pleasant prospect but upward; nor any thing whereon to fix my hope, but immortality.

"From the time I have had the happiness and honor of being with him, every day more and more convinced me he was the Christian. I saw, I loved, in him, the image of my Saviour, and thought myself the happiest of women in the possession of the most sympathizing and heavenly friend. My sorrow bears a due proportion. But it is alleviated, by that thought, 'United in God, we cannot be divided.' No: we are of one household still: we are joined in him, as our centre, 'of whom the whole family in heaven and earth is named.' It is said of New Testament believers, 'they are come to the spirits of just men made perfect:' to the glorious privilege of communion with the Church triumphant. But this is far more apparent to the eyes of celestial spirits than to ours, which are yet veiled with flesh and blood. Yet, as there is joy in heaven over one sinner that repenteth, and as the prayers of saints still on earth are represented by incense in the hands of the elders, I can only consider departed spirits and ministering angels as one innumerable company, continually surrounding us. And are they not as nearly united to their fellow-soldiers now as when they were in the body? What should hinder? Gratitude and affection are natives of heaven, and live for ever there. Forgetfulness is a property of mortality, and drops off with the body. Therefore they that loved us in the Lord will surely love us for ever. Can any thing material interrupt the sight or presence of a spirit? Nay,

> 'Walls within walls no more the passage bar,
> Than unopposing space of liquid air.'

7. "On the 17th his remains were deposited in Madeley churchyard, amid the tears and lamentations of thousands. The service was performed by the Rev. Mr.

Hutton, rector of Waters Upton, whom God enabled to pay a public tribute of respect to the memory of this great man, in a funeral sermon from Hebrews xiii. 7, and to speak in a pathetic manner to the weeping flock. In the conclusion, at my request he read the following paper:

"As it was the desire of my beloved husband to be buried in this plain manner, so, out of tenderness, he begged that I might not be present. And in every thing I would obey him.

"Permit me, then, by the mouth of a friend, to bear an open testimony to the glory of God, that I, who have known him in the most perfect manner, am constrained to declare that I never knew any one walk so closely in the ways of God as he did. The Lord gave him a conscience tender as the apple of an eye. And he literally preferred the interest of every one to his own.

"He was rigidly just, and perfectly loose from attachment to the world. He shared his all with the poor, who lay so close to his heart that, at the approach of death, when he could not speak without difficulty, he cried out, 'O my poor! What shall become of my poor!' He was blessed with so great a degree of humanity as is scarce to be found. I am witness how often he has rejoiced in being treated with contempt. Indeed, it seemed the very food of his soul to be little and unknown.

"His zeal for souls I need not tell you. Let the labours of twenty-five years, and a martyr's death in the conclusion, imprint it on your hearts. His diligent visiting of the sick occasioned the fever which, by God's commission, tore him from you and me. And his vehement desire to take his last leave of you with dying lips and hands, gave (it is supposed) the finishing stroke, by preparing his blood for putrefaction. Thus has he lived and died your servant. And will any of you refuse to meet him at God's right hand in that day?

"He walked with death always in his sight. About two months ago he came to me and said, 'My dear love, I know not how it is, but I have a strange impression death is near us, as if it were to be some sudden stroke upon one of us. And it draws out all my soul in prayer that we may be ready.' He then broke out, 'Lord, prepare the soul thou wilt call! And O stand by the poor disconsolate one that shall be left behind!'

"A few days before his departure he was filled with love in an uncommon manner. The same he testified as long as he had a voice, and continued to the end, by a most lamblike patience, in which he smiled over death, and set his last seal to the glorious truths he had so long preached among you.

"Three years, nine months, and two days, I have possessed my heavenly minded husband. But now the sun of my earthly joys is set for ever, and my soul filled with an anguish which only finds its consolation in a total resignation to the will of God. When I was asking the Lord, if he pleased, to spare him to me a little longer, the following promise was impressed on my mind, *Where I am, there shall my servants be, that they may behold my glory.* Lord, hasten the time."

"There is little need," says Mr. Wesley, "of adding any farther character of this man of God to the foregoing account, given by one who wrote out of the fullness of her heart. I would only observe that, for many years, I despaired of finding an inhabitant of Great Britain that could stand in any degree of comparison with Gregory Lopez or Mon. de Renty. But let any impartial person judge, if Mr. Fletcher were at all inferior to them? Did he not experience as deep communion with God, and as high a measure of inward holiness, as was experienced by either one or the other of those burning and shining lights? And it is certain his outward light shone before men with full as bright a luster as theirs. I was intimately acquainted with him for thirty years. I conversed with him morning, noon, and night, without the least reserve, during a journey of many hundred miles. And in all that time I never heard him speak an improper word, or saw him do an improper action. To conclude:--Within fourscore years I have known many excellent men holy in heart and life. But one equal to him I have not known; one so uniformly and deeply devoted to God. So unblamable a man in every respect I have not found either in Europe or America. Nor do I expect to find another such on this side eternity.

"Yet it is possible we may be such as he was. Let us then endeavor to follow him as he followed Christ."

But some may inquire, "Has not Mr. Wesley exceeded the truth in this testimony? Has he not given a too favourable representation of the character of his friend, influenced, perhaps, by the similarity of their views respecting the great subject of general redemption, and other subjects connected therewith, and by the very prompt and able manner in which Mr. Fletcher stood forth in defence of these views when attacked by Mr. Wesley's opponents?" I shall answer these inquiries by presenting the reader with an exactly similar testimony, borne by an eminent minister of Christ, whose sentiments, on these points of doctrine, were the reverse of those of Messrs. Wesley and Fletcher. This I shall do by inserting the following letter, which I received from a very pious and intelligent clergyman in May last, in consequence of his having lately read the first edition of this work:

"My Dear Sir:--Had not my time been very fully employed since I had the pleasure of seeing you in London, I should before now have fulfilled my promise in sending you the character which the late Rev. Mr. Venn, vicar of Yelling, gave me of the truly apostolic Mr. Fletcher. The testimony of Mr. Venn is the more valuable, as there were several points of doctrine in which he differed from Mr. Fletcher; and I believe he felt himself good deal interested in the support of several of those tenets which Mr. Fletcher publicly opposed. But difference of opinion on points respecting which good men probably never will be all agreed on earth, could not close the eyes of the great and good Mr. Venn against the extraordinary excellences of Mr. Fletcher, and therefore he spake of him with all the rapture and affection which preeminent graces will always excite in the breast of a true Christian. In the following narration I believe you will have nearly the words of Mr. Venn, as I was much impressed with his account of Mr. Fletcher, and wrote down what I remembered of it at the close of the day on which I heard it. With an expression in his countenance I shall not soon forget, making mention of Mr. Fletcher, he exclaimed, 'Sir, he was a luminary: a *luminary,* did I say?   He was a *sun.* I have known all the great men for these fifty years; but I have known none like him.   I was intimately acquainted with him, and was under the same roof with him once for six weeks; during which time I never heard him say a single word which was not proper to be spoken, and which had not a tendency to "minister grace to the hearers."   One time, meeting him when he was very ill of a hectic fever, which he had brought upon himself by his intense labour in the ministry, I said: "I am very sorry to find you so ill." Mr. Fletcher answered with the greatest sweetness, "Sorry, sir! Why are you sorry?   It is the chastisement of my heavenly Father, and I rejoice therein, as an expression of his love and affection toward me."'

"Mr. Venn being here asked whether Mr. Fletcher might not have been imprudent in carrying his labours to such an excess, answered, 'His heart was in them, and he was carried on with an impetus which could not be resisted. He did not look on the work of the ministry as a mere duty, but it was his pleasure and delight. Tell a votary of pleasure that his course of life will impair his property and health, and finally ruin him: he will reply that he knows all this; but he must go on; for life would not be tolerable without his pleasures. Such was the ardour of Mr. Fletcher in the ministry of the Gospel. He could not be happy but when employed in his great work.' Something having escaped one in the company which seemed to bear hard upon a particular body of Christians, Mr. Venn gave a solemn caution against evil speaking in these words:--'Never did I hear Mr. Fletcher speak ill of any man. He would pray for those that walked disorderly, but he would not publish their faults.'

"This I believe is the substance of what fell from Mr. Venn respecting the Rev. Fletcher, and the *manner* in which he spoke showed that his admiration of that great and good man was raised to the highest pitch. Indeed, Mr. Venn was a person peculiarly qualified to appreciate the value of Mr. Fletcher, as the ardor of his own zeal and devotion most nearly resembled that of Mr. Fletcher. He lived in very uncommon nearness to God, and, as I have been informed, made a most triumphant entrance into the kingdom of glory. I am, my dear sir, yours affectionately,

"_____."

A glowing description of Mr. Fletcher's character appeared in the Shrewsbury Chronicle of August, 1785 as follows:

"On the 14th instant departed this life, the Rev. John Fletcher, vicar of Madeley, in this county, to the inexpressible grief and concern of his parishioners, and of all who had the happiness of knowing him. If we speak of him as a man and a gentleman, he was possessed of every virtue and every accomplishment which adorns and dignifies human nature. If we attempt to speak of him as a minister of the gospel, it will be extremely difficult to give the world a just idea of *this great character*. His deep learning, his exalted piety, his never-ceasing labors to discharge the important duty of his function, together with the abilities and good effect with which he discharged those duties, are well known, and will never be forgotten in that vineyard in which he labored. His charity, his universal benevolence, his meekness and exemplary goodness, are scarcely equaled among the sons of men. Anxious to the last moment of his life to discharge the sacred duties of his office, he performed the service of the Church, and administered the holy sacrament to upward of two hundred communicants, the Sunday preceding his death, confiding in that almighty Power which had given him life, and resigning that life into the hands of Him who gave it, with that composure of mind, and those joyful hopes of a happy resurrection, which ever accompany the last moments of the just."

Epitaph of the Rev. J. Fletcher.

Here lies the body of

THE REV. JOHN WILLIAM DE LA FLECHERE
Vicar of Madeley,
Who was born at Nyon, in Switzerland,
September the 12th, 1729,
And finished his course, August the 14th, 1785,
In the village;
Where his unexampled labors
Will long be remembered.
He exercised his ministry for the space of
Twenty-five years
In this parish,
With uncommon zeal and ability.
Many believed his report, and became
His joy and crown of rejoicing;
While others constrained him to take up
The lamentation of the prophet,
"All the day long have I stretched out my hands
Unto a disobedient and gainsaying people;
Yet surely my judgment is with the Lord,
And my work with my God."
"He, being dead, yet speaketh."

(Joseph Benson, *The Life of the Rev. John W. De La Flechere*
[Chicago: The Christian Witness Co., 1925], 506-531)

Judith Perry:
A Teenaged Lass Made "Ripe For The Bridegroom"
(d. November, 1785)

"I buried," writes Mr. Wesley, "the remains of Judith Perry, a lovely young woman, snatched away at eighteen; but she was ripe for the Bridegroom, and went to meet him in the full triumph of faith" (John Wesley, *The Works of John Wesley*, IV [Grand Rapids: Zondervan Publishing House, 1958], 323).

What does Mr. Wesley mean by "the full triumph of faith"? First of all, he has in mind such a faith as "works by love." The love of God is shed abroad in the heart of one who is "in the full triumph of faith." This is accomplished "by the Holy Ghost given." The same Holy Spirit provides an assurance of having been made a child of God.

To Mr. Wesley, one who is in "the full triumph of faith" would also possess a consciousness of peace within—"even that 'peace of God which passeth all understanding.'" Such a peace "cannot," says he, "be fully and adequately expressed in human language." It can only be described as "an unspeakable calmness and serenity of spirit, a tranquility in the blood of Christ, which keeps the souls of believers, in their latest hour, even as a garrison keeps a city" (John Wesley, *The Works of John Wesley*, VII [Grand Rapids: Zondervan Publishing House, 1958], 432-33).

A Contrast of Final Testimonies

From the writings of Mr. Wesley and Mr. Fletcher, we share below contrasting scenes of the dying. We witness first those who expressed an agonizing consciousness of their soon entrance into the place of the damned, while the last is heard to utter assurances of happiness upon entrance into eternal felicity.

Mr. Voltaire, who died in 1778, was a French philosopher and infidel of the 18th century whose influence for evil was felt throughout Europe and places beyond. The following account is given in Mr. Wesley's *Journal* of this wicked and blaspheming man's last words.

> "Mr. Voltaire, finding himself ill, sent for Dr. Fronchin, first Physician to the Duke of Orleans, one of his converts to infidelity, and said to him, 'Sir, I desire you will save my life. I will give you half my fortune, if you will lengthen out my days only six months. If not, I shall go to the devil, and carry you with me.'" (John Wesley, *The Works of John Wesley*, IV [Grand Rapids: Zondervan Publishing House, 1958], 137)

In a letter written in 1769 to the Rev. Mr. Sellon, John Fletcher writes:

> I know two strong Calvinist believers, who lately took their leave of this world with "I shall be damned!" O what did all their professions of perseverance [or unconditional eternal security] do for them? They left them in the lurch. May we have the power of God in our souls, and we shall readily leave unknown decrees to others. (John Fletcher, *The Works of the Reverend John Fletcher*, IV [Salem: Schmul Publishers, 1974], 342)

On the evening of March, 1787, Mr. Wesley preached at Congleton to what he described as "a serious and well-established people." In this place he also found a Mr. ---, whom he thought to be just two months younger than himself. He described this unnamed man as "just a lamp going out for want of oil, gently sliding into a better world: He sleeps always, only waking now and then just long enough to say, 'I am happy'" ("Wesley, *The Works of John Wesley*, IV, 366").

In his sermon entitled, "Spiritual Worship," the founder of Methodism shows that true happiness is found in "knowing and loving God." Herein is a happiness that is "real, solid, and substantial. Then it is that heaven is opened in the soul, that the proper heavenly state, commences, while the love of God, as loving us, is shed abroad in the heart …." He then goes so far as to say that "every [true] Christian is happy; and that he who is not happy is not a Christian: Seeing if he was a real Christian, he could not but be happy.

> But I allow an exception here in favour of those who are under violent temptation; yea, and of those who

are under deep nervous disorders, which are, indeed, a species of insanity. The clouds and darkness which then overwhelm the soul suspend its happiness; especially if Satan is permitted to second those disorders, by pouring in his fiery darts. But, excepting these cases, the observation will hold, and it should be well attended to,--Whoever is not happy, yea, happy in God, is not a Christian. (John Wesley, *The Works of John Wesley*, VI [Grand Rapids: Zondervan Publishing House, 1958], 433-34)

Those who endeavor to persuade their hearers of holiness without happiness are false prophets. Holiness and happiness can never be separated.

Charles Wesley's Peaceful Death And Lasting Legacy
(d. March, 1788)

Charles Wesley, A. M. was born the youngest son of Rev. Samuel Wesley, rector of Epworth and his wife, Susannah. He was a graduate of St. Peter's College, Westminster as well as Christ Church College, Oxford and ordained an Anglican priest in 1735.

Adam Clarke refers to him as "a good man, a powerful preacher, and the best Christian poet, in reference to hymnology, that has flourished in either ancient or modern times." Most of the hymns sung by early Methodists were composed by him and it could be wished that all who today claim to be Wesleyan Arminian in their theological persuasion would make a practice of using more of his hymns in services of worship.

The Rev. Henry Moore was once asked by T. Marriott, Esq., "for the distinctive characteristics of ... John and Charles Wesley, as preachers, replied: 'John's preaching was all principles; Charles's was all aphorisms'" (Adam Clarke, *Memoirs of the Wesley Family* [New York: Lane & Tippet Publishers, 1848], 597, 598).

"For twenty years," writes D. M. Jones, "Charles Wesley had been among the greatest of missionary preachers, superior to his brother John in the intensity of his emotional appeal, and in this respect ranking second only to Whitefield himself."

It was in the year 1756, however, that "he ceased the itinerant journeys by which he had carried the gospel through England and Ireland, and devoted himself to a general superintendence of the Methodist societies in London and Bristol, and to his incessant work as a writer of hymns." Why did Charles cease actively as a traveling preacher thirty-five years before death caused a termination of his brother's itinerancy? Reasons that have been most often offered are "his own delicate health and advancing years," together with "the claims of his wife and young family."

The last days and final hours of this good man are described below, taken from a biography written by D. M. Jones entitled, *Charles Wesley: A Study.*

> At the beginning of February 1788 [the Rev. Charles Wesley was obviously failing fast, though he still went out.] On the 18th February he had a cordial note from his brother—
>
> "Dear brother, you must go out every day.... Do not die to save charges. You certainly need not want anything so long as I live."
>
> The young Wesleys [sons of Charles] had been wayward and difficult: for we find John admonishing his brother to be master in his own house. He had written in a previous letter: "I shall shortly have a word to say to [nephew] Charles or his brother or both."
>
> On March 7th he wrote to Sarah Wesley,

recommending "ten drops of elixir of vitriol in a glass of water" as a remedy. It was his harmless mania to prescribe for all his friends. He goes on, "Now, Sally, tell your brothers from me that their tenderly respectful behaviour to their father (even to asking his pardon if in anything they have offended him) will be the best cordial for him under heaven. I know not but they may save his life thereby. To know that nothing will be wanting on your part gives great satisfaction to, my dear Sally, yours very affectionately."

John Wesley advised the family to call in Dr. Whitehead, who afterwards wrote his life. "I visited him several times" (said Whitehead) "in his last illness, and his body was indeed reduced to the most extreme state of weakness. He possessed that state of mind which he had been always pleased to see in others, unaffected humility and holy resignation to the will of God. He had no transports of joy but solid hope and unshaken confidence in Christ, which kept his mind in perfect peace."

He was now so weak that he could not retain nourishment, but John Wesley still wrote hopefully from Bristol. He could not believe that the bond of so many years was about to be snapped. "Let prayer be made continually, and probably he will be stronger after this illness than he had been these ten years. Is anything too hard for God?"

A short time before Charles Wesley died he called his wife to him and dictated these lines, the last he ever composed—

> In age and feebleness extreme,
> Who shall a helpless worm redeem?
> Jesus, my only hope Thou art,
> Strength of my failing flesh and heart.
> O, could I catch a smile from Thee
> And drop into eternity!

He called his son Samuel to his bedside and said, *"Omnia vanitas et vexatio spiritus praeter amare Deum et Illi servire."*

At other times he spoke tenderly of his boys, told his daughter to trust in God and that He would never forsake her, and prayed with tears for all his enemies.

The end came on March 29th, 1788, and on April 5th Sarah Wesley wrote to his brother—

"For some months past he seemed totally detached from earth. He spoke very little nor wished to hear anything read but the Scriptures.... All his prayer was, 'Patience and an easy death.' He told my mother the week before he departed, that no fiend was permitted to approach him, and said to us all, 'I have a good hope.'

"When we asked him if he wanted anything, he frequently answered, 'Nothing but Christ.'

"Some person observed that the valley of death was hard to be passed. 'Not with Christ,' replied he.

"On March 27th, after a most uneasy night, he prayed as in an agony, that he might not have many such nights. 'O my God,' said he, 'not many.'

"The last few days he was scarcely conscious; he was eager to depart, and if we moved him or spoke to him, he answered, 'Let me die. Let me die.'

"When your kind letter came [to Charles] (in which you affectionately tell him that you will be a father to him and to my brother Samuel) I read it to my father. 'He will be kind to you,' he said, 'when I am gone. I am certain your uncle will be kind to all of you.'

"The 28th, my mother asked if he had anything to say to us. Raising his eyes he said, 'Only thanks, love, blessing.'

"The last morning, which was the 29th of March, being unable to speak, my mother entreated him to press her hand if he knew her, which feebly he did.

"His last words which I could hear were, 'Lord—my heart—my God.' He then drew his breath short, and the last so gently that we knew not exactly the moment when his happy spirit fled.

He was buried, by his own request, in the churchyard of the old church of St. Marylebone. We have it on the authority of John Pawson that he sent for the parson of the parish where he lived and said, "Sir, whatever the world may have thought of me, I have lived and I die in the communion of the Church of England, and I will be buried in the yard of my parish church."

The pall was borne by eight clergymen of the Church of England. The place where he was interred is now marked by the monument erected by the Methodist Conference of 1858, as a token of "respect and reverence" for the brother of "the Founder (under God) of the Methodist Connection." One face of the obelisk bears the inscription which was engraved on the original tombstone, including the following verse from a hymn which he himself had written in memory of a friend—

> "With poverty of spirit blest,
> Rest, happy saint, in Jesus rest,
> Thy labours of unwearied love,
> By thee forgot, are crowned above,
> Crowned, through the mercy of thy Lord,
> With a full, free, immense reward."

It is interesting to compare with Pawson's remarks the estimate given of Charles Wesley by another of the preachers, William Bradburn, who preached his funeral sermon at City Road on Sunday, April 6th, "to an inconceivable concourse of people of every description."

"Mr. Charles Wesley died just as any one who knew him might have expected. He had no disorder but old age. He had very little pain. His mind was calm as a summer evening.... He always seemed fearful of suffering something dreadful before death. I think he was quite disappointed, for no one could pass easier out of time than he did.

"… His soul was formed for friendship in affliction, and his words and letters were a precious balm to those of a sorrowful spirit. He was courteous without dissimulation, and honest without vulgar roughness. He was truly a great Christian without any pompous singularity, and a great divine without the least contempt for the meanest of his brethren."

But the most eloquent of all tributes to the dead poet was paid without words a fortnight after his death, when John Wesley, preaching at Bolton, gave out the hymn "Wrestling Jacob" for the congregation to sing. When the bereaved old man, eighty-five years of age, came to the lines—

"My company before is gone
And I am left alone with Thee,"

he sat down in the pulpit, covered his face with his hands, and burst into tears, while the whole congregation wept with him.

The following notice from the pen of John Wesley, and marked by his usual terseness, appeared in the "Minutes of Conference" for 1788.

"Mr. Charles Wesley, who after spending fourscore years with great sorrow and pain, quietly retired into Abraham's bosom. He had no disease, but after a gradual decay of some months, 'the weary wheels of life at last stood still.' His least praise was his talent for poetry, although Dr. Watts did not scruple to say that the single poem, 'Wrestling Jacob,' was worth all the verses he himself had written."

John Wesley, and the Methodist people after him, provided for the widow and daughter of Charles Wesley. Mrs. Wesley died in London in 1822, at the great age of ninety-six. Her daughter Sarah, who never married, only survived her six years. Charles Wesley the younger had an honourable career as an organist and composer, though he never fulfilled the extraordinary promise of his childhood. The career of Samuel Wesley and of his son Samuel Sebastian belong to the history of English music. (D. M. Jones, *Charles Wesley: A Study* [London: Skeffington & Son, Ltd, nd.] 255-261)

Robert Windsor:
Died Praising God
(d. February, 1790)

"I preached," writes Mr. Wesley, "the funeral sermon of that saint of God, Robert Windsor, many years a burning and a shining light. He was born a few months after me; was a prudent, serious, diligent man, full of mercy and good fruits; without partiality, and without hypocrisy. He seemed on the brink of death some months ago; but was suddenly raised up again; praised God without ceasing a few days; and then laid down, and died" (John Wesley, *The Works of John Wesley*, IV [Grand Rapids: Zondervan Publishing House, 1958], 479).

The man Mr. Wesley describes above had doubtlessly been perfected in love. He or she who has attained Christian perfection possesses, according to Mr. Wesley, "'the mind which was in Christ,' enabling us to walk as Christ walked." In other words, to be inwardly and outwardly devoted to God; all devoted in heart and life (John Wesley, *The Works of John Wesley*, XI [Grand Rapids: Zondervan Publishing House, 1958], 444).

How glorious it is for one to spend the last few day of life praising God without ceasing so as to face death victoriously as did this man, Robert Windsor.

Mr. Wesley's Final Testimony
And Victorious Departure
(d. March, 1791)

On his 87th birthday, Mr. Wesley records in his *Journal* a review of his physical condition. He claimed to have "found none of the infirmities of old age" during the first eighty six years of his life. Now, however, his "eyes had become so dim that no glasses would help." His strength had likewise quite forsaken him "and probably," as he concluded, "will not return in this world: but I feel no pain from head to foot: only it seems, nature is exhausted, and humanly speaking, will sink more and more, till

The weary springs of life stand still at last."

"This," says Dr. Whitehead, "at length was literally the case; the death of Mr. Wesley, like that of his brother Charles, being one of those rare instances in which nature, drooping under the load of years, sinks by a gentle decay."

For several years preceding his death, this decay was, perhaps, more visible to others than to himself, particularly by a more frequent disposition to sleep during the day, by a growing defect in memory, a faculty he once possessed in a high degree of perfection, and by a general diminution of the vigour and agility he had so long enjoyed. His labours, however, suffered little interruption; and when the summons came, it found him, as he always wished it should, in the harness, still occupied in his Master's work!

Until his final illness he continued active in writing, travel, preaching and visiting various Methodist societies, "exhorting them to *love as brethren, to fear God, and honour the king,* which he wished them to consider as his last advice." He then would often conclude his exhortations with the quoting of the following verse:

> 'O that, without a lingering groan
> I may the welcome word receive;
> My body with my charge lay down,
> And cease at once to work and live.'

The day finally came when the aged founder of Methodism arrived home to leave it again no more alive. "His friends were struck with the manner of his getting out of the carriage, and still more with his apparent weakness when he went up stairs and sat down in his chair. He now desired to be left alone, and not to be interrupted by any one, for half an hour." Later in the day he wished to lie down and it became evident to those around him that he was seriously ill. Dr. Whitehead was then called to attend him. The next morning "he looked quite cheerful, and repeated the latter part of the verse, in his brother Charles's Scripture Hymns, on *'Forsake me not when my strength faileth,'* viz.—

> 'Till glad I lay this body down,
> Thy servant, Lord, attend;
> And, O! my life of mercy crown
> With a triumphant end.'"

Eight years before, Mr. Wesley had suddenly become quite ill during the 1783 Bristol conference. Neither he nor those in attendance with him had thought he could recover. In the midst of this uncertainty, he expressed to a close friend,

> "I have been reflecting on my past life: I have been wandering up and down, between fifty and sixty years, endeavouring, in my poor way, to do a little good to my fellow-creatures; and now it is probable that there are but a few steps between me and death; and what have I to trust to for salvation? I can see nothing which I have done or suffered, that will bear looking at. I have no other plea than this,
>
> > 'I the chief of sinners am,
> > But Jesus died for me.'"

Now, while in this his final illness, he was heard to say, "There is no need of more; when at Bristol my words were,

> 'I the chief of sinners am,
> But Jesus died for me.'

"One said, 'Is this the present language of your heart, and do you now feel as you did then? He replied, 'yes.' When the same person repeated,

> 'Bold I approach the eternal throne,
> And claim the crown, through Christ, my own;'

and added, 'tis enough. He our precious Immanuel has purchased, has promised, all;' [Wesley] earnestly replied, 'He is all! He is all!'"

Two days before his release and in the midst of great weakness, he astonished all who were present by singing,

> 'I'll praise my Maker while I've breath,
> And when my voice is lost in death,
> Praise shall employ my nobler powers;
> My days of praise shall ne'er be past,
> While life, and thought, and being last,
> Or immortality endures!'

On several occasions he desired all that were in the house to "pray and praise." A little after one of these sessions of prayer, he was observed to be trying to speak, but could not.

> "Finding they could not understand him, he paused, a little, and then, with all the remaining strength he had, cried out, *The best of all is, God is with us,* and, soon after lifting up his dying arm in token of victory, and raising his feeble voice with a holy triumph not to be expressed, he again repeated the heart-reviving words, *The best of all is, God is with us.* At another time he said, 'He causeth his servants to lie down in peace.' Then pausing a little, he cried, 'The clouds drop fatness!' and soon after, 'The Lord is with us, the God of Jacob is our refuge!'"

On the day of his death, "… the closing scene drew near. Mr. Bradford, his faithful friend, prayed with him, and the last words he was heard to articulate were, 'Farewell!'"

"The following is the inscription on the marble tablet erected to his memory in the chapel, City-road":--

Sacred to the Memory
OF THE REV. JOHN WESLEY, M.A.

Sometime Fellow of Lincoln College, Oxford;

A Man of Learning and sincere Piety
Scarcely inferior to any;
In Zeal, Ministerial Labours, and extensive Usefulness,
Superior, perhaps, to all Men,
Since the Days of St. Paul.
Regardless of Fatigue, personal Danger, and Disgrace,
He went into the highways and hedges,
Calling sinners to Repentance,
And Publishing the Gospel of Peace.
He was the Founder of the Methodist Societies,
And the chief promoter and Patron
Of the Plan of Itinerant preaching,
Which he extended through Great Britain and Ireland,
The West Indies and America,
With unexampled Success.
He was born the 17th of June, 1703;
And died the 2d of March, 1791,
In sure and certain hope of Eternal Life,
Through the Atonement and Mediation of a Crucified
Saviour.
He was sixty-five years in the Ministry,
And fifty-two an Itinerant Preacher:
He lived to see, in these Kingdoms only,
About three hundred Itinerant,
And one thousand Local Preachers,
Raised up from the midst of his own People;
And eighty thousand Persons in the Societies under his care.
His Name will be ever had in grateful Remembrance
By all who rejoice in the universal Spread
Of the Gospel of Christ.
Soli Deo Gloria.

(Richard Watson, *The Life of the Rev. John Wesley, A. M.* [New York:
W. Disturnell Publishers, 1834], 286-296.)

Duncan Wright:

Found The Valley Of Death "All Clear," And "All Light"
(d. May, 1791)

For some twenty years, Duncan Wright served as a preacher of God's Word within the Methodist Connection. He was described as "an old faithful labourer in the vineyard of the Lord. Gravity and steadiness were two eminent parts of his character." He was further described as "a truly upright and pious man, a faithful defender of the Word of God, an ardent lover and conscientious observer of the Methodist discipline …" (John Telford, ed., *Wesley's Veterans*, II [Salem: Schmul Publishers, 1976], 49, 50).

The account of Mr. Wright's sickness and death, hereby abbreviated and edited below, was originally provided by the Rev. James Creighton, who was a witness of both.

In early winter of 1790, Mr. Wright caught cold by exposing himself to the early morning air on his way to the City Road Chapel. The infection settled in his lungs and caused a rapid decline of health and strength. "He struggled through the winter with great difficulty, and when attending Mr. Wesley's funeral, March 9, 1791, said it was most probable that he should be the next that should be laid in that vault, which proved to be the fact."

The "vault" referred to is located in the yard behind the City Road Chapel in London. It is comparatively large and after the burial of Mr. Wesley, several of his preachers and one of his sisters were, over a period of years, buried in the same vault with him.

Mr. Creighton says that for a change of air, Mr. Wright came to his house at the beginning of April. He was, at that time, suffering from "a violent pain in both his sides, so as not to be able to lie on either of them, nor yet on his back, as his cough was exceedingly troublesome." Every night his fever became "high and his pulse quick." As each morning approached, he would fall "into a sweat, which gave him a little temporary ease." Such was his condition for a couple weeks. Then it was that "he was seized one night with an uncommon and violent pain, which he supposed to be a symptom of immediate death: he therefore called me up," says Mr. Creighton, " as I had been in bed for some time. I sat and conversed with him till morning, and indeed it was a truly profitable time to me."

Although his pain was excruciating, his voice seemed quite strong. He spoke much as one in full triumph of faith. Mr. Creighton says that he "did not think death was so near as" his friend thought himself to be.

> … He related to me much of what he then felt, though it was impossible to find language fully to express it, and he told me a great part of his experience for thirty years back. In the year 1762, he said that he "had entered into a superior light and greater liberty than he had ever enjoyed before." Previous to this time, he said that he had "walked in a kind of darkness; but ever since that time had walked constantly in the light of God's countenance, and would not be satisfied any day

without a direct and clear witness of his acceptance."

Each evening at seven o'clock, he desired, according to a long standing custom of his, "to be left alone [at that time] in order that he might commune and wrestle with God." He spoke of one such evening when "the Lord filled him with such consolation and such joy as was unspeakable, which he looked upon as a token that God would shortly take him to Himself."

"While I felt [said he] the mighty operation of the Spirit my whole frame was agitated in a most wonderful manner; but I did not desire the Lord to stay His hand, for I knew He could support me under this mighty outpouring of His Spirit." While lingering in his illness, he said, "I had many promises ... that He would sprinkle me with clean water, and now He gives me a full manifestation of it. I am a witness that the blood of Christ does cleanse from all sin." Though he did not desire that anything be said of him at his funeral, he was willing "for their encouragement" that the people be assured that the Lord has finished His work and that He has cleansed, and filled me with Himself.

He then continued to express himself in the following words:

> O the goodness of God to a poor sinner! Can there be a greater proof of the immortality as well as of the activity of the soul in its state of separation than this which I now feel! Surely it cannot be that the soul will sleep till the resurrection. I used sometimes to reason about the doctrine of materialists, and about persons who were restored from drowning; but now all my doubts are vanished. O what a weight of glory will that be, when Thy weight of grace, O Lord, is now so great! The Lord sets my poor heart at ease, though it is now burning with a fever. Some nights ago He told me that He would do

more for me than I could ask or think. O that the world might taste and see what I now experience! O, I could sing, if I had strength! The Lord maketh my very bones to rejoice. O how kind, how merciful art Thou! Hast Thou not made up all at last? This is not mere imagination or the effects of a disordered brain! No, no, what I now feel is better than crowns or thrones!

> O that the world might taste and see
> The riches of His grace!
> The arms of love that compass me
> Would all mankind embrace.

I often used to sing these words:

> Happy, if with my latest breath
> I may but gasp His name!
> Preach Him to all, and cry in death
> Behold! Behold the Lamb!

O, I can now do it; He does enable me, a poor worm, to do it, who endeavoured, in my little way, to preach Him, and point others to Him.

On another occasion "he repeated 'Jesus, Thou art all compassion,' &c., and then added, 'I pass through the valley of death; but it is not dark—all is clear, all is light about me.'"

Mr. Creighton tells of "another remarkable night, which," says he, "was chiefly spent in intercession, and that in a most astonishing manner." He gave an account of it in the morning, telling "…how the whole world seemed as it were spread before him. First he prayed for his wife and near relations, then the Methodist Connexion, then the Jews, infidels, and heathens of all sorts; that they might shortly be brought in, and taste the sweetness of redeeming grace."

He had an ear for music and during his illness, often sang the "following lines … with a shower of tears":

> O might I with Thy saints aspire,
> The meanest of that dazzling choir,
> Who chant Thy praise above;
> Mixt with the bright musician band,
> May I a heavenly harper stand,
> And sing the song of love!
>
> O might I die that awe to prove,
> That prostrate awe that dares not move
> Before the great Three-One!
> To shout by turns the bursting joy
> In songs around the Throne!

Some of the last lines which he was able to repeat were these:

> When from the dust of death I rise
> To claim my mansion in the skies,
> This, this shall then be all my plea,
> Jesus hath lived, hath died for me!

There was always with him a spirit and expression of much thankfulness for any respite from pain. No word was ever "dropped from him that bore the most remote implication of murmuring or complaining." He mentioned how suitable to his case that hymn was, and the peculiar sweetness there was in it:

> My sufferings all to Thee are known.

"He generally expressed himself with a smile, even when he felt very great pain in both his sides, and through his whole body." On one occasion, "he expressed something like fear lest the enemy might

337

be permitted to [sorely] attack" him before his final departure, "and mentioned the case of Thomas Walsh. 'If so great and pious a man,' said he, 'had such a conflict, and was in some degree of darkness not long before his death, what may I not expect?'"

As it turned out, "...the enemy was permitted [once more] to buffet ... and harass him with strange thoughts." Of this "he was eager to relate the circumstances ... the night before he died." To Mr. Creighton, this "appeared to arise partly, or chiefly, from the debilitated state of his body and weakness of his head, of which the enemy strove to take advantage; but the crafty foe was finally put to flight by Him who shed His blood to save sinners."

Mr. Creighton says that when he went in to see him the next morning, he was asked how he felt. His reply was, "I am getting more rest." "Yes," said his friend, "and you will shortly get more—you will soon enter into a glorious rest." Later in the day "he said to his wife, 'Jesus is come!—He is now in my heart: now let me muse awhile.'" To the very last he continued quite "sensible, and sunk gradually with a serene and placid countenance, into the arms of the Redeemer, and expired without a sigh or a groan." Several of his friends were present, "commending his spirit into the hands of Him who gave it." He had "just completed the fifty-fifth year of his age." ("ibid., 43-50")

Jasper Robinson:
A Dying Methodist Preacher Who Was
"Blessed With Utmost Tranquility"
(d. 1797)

Jasper Robinson was born in December of 1727. He first became acquainted with the people called Methodists in 1760. He joined their fellowship, diligently attended class meetings, participated in all the means of grace and missed no opportunity of hearing the preaching. Under the preaching of Mr. Wesley he was soundly converted, by which he "received a large effusion of the Holy Spirit, and seemed changed throughout the whole man." He first set out as a traveling preacher in 1776. During the next twenty-two years he served as a local and traveling Methodist preacher in numerous places in both England and Scotland.

Mr. Pawson, who was a colleague, spoke of him as "a pattern of solid piety and serious godliness, and remarkably zealous for the glory of God and the salvation of souls. He was exceedingly useful as a class-leader, and likewise in visiting the sick and the poor. Very few have excelled him in these labours of love."

As Mr. Robinson approached the age of three-score years and ten, physical weakness accompanied with shortness of breath made it impossible for him to continue preaching. One by the name of George Dermott was a witness of his final days.

> On the 24th [of November] we got him home, and I found him labouring under a very great difficulty of breathing, and evidently sinking under his affliction, but perfectly resigned to the will of God, whether for life or death. Not a single murmur was ever heard from him at any time. A friend asked him how he felt when [first] he thought himself dying.... He answered, "I felt something of apprehension respecting the pains and feelings of nature; but I had no fear at all beyond death."
>
> A little while before he was taken ill, he dreamed one night that the chariot of Israel was come to convey him away, in which was the happy spirit of the late venerable Hanby, and another old preacher who was gone to glory.
>
> He expressed himself infinitely thankful that he had only his bodily affliction to endure, and heartily praised God for all His mercies; especially for the strong confidence he had in the Redeemer, and the blessed prospect, through faith in his name, of a glorious immortality.

A couple of days later, Mr. Dermott mentions having prayer with his dying friend, "in which," says he, "his whole soul appeared to be drawn out after God." Several more days passed by with a noticeable increase in his weakness. However, "Not the shadow of discontent ever made its appearance in him at any time." Some days later several visiting friends spent time in prayer with him. As they knelt around his bed, it was said that, "The room seemed to be filled with the glory of God, and their hearts were as melting wax while bowed before Him."

Several more days passed by in which Mr. Robinson was found to have become exceedingly weak. He was, nevertheless, "still able to converse a little." After Psalms 31 and 36 together with John 14 were read to him by Mr. Dermott's wife and daughter, he said, "Who could have thought that I should have such ease of body and mind in such circumstances?" Although he was restless by reason of his heavy afflictions, he nevertheless "accounted them light, and only for a moment." He was then heard to say, "I have often thought where I shall die"; and added, "For me to live is Christ, and to die is gain."

On the last day of his life he joined in prayer with great fervency of spirit. His Amens pierced our very hearts; and his soul was filled with the love of God. He said, "I am quite clear from all distressing doubts respecting my acceptance with God. I feel as free from condemnation as if I had never sinned at all." Indeed, throughout his affliction, he was wonderfully preserved from the power of the enemy, who was never permitted to approach him; but the Lord blessed him with the utmost tranquility. "The Lord," said he, "encompasses me about with mercies, and He makes all my bed in my sickness. I have no uneasiness respecting my soul: it is my bodily trouble only that I feel."

Near evening he repeated these opening words from a hymn by Isaac Watts:

I'll praise my Maker while I've breath, &c.

341

> And looking up, he said, to my daughter, "Remember, you must die!" The next morning ... about five o'clock, his happy soul took its flight to the kingdom of glory without a sigh or groan.

George Dermott took an affectionate leave of his much esteemed friend by assuring the reader that "His memory will long be precious to all the churches where he has laboured. He was always the Christian," continues Mr. Dermott, "and lived and died a witness of the full salvation of God. The last words he had written in his *Journal* were, 'Thanks be to the Lord for all His mercies!'" George Dermott then closed his account by expressing this fervent wish: "O, may I live and die like Jasper Robinson!" (John Telford, ed., *Wesley's Veterans*, VI [Salem: Schmul Publishers, 1976], 221-233).

William Hunter:

"Precious Christ! Precious Jesus! What A Sight Is This!"
(d. August, 1797)

In a letter to Mr. Wesley, William Hunter described his first experience of salvation. He wrote:

"When I was about sixteen, I heard Mr. Hopper: as soon as he began to speak, his words affected me deeply, not with terror, but with love." William then says that he had "a taste of heaven; it seemed as though I was created anew; there was a wonderful change in my tempers and conduct; I laid aside everything that I thought was contrary to the will of God, and practiced all religious duties. I attended preaching on all occasions, and felt much sweetness therein, and love to those that I believed were devoted to God ...."

"When I had thus found the goodness of God to my own soul, I could not forbear speaking of it to others; and the Lord gave me wonderful light and courage in His blessed work." William continued to testify of the help given him "to reprove sin, wherever [he] met it, with humility, meekness, and much prayer."

He took occasion, at times to gather "a few poor people together, and [talk] to them about their souls. I often read the Scriptures to them, and sometimes made some remarks thereon. The Lord was pleased to bless my weak endeavours among them; ....."

In the year 1767, at the London Conference, he was recommended for the work of an itinerant preacher. In the ensuing years he ministered with much success in the circuits of Barrnard Castle, Yarm, Hull, York, Scarborough and Thirsk.

Shortly before Mr. Hunter's last illness, He gave the following testimony and exhortation.

> I desire to give Him all the glory [for the work of God in my heart]. But I have great cause to be ashamed before Him for my unfaithfulness. I feel I need His grace every moment. I stand by faith; I have as much need of Christ as ever; I may truly say,
>
> > Every moment, Lord, I want
> > The merit of Thy death.
>
> Glory be to His name, I find my soul united to Him, and my heart cries, "None but Christ!" I am kept by His power; I enjoy salvation; my heart is fixed, my anchor is sure and steadfast. I believe nothing shall separate me from the love of God which is in Christ Jesus.
>
> I conclude with saying, Though the whole of our salvation is from the Lord, yet He deals with us as rational creatures. He gives us light and conviction of our lost state; then the heart is humbled, and the soul bows before Him. He then speaks peace. This is done in a moment, and faith in the soul is root of all Christian holiness. Thus the work of sanctification

is begun in the heart, and the person is in a capacity of living to God, and growing in grace. If He finds us faithful in a little, He shows us there is a state of greater liberty provided for us. The soul being open to the divine teaching, He shows us our want of this. We seek it with our whole heart, and He is pleased to put us in possession of it. This too is generally given in a moment, and perfectly frees the mind from all evil tempers, and enables us to love the Lord with all our hearts, and our neighbour as ourselves.

Being thus perfected in love, we are much more qualified to grow in grace and in the knowledge of our Lord and Saviour Jesus Christ than ever. O precious salvation! Let me ever be a witness of it!

Mr. Thomas Dodd sent Mr. Mather the following account of Mr. Hunter's "last affliction and death":

On the 17th of July, 1797, Mr. Hunter came to my house, having previously wrote him to come and take care of the society at Nenthead in my absence, being then at Tynemouth for the benefit of my health. When I came home on the 27th, I was struck with Mr. Hunter's appearance, which was greatly altered from the last time I saw him, which was on the 13th of April. On inquiring how he was, he said, "Very poorly"; and intimated he was much exhausted by meeting the classes, and preaching twice on the Sunday before. At night he preached for the last time, from Matt. xxiv. 44, "Be ye also ready"; and made many excellent remarks upon the subject, to which the people seriously attended, as unto the words of a dying man. In the morning he looked refreshed and pleasant, though very weak, and in the course of the day frequently walked out with me; but towards evening he began to breathe with difficulty. About one o'clock in the morning he called us up, and said, "I am almost dead." I was greatly affected with his humble, quiet, composed confidence in God. The preacher and the Christian shone with peculiar luster; it was evident that he possessed what he had long been with holy fervour inculcating upon others.

In the morning he got up about nine o'clock, and came downstairs; but it was too plain that his dissolution was approaching apace. On the 30th he breathed with less difficulty, and the fever was much abated; which I attributed to his drinking plentifully of lemonade. When he spoke, which was but seldom, his words were solemn and affecting. On Monday, the 31st, he frequently forgot himself, and had various symptoms of death about him. I was afraid he would lose his senses for want of sleep, having had none for four or five days. August 1st, he frequently said, "I am a monument of God's goodness: glory be unto His name for ever and ever!" In the evening he said, "The Lord is my strength and my song; He also is become my salvation"; and added, "The Lord be praised for ever and ever." "I am a monument of God's rich mercy." I asked, "If you die with us, shall a funeral sermon be preached on the occasion?" He answered, "Yes, and you must preach it." I requested he would name a portion of Scripture. After a short pause, he said, "I have fought a good fight, I have finished my course, I have kept the faith. Henceforth there is laid up for me a crown of righteousness, which the lord, the righteous Judge, shall give me at that day" (2 Tim. iv. 7, 8). A person present happening to say, "Mr. Hunter gets no sleep"; he replied, "Sleeping or waking, all is well: glory be to God for ever!" About ten he gave out his favourite hymn,

I long to behold Him arrayed.

He then prayed with great fervor.

On the 2nd the pins of the tabernacle seemed to slacken apace, and the pitcher was ready to break at the fountain, and all the animal powers were almost exhausted, and refused to do their respective offices. In the evening, when I sat down by him, he frequently took my hand in his, and attempted to say something respecting the divine law, but was not able to speak. At length he cried out aloud, "Glory be to God, He has fulfilled all righteousness! If this was not included in His obedience, it would be imperfect; and then what should we do?" His whole salvation he rested on the merits of the Redeemer. While the bed was making, he sat in a chair, and desired we would sing the above-mentioned hymn; which was done in a solemn manner, during which his happy soul was swallowed up in the love of God. He then prayed with an holy fervour and devotion suitable to the occasion. About one o'clock in the morning we were called up to see him die; but he got over this struggle, and lay in quiet slumbers till eight o'clock. When I entered the room, he said, "There is much to do before we can die; but I have no fear; my whole heart is devoted to God; I have not followed cunningly-devised fables." When any persons came to see him, he was very particular in recommending to them the service of God, with all its attendant comforts; nor did he suffer any to depart without pouring out his solemn benediction upon them. He frequently repeated Mr. Wesley's hymn [the same hymn, composed by Dr. Watts and sung by Mr. Wesley on his death-bed],

> I'll praise my Maker while I've breath.

He would then burst into tears of joy; and, taking my hand and kissing it, said, "Oh how I love you, my brother!" Coming out of a short slumber, and fixing his eyes on the opposite side of the room, he cried out, "Precious Christ! Precious Jesus! What a sight is this! A poor unworthy creature dying, full of faith and joy in the Holy Ghost." Adding,

> A feeble saint shall win the day,
> Though death and hell obstruct the way.

When he was raised up to drink a little wine-and-water, he said with an air of holy triumph, "O grave, where is thy victory? O death, where is thy sting?" In the evening he attempted frequently to whisper something weighty respecting the goodness of God; and got out, "Offer me up to God in prayer." About nine o'clock he whispered in my ear, "Pray and praise." And indeed, when we prayed in his presence, the glory of God filled the place. He would often whisper, "When will my Lord come?" and when I observed, "God's time is a good time," he replied, "All is well; all is well."

On Saturday, when I entered the room, he took my hand, but could not speak. Asking him if he felt much pain, he laid his hand upon his right breast. Through the whole of Mr. Hunter's affliction there appeared such perfect resignation to the will of God that I durst not pray for life or death; but that God would treat His servant according to the good pleasure of His unerring goodness. On Wednesday he desired that the preachers might be informed of his case and situation. I asked if he meant the preachers then assembled in Conference. He replied, "All of them: let them know I have never varied from the Methodist doctrine and discipline, from my first setting out." Whenever he had an interval of ease, he discovered much patience and humility, and was a pleasing ornament of his profession. On the 9th, after prayer in the evening, as I was sitting by him, I happened to say, "What has the world to call happiness, compared to this?" not thinking that he heard me; but he replied, "It is all a cheat." I then asked if he had much pain. He laid his hand as usual on his right breast, and said, "But all is well." His whole deportment fully evidenced undissembled piety and true godliness. On Thursday my wife asked him if he was desirous of being gone. He answered, "I am passive." He said little more till the evening, when all the powers of his soul seemed deeply engaged with God and eternal things.

"On Saturday morning, the 12th, at four o'clock; those who sat up with him called us up to see him depart. When I entered the room, I asked if he knew me. He whispered, 'Yes.' I said, 'Is God present with you?' He replied three times, 'Oh yes.' Upon wetting his lips, he said, 'Glory be to God! We should praise Him for everything.' In the evening he took a cup of cocoa; and, after changing his linen, he was blessed with an interval of ease, and looked pleasant and cheerful. I read to him, in a slow soft manner, the 32nd and 35th chapters of Isaiah; and observed on the conclusion, 'How beautiful is the Word of the Lord!' He lifted up his hands and eyes, and cried, 'May all the ends of the earth praise Him!' Sunday, the 13th, he appeared on the threshold of eternity. I said to him, 'Sir, you are very weak this morning.' 'Yes,' he replied; 'but the Lord is strong: glory be to His precious name for ever!' In the evening he nearly fainted. When he opened his eyes, he whispered, 'All is well; there is nothing wrong.' When I prayed by him, he was perfectly sensible, and exerted his remaining strength in hearty amens. I put my hand into his, when leaving the room, and asked if he knew me. He answered, in a broken whisper, 'Very well.' He then, as well as he was able, blessed the children present, and exhorted them to seek the Lord. About four in the morning of the 14th I was hastily called; and after being a few minutes in the room, the happy spirit of this blessed man of God took its flight into the regions of eternal repose. Thus died, as he had lived, Mr. William Hunter, full of divine peace, love, and joy.

During the seventeen days of his affliction the enemy was not permitted to approach him, for perfect love cast out fear; and, in the fullest sense of the word, he rejoiced evermore, prayed without ceasing, and in everything gave thanks unto God. I said in my heart, and with my whole heart, 'Blessed are the dead that die in the Lord! Let my last end by like his!'" (John Telford, ed., *Wesley's Veterans*, IV [Salem: Schmul Publishers, 1976], 171-75; 180-87)

John Furz:

A Story Of Mighty Conversions And Glorious Deaths
(d. 1800)

As a young man, John Furz endured the symptoms of deep conviction which lasted intermittently for several years. He often found himself overcome with terror, fearing that hell should be his final destiny. Upon leaving the church sanctuary one Sunday morning, he was convinced that he lacked that faith necessary for his soul's salvation. He felt assured within himself that he would surely be damned. When reaching the church door, he could refrain himself no longer. Bursting into a flood of tears, he cried aloud. Members of the congregation came about him and asked why he wept so. He replied, "I shall go to hell; for I do not believe." One of them answered, "Young man, if you go to hell, no one in the town will go to heaven."

He continued in a state of despair for nearly two more years. His sleep and appetite often departed from him. The heaviness of his soul had such an adverse effect upon his physical health that he was observed wasting away with an accompanying weakness of physical strength. There were times when he feared that "the earth would open and swallow him up or that infernal spirits would be permitted to drag him to the bottomless pit."

While in a spirit of prayer one night, "a strong desire constrained [him] to ask, 'Are there no bowels of mercy for me?' Before I could utter it," said he, "I heard a small, still voice, saying, 'Thy sins are forgiven thee.'" In the following words he shares his experience as a new born babe in Christ.

> What a change did I feel! My sorrow was turned into joy; my darkness into light! My soul was filled with love to God for His unspeakable mercies. Now I did indeed draw water out of the wells of salvation. Yea, a fountain was opened in my heart, springing up into everlasting life. My tongue could not express the feelings of my heart; I was lost in speechless rapture. I now knew what it was to believe: I knew on whom I believed—even on Him that justifieth the ungodly. Being justified by faith, I was at peace with God, through our Lord Jesus Christ. My bands were broken in sunder, and my captive soul was set at liberty.
>
> I that before was dead in trespasses and sins was now made alive to God. I sat in heavenly places with Christ Jesus. I was as in a new world. If I walked out into the open field, everything showed forth the glory of God. If I looked at the sun, my heart said, My God made this, not for Himself but for us. If I looked on the grass, the corn, the trees, I could not but stand and adore the goodness of God. My Bible also was become a new book; it was sweeter to my soul than honey to my tongue. I had near communion with God day and night. And oh how I longed for all the world to know what I knew!

Mr. Furz was not content to keep his newfound joy to himself. It was not long before opportunities arose for his sharing that which God had done for his soul. His conversion was wrought with such a mighty baptism of the Holy Spirit that he was soon exhorting others to flee from the wrath to come and eventually became one of Mr. Wesley's itinerant preachers. He traveled by horseback many years in the Methodist Connection and was recognized as "a zealous defender of [its] purest doctrines."

After marrying a young woman who had impressed him as one possessing a religious turn of mind, he was soon convinced of his mistake. He found to his dismay that she possessed a love for lavish attire and was careless concerning the sacred observance of the Lord's Day. Furthermore, she refused to kneel with her husband when he led in prayer. Her ill temper came to a head one Sunday morning as he descended the stairs on his way to church and sacrament. When reaching the foot of the stairs she, without warning, struck him across the face, breaking out one of his teeth. "She [then] stepped back, sat down in a chair, and wept aloud, saying, 'Lord, I cannot help it, I am so tempted by the devil.'" Her husband went to her, put his tooth in her lap and returned to his room in silence. Mr. Furz says, "It was a sorrowful day with her." Upon his coming down the stairs the next morning he found his wife weeping and asking, "Can you forgive me?" As he moved toward the door, she said, "For God's sake, do not leave me." His response was, "It is God against whom you have sinned." She wept aloud. Her husband spent the next three hours walking in the fields praying for her. When he returned home he found that "God had spoken peace to her soul. Nothing," says he, "would satisfy her, but I must sit on her knees, and hear her praise God. I believe she never lost His love from that hour, but was daily growing in grace." Mr. Furz continues this account by writing a laudable tribute to his wife.

He says that when he from this time "set out as a traveling preacher, leaving my children to her care, she never once asked me when I should come home; but in her letters said, 'I find difficulties, but let not that distress you. I am content. Go straight forward in the work that God has called you to.'"

The time came when Mr. Furz was informed of his wife's illness. He rode "seventy miles," as he said, "in one of the shortest days to see her." When he arrived and had softly stepped to her bed side, she looked at him, and said,

> "My dear husband, I am going to Abraham, to Isaac, and Jacob. I am going to all the prophets, and to the spirits of just men made perfect. I am going to my dear Jesus"; and added,

> > 'Not a doubt can arise,
> > To darken the skies,
> > Or hide for a moment my Lord from my eyes.

> No, not for a moment!' She then paused awhile, and said,

> > 'Hark! Hark how they shout
> > All heaven throughout!

> Lord, let me come up!' and so departed. I found her clothes had been sold to procure her necessaries in time of affliction. So that naked as she came into the world, naked did she return.

When Mr. Furz had for some years traveled as an itinerant preacher, instrumentally bringing many to a saving knowledge of the Savior, he of sudden became violently ill. None expected that he should recover. He heard one of those near his bedside say, "'Now he is going.' Meantime," says he, "the cry of my heart was, 'Lord [wholly] sanctify me now or never.' In that instant I felt the mighty power of His sanctifying Spirit.'" As he described it, there "'came down into my soul as a refining fire, purifying and cleansing from all unrighteousness. And from that instant I began to recover.'" He confessed that previously, he was "easily provoked." This had caused him to fear that after preaching to others he should be a castaway. Now, however, he praised God that he felt "no anger, no pride, no self-will: old things are passed away. All things are become new. Now I know, he that dwelleth in love, dwelleth in God, and God in him!"

John Furz is recorded to have traveled as a Methodist preacher for many years. It is said that into his old age, "he retained his piety, and closed his life in holy triumph, having fought the good fight of faith." (John Telford, ed., *Wesley's Veterans*, V [Salem: Schmul Publishers, 1976], 199-228)

Alexander Mather:
"A Father To The Preachers"
(d. August, 1800)

It was while hearing a sermon preached by Mr. John Wesley that Mr. Mather felt his heart set at liberty, "removing," as he says, "my sins from me as far as the east is from the west—which the very change of my countenance testified before my tongue could utter it." He continues in the following words to tell of this initial but mighty work of God in his heart.

"[M]y load was gone and I could praise God from the ground of my heart, all my sorrow, and fear, and anguish of spirit being changed into a solid peace." So it was that by the "foolishness of preaching," his conversion was both scriptural and solidly effectual. He had experienced a marvelous regeneration—a resurrection of the soul from spiritual death to spiritual life.

Sometime after his conversion he was assigned the leadership of a band and then a class. When he later felt in his heart a strong conviction that he must preach, he had no rest day nor night until, by contacting Mr. Wesley, he was able to express just what he felt. Mr. Wesley responded by warning him thus:

To be a Methodist preacher is not the way to ease, honour, pleasure, or profit. It is a life of much labour and reproach. They often fare hard, often are in want. They are liable to be stoned, beaten, and abused in various manners. Consider this before you engage in so uncomfortable a way of life. [Mr. Mather] replied [that he] had no desire to engage therein unless it was the call of God, and ... did not regard what [he] suffered in doing the will of God.

Alexander Mather laboured for forty-three years as a traveling preacher in the Methodist Connexion. During his long years of ministry he was known to have preached in most Methodist circuits within the kingdom and was very useful in them all. "As he laboured in dependence on divine grace, He who sent him did not suffer him to labour in vain, but gave him many seals to his ministry." It is said that by his preaching "many were awakened, many justified, and believers in general edified ... wherever he came."

It was also said that he became "a perfect master of all the minutiae of the doctrines of and discipline of Methodism. Hereby he was enabled, from a principle of duty and conscience, to afford Mr. Wesley very considerable assistance in the superintendence of the societies." The wisdom, courage, experience and perseverance he manifested while laboring in the Connexion rendered him an invaluable friend to all his colleagues and a valuable leader in the advancement of the Methodist societies. He became under Mr. Wesley a "father to the preachers."

One informs us that he "bore a faithful testimony against that dangerous error that a man may be in a state of favour and acceptance with God and yet have no evidence of it." The claim was made that "He constantly and strongly insisted upon the knowledge of salvation by the remission of sins and the abiding witness of the Holy Spirit, and clearly proved these precious doctrines by the express testimony of the holy Scriptures." This emphasis of early Methodist teaching, by the way, has been greatly neglected in later times.

His personal testimony to entire sanctification or Christian perfection is worthy of note. Concerning this, he writes,

> What I had experienced in my own soul was an instantaneous deliverance from all those wrong tempers and affections which I had long and sensibly groaned under, an entire disengagement from every creature with an entire devotedness to God: and from that moment I found an unspeakable pleasure in doing the will of God in all things. I had also a power to do it, and the constant approbation both of my own conscience and of God. I had simplicity of heart and a single eye to God at all times and in all places, with such a fervent zeal for the glory of God and the good of souls as swallowed up every other care and consideration. Above all, I had uninterrupted communion with God, whether sleeping or waking. O that it were with me as when the candle of the Lord thus shone upon my head! While I call it to mind my soul begins to wing its way toward that immediate enjoyment of God. May it never be retarded, but press into the glorious liberty, which is equally free for all the sons of God.

When Mr. Mather came down to the end of life, it was with much patience and resignation, he supported the tedious, complicated and painful affliction wherewith it pleased God to exercise and perfect him. "For it was necessary," says one, "that he, like his Master, should

be perfected through sufferings." One has described this final period
of his life in the following words:

> His sufferings, indeed, for some years have occasionally
> been great, but for six or eight months nearly
> uninterrupted. At the time I last saw him ... his
> affliction was great indeed. And what I was then a
> witness to I shall never forget. The moment his dear
> friend Mr. Pawson and I entered the room his pale face,
> his emaciated body, and his death-like appearance struck
> and affected us exceedingly, and for some minutes we
> both remained silent, and wept. At length he attempted
> to address us; and with a low whisper, not being able
> to speak above his breath, he said, "Through the mercy
> of God I have got hither by a miracle; but why I am
> here I know not, for I seem to be of no use." I said,
> "You are here that you may be an example of patience,
> by suffering the will of God, as you have long been of
> diligence in doing it. And doubtless you find this a
> harder duty than the other." "Indeed I do," said he;
> "but I find the grace of God sufficient for this also." He
> then expressed himself in the most clear, pertinent, and
> feeling manner concerning our redemption by Christ,
> as I have mentioned above, and of his whole dependence
> being on this alone and not on anything he had done
> or suffered for salvation. We were both much affected
> while he discoursed on this subject. After this he spoke
> concerning the Methodist Connexion in a way which
> showed how much his soul was wrapped up in the
> prosperity of it, and gave us many cautions and advices,

urging us especially to attend, at the Conference, to the state of the poor preachers, many of whom, he said, he knew to be in great want and distress. After he had quite spent himself with speaking to us on these and some other subjects, we kneeled down to pray, as we had reason to believe, for the last time. But we could not speak much. We could do little more than weep in silence, and gave vent to our tears and sighs. We then bade him farewell.

In patience and resignation he continued from the first attack of his disorder. He retained his confidence in God, and his hope of everlasting life, to the very last. To a much esteemed friend he testified as follows:

I have nowhere to look, nor anything else to depend upon for salvation, but Christ, and my confidence in Him is firm as a rock. My faith has frequently been assaulted during my affliction in an unusual manner, but it has never shrunk in the least degree. I feel a blessed evidence of my acceptance, and a sacred sense of God's presence being with me always. How comfortable are these words, "Him that cometh to me I will in no wise cast out." "God so loved us, that He gave His only Son' to be the propitiation for us. There is no other name, no other Redeemer; on Him my soul relies. Mine is a hope of more than forty years: it cannot easily be shaken."

Days later he was found to be "in extreme anguish" and was heard to say, "I long to be gone, I long to be gone." He thus desired those around him to pray for his dismissal. After prayer was made he was reminded that the desire to be released from this life and its discomforts "could only be asked with submission." He sweetly and reverently answered, "With great submission; with great submission." After pausing awhile he said, "I am happy in Jesus, but my sufferings are very great," and added:

> Rivers of life divine I see,
> And trees of paradise.

Then with expression of great longing he said, "O, let me be there— I'll be there, there, there! O that it might be this night! O, hide me among these trees! Here may I have an abiding place!"

> Tis there, with the lambs of Thy flock,
> There only I covet to rest.

"But," said he in a reverential tone, "if I may not have the privilege, the happiness, the honour of being with Thee this night, may I be resigned to Thy will. O that exercise of praise and thanksgiving! It has," he continued, "been the delight of my soul, my chief exercise on earth. I have loved Thy word, Thy law, Thy people, and I still love them." In a spirit of continued resignation, he said:

> Let it not my Lord displease,
> That I would die to be His guest.

Jesus answers, "Thou art all fair, My love; there is no spot in thee. Arise, My love, My fair one, and come away." Jesus has made me all fair. Again, when labouring under the most extreme pain, anguish, and anxiety (for his complicated afflictions racked his body with the most torturing sufferings, and bowed down his formerly strong spirits with the heaviest depression), he most affectingly cried out, "O God, my heart is broken within me. Why are Thy chariot-wheels so long in coming? Lord, grant me patience"; and then, as though his prayers were immediately answered, he calmly said:

> To patient faith the prize is sure,
> And they that to the end endure
> The cross, shall wear the crown.

Another night of inexpressible suffering was passed, followed by a little time of slumber and silent composure. Upon awakening, however, he seemed surprised to find himself still in the body, and said,

"Why did you call me back? I have been in Paradise. As surely as I shall go there again, I have been in heaven this morning." Then, after taking leave of, and giving his dying advice to, the family, he turned to Mrs. Mather and said, "As for you, my dear, I can say nothing to you that I have not already said; but" (pointing to the Bible) "that book is yours, and the Author of it." On this night, amongst many other heavenly breathings, [he was heard] to say, "O Jesus, whom I have loved, whom I do love, in whom I delight, I surrender myself unto Thee." This was a night of peculiar affliction, which he bore with the utmost degree of Christian patience.

On the day of his release and about two hours before his departure, he was heard to utter these final words:

"I now know that I have not sought Thee in vain; I

have not—I have not—I have not." And then, "O Thou that causedst light to shine out of darkness, shine upon my soul with the light of the knowledge of the Son of God. That name above every other name for ever dear, it dispels all my fears. O, proclaim, proclaim Jesus! Tell me, shall I be with Him this night?" On being answered, "Yes, there is no doubt of it," he cried out, "He that I have served for near fifty years will not forsake me now. Glory be to God and the Lamb, for ever and ever! Amen! amen! amen!"

It was not long thereafter that his voice began to fail and he spoke very little so as to be heard. The motion of his lips, however, gave indication that he was engaged in silent prayer. After this he fell "into a sweet slumber, and silently and almost imperceptibly breathed his soul into the arms of his loved and adored Redeemer." (John Telford, ed., *Wesley's Veterans*, II [Salem: Schmul Publishers, 1976], 78-155)

John Pawson:
Wanted Only Jesus And Death
(d. March, 1806)

John Pawson began proclaiming the good news of the Gospel in the year 1761. For the next forty-five years he was a highly respected Methodist preacher. As a leader among his fellow laborers, he was held in much esteem. His mental abilities were strong and his preaching greatly effective. The following is an edited account of his last days and departure to a better world.

He preached his last sermon on February 3, 1806, in Wakefield. Physical illness now became so severe that it became impossible for him to continue labouring in the ministry. Shortly after, he began to be confined to his room, being now attacked by an internal inflammation. "From this period, he appeared to be fast approaching the borders of the grave. This [however], was to him a source of consolation, and he frequently declared that when his pain was most acute, his confidence in God was strongest."

Several days later he "exhorted those ministers who were present to insist especially on the necessity of enjoying the witness of the Spirit, and holiness of heart, and then declared that the only foundation of his hope was the infinite merits of the Lord Jesus." Later in the same day he was heard to say, "'All will be well soon. I can speak of my funeral as cheerfully as of my wedding.'"

While in conversation with a friend, the necessity of doing all things to the glory of God was discussed. As a personal illustration of this, "he declared that he had never purchased a single article since his conversion but with an eye to eternity, and said, 'I have nothing to do: all is ready.'"

In the presence of several friends, he expressed, "in the most elevated and forcible language, his glorious prospects into eternity" and then "he began to pray with the utmost fervency for the Conference, that they might abide by their original doctrines." He also, "in a most affecting manner, [prayed] for his wife, that the Lord would enable her cheerfully to resign him into His hands, and support her through this trying scene; and then for every individual present."

In spite of his weakness he, upon the request of Mrs. Pawson, "baptized a child belonging to a particular friend." It is said that he did this "with perfect recollection and presence of mind." To those present it proved to be a most "affecting sight, and a most solemn season."

It was his desire that one who was present send a message to the congregation at Birstall.

> "Give my love to the congregation and tell them I am
> going to my precious Saviour; the heaven of heavens is
> open to my view, I have nothing on my mind; I have
> nothing to do but die. I have long been sailing to this
> fair haven. Sometimes the seas have been rough and
> tempestuous; Satan has often tried to raise a storm, if
> possible, to overset my little bark; but this he could
> not [do]. No, no; now Satan hath no business with
> me; he appears to have quitted the field, and given it

up as a lost case." At another time he spoke to this effect: "All the powers of darkness will never be able to extinguish the flame of divine love that burns within." Soon afterwards he said, "It is enough; Christ died for me; I am mounting up to the throne of God." Then he broke out into most rapturous strains of praise; and, clasping his hands, said, "I know I am dying; but my deathbed is a bed of roses; I have no thorns planted upon my dying pillow."

Sometime later, he spoke of death with much cheerfulness, and, when feeling his pulse, wondered why his Master should delay His coming:

"I have no dread; all is prepared; death is welcome." A few hours after this, he again committed his wife into the hands of God, telling her she would soon follow, and that the Lord would be her refuge and strength. Feeling himself exceedingly weak, he said, "I am on the verge of eternity." and with his utmost remaining strength exclaimed, "Victory, victory, victory, through the blood of the Lamb! Let my soul now take its everlasting flight." After this he sung the following verse from one of his favourite hymns:

> O! could we but our doubts remove,
> Those gloomy doubts that rise;
> And see the Canaan that we love,
> With unbeclouded eyes!

"Doubts, gloomy doubts! Where are they? I know nothing of gloomy doubts; I have none. Where are they gone?" To him a friend replied, "I suppose they are fallen at the foot of the cross, where Bunyan's Pilgrim lost his burden." "O!" said our reverend father, "but I am now upon the Delectable Mountains; and with the Shepherd's spying-glass I view the heavenly country." At this time there appeared a favourable change in his complaint, which continued ten days; during which period, through extreme debility, he was incapable of speaking much; but what he said was strongly expressive of his happy state. "I have," said he, at one time, "neither pain, sickness, sorrow, nor a wish to live or die. All is well. "

> My Jesus to know, and feel His blood flow,
> 'Tis life everlasting, 'tis heaven below.

"Yes, heaven already is begun, everlasting life is won, is won, is won! I die a safe, easy, happy death. Thou, my God, art present; I know, I feel Thou art. Precious Jesus! Glory, glory be to God!'

Sunday, 16.—Having passed through a very painful night, he said he thought two more such would carry him off; but added, "All is well; my life is hid with Christ in God: and you, my dear partner, will soon follow me." He then, with peculiar energy, spoke the following lines:

> Trembling, hoping, ling'ring, flying,
> O the pain, the bliss of dying!

Monday, 17.—Being asked if he wanted anything, he replied, "I want nothing but my blessed Jesus, and death. But I have Him now: thanks be to God, Christ is mine. I am dying, but I shall live for ever. Christ is all in all to me: death is indeed desirable; but all the days of my appointed time will I wait till my change come." One present said, "You will have a blessed change." "Yes," said he, "I know I shall." To one who came to see him, he said, "My kind friend, I am drawing fast to a conclusion. O my Jesus, it is all light and glory! I am completely happy; completely happy."

On Tuesday, 18, suffering much from difficulty of breathing, he said,

"Dying work is hard work: but now my strength fails, God is the strength of my heart, and my portion for ever; yes, for ever and ever. Christ is my Saviour, my All. Help me to render unto Thee the praise so justly due to Thine excellent name for the support I feel. Thou dost not suffer me to faint; no;

> From Zion's top the breezes blow,
> Refreshing all the vales below.

About eleven o'clock at night he began to be much worse; respiration was exceedingly difficult, and he appeared to suffer much pain.

Early on Wednesday morning, he said to his nephew and fellow labourer, who sat by his bedside, "I feel I am dying, but must get up and die in my chair." Soon after he was seated, he said, "Now kneel down, both of you, and pray that I may be released, if it be the will of the God." After they had prayed, he took hold of the hand of each of them, and gave them his dying blessing. He then lifted up his hands and eyes to heaven, and said,

371

"Lord Jesus, receive my spirit." Soon after he was again put into bed, and said, "My God! my God! my God!" These were the last words he distinctly uttered. He was now incapable of speaking, and sunk very fast, but was perfectly sensible to the end. He died about twenty minutes past nine o'clock in the morning, apparently without any struggle or pain, in the sixty-ninth year of his age, and forty-fourth of his ministry; leaving a most glorious testimony that he was gone to be for ever with the Lord.

Mr. Pawson's funeral sermon was preached by Mr. Benson in City Road Chapel, London. (John Telford, ed., *Wesley's Veterans,* IV [Salem: Schmul Publishers, 1976], 1-121)

George Shadford:
An Old Preacher Who Was Happy To Hear He Was About To Die
(d. March, 1816)

It is said of Mr. Shadford that he "prayed and preached till disease and infirmity arrested him in his career. After having traveled for twenty-three years," he retired from active itinerancy. He did not, however, "bury himself in obscurity, or sink into indolence." He happily showed "the same unabated love for the souls of men and the prosperity of the Church of God which he had done during the vigor of his health. He neither outlived his piety nor his usefulness." To all who knew him well, "it was evident … that he enjoyed communion and fellowship with God, and was ripening for eternal glory." In his retirement he became leader of two classes. The members therein "had a high opinion of his piety, and, when assembled round him, hung upon his lips, eagerly expecting some word of instruction or comfort, for they had no doubt that God would make him an honoured instrument for their good." It is said that when meeting with his classes, he "was remarkably conciliating; there was nothing rough or austere in his manner." With a gracious spirit "he blended the most benevolent feelings with faithfulness, and never appeared satisfied unless all the people under his care loved God with all their hearts, with all their strength, and with all their might. To these his advice was, 'Grow in grace.'"

The following account of Mr. Shadford's last illness and death is provided by Rev. John Riles.

> On Monday ... Mr. Shadford dined with his affectionate friend Mr. Blunt, in company with his brethren. He then appeared in tolerable health, and ate a hearty dinner. In the course of the week he felt indisposed, from a complication of diseases. He was under no apprehension at this time that his departure was so near, as he had frequently felt similar affections, and by timely applications to his medical friend, Mr. Bush, had been relieved. On Friday, March 1, he with some difficulty met his class, and afterwards said it was impressed on his mind that he should never meet it more. On the Sunday afternoon I called to inquire about his health, when he said with unusual fervour:
>
> > To patient faith the prize is sure;
> > And all that to the end endure
> > The cross, shall wear the crown.
>
> His mind seemed fully occupied with the great and interesting realities of eternity, and he had no greater pleasure than in meditating and talking of the dying love of Christ. On the Lord's day morning, March 10, before I went to the chapel, I called to see him, and found he had slept most of the night; from this we flattered ourselves the complaint had taken a favourable turn, and were in hopes of his recovery. But when the doctor called he said the disease was fast approaching

to a crisis, and it was impossible for him to recover. Upon this information Mr. Shadford broke out in a rapture, and exclaimed, "Glory be to God!" Upon the subject of his acceptance with God, and assurance of eternal glory, he had not the shadow of a doubt. While he lay in view of an eternal world, and was asked if all was clear before him, he replied, "I bless God it is"; and added, "Victory, victory, through the blood of the Lamb!" When Mrs. Shadford was sitting by him he repeated, "What surprise! What surprise!" I suppose he was reflecting upon his entrance into the presence of his God and Saviour, where every scene surpasses all imagination, and the boldest fancy returns weary and unsatisfied in its loftiest flights. Two friends, who were anxious for his recovery, called upon him; and when they inquired how he was, he replied, "I am going to my Father's house, and find religion to be an angel in death." A pious lady in the course of the day was particularly desirous of seeing him, and she asked him to pray for her. He inquired, "What shall I pray for?" She said, "That I may meet you in heaven, to cast my blood-bought crown at the feet of my Redeemer." He said with great energy, "The prize is sure." His pious sayings were numerous, and will long live in the recollection of many; but a collection of them all would swell this article beyond due limits. His last words were, "I'll praise, I'll praise, I'll praise!" and a little after he fell asleep in Jesus, on March 11, 1816, in the seventy –eighth year of his age.

"For nearly fifty-four years Mr. Shadford had enjoyed a sense of the divine favour. His conduct and conversation" gave sufficient evidence of the "truth of his profession. For many years he had professed to enjoy that perfect love which excludes all slavish fear; and if Christian tempers and a holy walk are proofs of it, his claims were legitimate." He maintained "a humble dependence upon the merits of the Redeemer" while steering "clear of both Pharisaism and Antinomianism: his faith worked by love. Truly happy himself, there was nothing forbidding in his countenance, sour in his manners, or severe in his observations." In the presence of others "his company was always agreeable, and his conversation profitable. If there was anything stern in his behaviour, it was assumed to silence calumniators and religious gossips. In short, he was a man of prayer and a man of God." (John Telford, *Wesley's Veterans*, II [Salem: Schmul Publishers, 1976], 213-216)

Adam Clarke:

Died Putting On His Armour
(d. August, 1832)

It is understandably granted that few would wish to suffer a lingering death, particularly if it should be accompanied with severe pain and bodily affliction. Nor is it commonly desired that one's last illness should require a great burden of care and expense to be borne by family members. However, is it altogether wise for the godly to wish and pray for death to be *sudden?*

Adam Clarke, gloriously converted at an early age, became one of the most effective of Mr. Wesley's traveling preachers. In process of time he proved to be an outstanding student and exponent of the sacred Scriptures. Shared below are his personal thoughts and desires concerning the subject of sudden death. It is hoped that the reader will find his comments worthy of serious consideration.

> The sentence, frequently applied to the death of the righteous, "sudden death is sudden glory," is a foolish expression: *no* man should desire to be taken off at a moment's warning: when *my* time comes to go the way of all the earth, I should pray not to be taken *suddenly* into the presence of my God; gladly would I have

time to brace on my armour, and to take my shield; then would I meet and struggle with the monster, in the power of my Redeemer, and to the last gasp, death though conqueror, should possess no *victory* over Adam Clarke.

As it turned out, Dr. Clarke received his wish. The last and fatal illness proved to be an attack of cholera. His death, at the age of 72, was neither a protracted one nor his illness severely painful. And in accordance with his desire, he was providentially given several hours of consciousness before taking his last breath. Following announcement of the medical diagnosis, one who was present at his bedside remarked, "My dear doctor, you must put your soul into the hands of your God, and your trust in the merits of your Saviour." In reply, he could but faintly utter the words, "I do, I do." While his physical powers continued to decline and his speech finally left him, his knowledge of persons around him continued to be evident. From the posture and position of his hands, it was clear to all who were present that he was indeed "bracing on his armour and taking his shield." (J. J. B. Clarke, ed., *An Account of the Infancy, Religious and Literary Life of Adam Clarke* [New York: B. Waugh and T. Mason Publishers, 1833], 222, 239)

A Methodist Tombstone Witness

The following notation was included in the 1780 Methodist Hymnbook and frequently found on early 19th century Methodist tombstones.

Pass a few swiftly fleeting years,
And all that now in bodies live
Shall quit, like me, the vale of tears,
Their righteous sentence to receive.

But all, before they hence remove,
May mansions for themselves prepare
In that eternal house above-
And, O my God, shall I be there?

Concluding Observations

While witnessing the dying testimonies of eighteenth century Methodists, we are constrained to conclude that the doctrines they heard preached and taught were, when fully embraced, more than sufficient to bring them safely "through the valley of the shadow of death" to a glorious and heavenly inheritance. All of this, to be sure, was and still is possible through grace alone.

It becomes clear that early Methodists unhesitatingly believed in a religion of the heart. It is popular in today's evangelical and holiness circles to openly devalue what they like to call "feelings" in Christian experience. However, Christianity without an inward awareness of God was unacceptable to early Methodists. An assurance of sins forgiven and a conscious evidence of the fruit of the Spirit were important. Yes, faith was ever the means by which inward enjoyment of God was made possible, but a truly saving faith was always productive of God's "love shed abroad in the heart by the Holy Ghost given" together with "a peace that passeth all understanding."

The testimony of John Murlin who was one of Mr. Wesley's itinerant preachers is an example of this early Methodist view of heart religion. He writes,

I bless God I can say to His glory I do find a constant communion with Him. And I pay no regard to those who tell us, "You must come from the mount, and you must not mind your frames and feelings." No! If I have the peace of God, do I not feel it? If I do not feel it, I have it not. And if I do not feel joy in the Holy Ghost, it does not exist. And shall I not feel it more and more if I go on from faith to faith, if I daily "grow in grace" (as I trust I shall), "and in the knowledge of our Lord Jesus Christ"? (John Telford, ed., *Wesley's Veterans*, II [Salem: Schmul Publishers, 1976], 163-64)

In his "Essay on Truth," the Rev. John Fletcher once wrote that "when living faith ceases to 'work,' it dies away, as the heart that ceases to beat; it goes out, as a candle that ceases to shine."

Later in the same discourse, the saintly Fletcher assures us that he is "no judge of what passes in the breasts of [others]; but, for my part," says he, "I never feel faith more strongly at work than when I wrestle not only with flesh and blood, but with the banded powers of darkness." He then reminds us that "None but a dead man is quite destitute of frame and feeling" (John Fletcher, *The Works of the Reverend John Fletcher*, I [Salem: Schmul Publishers, 1974], 543-44).

It is observed, moreover, that early Methodists who died happy had the Spirit's witness that sins were forgiven and the heart cleansed. Mr. Wesley was a strong advocate of the doctrine of assurance through the witness of the Spirit. He produced no less than three sermons on the subject, basing the truth thereof on Romans 8:16 and Galatians 4:6. In his *Plain Account of Christian Perfection,* he produced helps to a fuller understanding of this truth. For instance, while once in conference with his preachers he was asked how one could know that he was entirely sanctified and saved from inbred sin. He answered,

> I can know it no otherwise than I know that I am justified. "Hereby know we that we are of God," in either sense, "by the Spirit that He hath given us."
>
> We know it by the witness and by the fruit of the Spirit. And, First, by the witness. As, when we were justified, the Spirit bore witness with our spirit, that our sins were forgiven; so, when we were [entirely] sanctified, He bore witness that [inbred corruption was cleansed] away. Indeed, the witness of [entire] sanctification is not always clear at first (as neither is that of justification); neither is it afterwards always the same, but like that of justification, sometimes stronger, and sometimes fainter. Yea, and sometimes it is withdrawn. Yet, in general, the latter testimony of the Spirit, is both as clear and as steady as the former. (John Wesley, *The Works of John Wesley*, XI [Grand Rapids: Zondervan Publishing House], 420)

Mr. Wesley further enforces the importance of a believer's receiving the witness of the Spirit in the following words:

> In the hour of temptation, Satan clouds the work of God, and injects various doubts and reasonings, especially in those who have either very weak or very strong understandings. At such times, there is absolute need of that witness, without which, the work of sanctification not only could not be discerned, but could not longer subsist. Were it not for this, the soul

could not then abide in the love of God; much less could it rejoice evermore, and in every thing give thanks. In those circumstances, therefore, a direct testimony that we are [entirely] sanctified, is necessary in the highest degree. *("ibid., 420")*

Close observation reveals that early Methodists followed Scriptural methods in their seeking of both initial salvation and Christian perfection. The "altar call" and "mourner's bench" were not yet known in the days of the great Wesleyan revival. These human innovations would not appear until later in the next century. We have noticed that some received assurance that they were newly born of the Spirit during the preaching of a sermon, the singing of a hymn, or while participating in the Lord's Supper. Some received assurance of sins forgiven while in prayer alone, others while engaged in corporate supplication. Still others received the blessing when baptized.

Repentance toward God and faith in our Lord Jesus Christ are Scriptural steps by which all seekers find justification and regeneration. However, the faith that saves, according to Mr. Wesley, "is the gift of God. No man," says he, "is able to work it in himself. It is a work of omnipotence. It requires no less power thus to quicken a dead soul, than to raise a body that lies in the grave. It is a new creation; and none can create a soul anew, but He who at first created the heavens and the earth" (John Wesley, *The Works of John Wesley*, VIII [Grand Rapids: Zondervan Publishing House, 1958], 5).

The modern holiness movement promises the experience of entire sanctification to all seekers if they but obey the injunction of Romans 12:1. And though we can be sure that entire sanctification would never be attained without total dedication and presentation of one's body as a living sacrifice unto God, early Methodists were aware of yet another important condition that is too often overlooked in today's holiness circles. That condition is found in 1 John 1:9: "If we confess our sins, he is faithful and just to forgive us our sins, and to cleanse us from all unrighteousness." We share below a portion of Adam Clarke's commentary on this verse:

> If, from a deep sense of our guilt, impurity, and helplessness, we humble ourselves before God, acknowledging our iniquity, his holiness, and our own utter helplessness, and implore mercy for his sake who died for us; *he is faithful*, because to such he has *promised* mercy, **Psalm 32:5; Proverbs 28:13;** *and just*, for Christ has died for us, and thus made an atonement to the Divine justice; so that God can now be just, and yet the justifier of him who believeth in Jesus ... Not only to forgive the sin, but to *purify the heart.*
>
> OBSERVE here, 1. Sin exists in the soul after two modes or forms: (1.) In *guilt*, which requires *forgiveness or pardon.* (2.) In *pollution*, which requires *cleansing.*
>
> 2. *Guilt*, to be forgiven, must be *confessed;* and *pollution*, to be *cleansed*, must be also *confessed.* In order to *find* mercy, a man must *know* and *feel* himself to be a *sinner*, that he may fervently apply to God for pardon; in order to get a *clean heart*, a man must know and feel its depravity, acknowledge and deplore it before God, in order to be *fully sanctified.*
>
> 3. Few are pardoned, because they do not feel and confess their sins; and few are sanctified or cleansed from all sin, because they do not feel and confess their own sore, and the plague of their hearts.

4. As the blood of Jesus Christ, the merit of his passion and death, applied by faith, purges the conscience from *all dead works*, so the same *cleanses the heart* from *all unrighteousness....*

Another observation which cannot escape the attentive reader is that early Methodists who died gloriously were altogether without fear. The Apostle John assures us that "There is no fear in love; but perfect love casteth out fear: because fear hath torment. He that feareth is not made perfect in love" (John 4:18). Adam Clarke's comments on this verse are instructive.

The man who feels that he loves God with all his heart can never *dread* him as his *Judge*. As he is now made a partaker of his Spirit, and carries a sense of the Divine approbation in his conscience, he has nothing of that *fear* that produces *terror* or brings *torment*. The *perfect love*-that fullness of love, which he has received, *casteth out fear*-removes all terror relative to this day of judgment, for it is of this that the apostle particularly speaks. And as it is inconsistent with the gracious design of God to have his followers miserable, and as he cannot be unhappy whose heart is full of the love of his God, this love must necessarily exclude this fear or terror; because that brings *torment*, and hence is inconsistent with that happiness which a man must have who continually enjoys the approbation of his God.

He who is still uncertain concerning his interest in Christ; who, although he has many heavenly drawings, and often sits with Christ some moments on a throne of love, yet feels from the evils of his heart a dread of the day of judgment; *is not made perfect in love*-has not yet received the abiding witness of the Spirit that he is begotten of God; nor that fullness of love to God and man which excludes the *enmity* of the *carnal mind*, and which it is his privilege to receive. But is the case of such a man *desperate?* No: it is neither *desperate nor deplorable*; he is in the way of salvation, and not far from the kingdom of heaven. Let such earnestly seek, and fervently believe on the Son of God; and he will soon ... purge out all the old leaven, and fill their whole souls with that love which is the fulfilling of the law. He who is not yet perfect in love may speedily become so, because God can say in a moment. *I will, be thou clean; and immediately his leprosy will depart.* Among men we find some that have neither love nor fear; others that have fear without love; others that have love and fear; and others that have love without fear.

1. Profligates and worldly men in general, have neither the fear nor love of God.

2. Deeply awakened and distressed penitents have the fear or terror of God without his love.

3. Babes in Christ, or young converts, have often distressing fear mixed with their love.

4. Adult Christians have love without this fear; because fear hath torment, and they are ever happy, being filled with God....

1. We must not suppose that the love of God shed abroad in the heart is ever *imperfect in itself*; it is only so in *degree*. There may be a *less or greater degree* of what is *perfect* in itself; so it is with respect to the love which

the followers of God have; they may have *measures* or *degrees* of perfect love without its *fullness*. There is nothing *imperfect* in the love of God, whether it be considered as existing in himself, or as communicated to his followers.

2. We are not to suppose that the love of God casts out *every kind of fear* from the soul; it only casts out that which has *torment*. 1. A *filial fear* is consistent with the highest degrees of love; and even necessary to the preservation of that grace. This is properly its guardian; and, without this, love would soon degenerate into listlessness, or presumptive boldness. 2. Nor does it cast out that *fear* which is so necessary to the *preservation of life*; that fear which leads a man to *flee from danger* lest his life should be destroyed. 3. Nor does it cast out that *fear* which may be engendered by *sudden alarm*. All these are necessary to our well-being. But it destroys, 1. The fear of *want;* 2. The fear of *death;* and 3. The fear of terror of *judgment*. All these fears bring torment, and are inconsistent with this perfect love.

We finally observe that Christian perfection was commonly experienced and enjoyed by dying saints of early Methodism. Methodists, however, were not the first to teach and embrace such a doctrine. The terms "perfect," "perfecting," and "perfection" are repeatedly used by New Testament writers. Early Apostolic Fathers such as Clement of Rome, Ignatius of Antioch, and Polycarp of Smyrna faithfully followed the Apostles in their teaching of Christian perfection. It was found that divine love filling the heart had the power to expel all pride, anger, carnal desires and self-will. Mr. Wesley writes:

I know many that love God with all their heart. He is their one desire, their one delight, and they are continually happy in Him. They love their neighbor as themselves. They feel as sincere, fervent, constant a desire for the happiness of every man, good or bad, friend or enemy, as for their own. They rejoice evermore, pray without ceasing, and in everything give thanks. Their souls are continually streaming up to God, in holy joy, prayer, and praise. This is a point of fact; and this is plain, sound, Scripture experience. (John Wesley, *The Works of John Wesley*, XI [Grand Rapids; Zondervan Publishing House, 1958], 418)

While knowing and loving God, while seeking and finding all their delight in Him, it is little wonder that early Methodists were found happy in both life and death.

Bibliography

Benson, Joseph. *The Life of the Rev. John W. De La Flechere*. Chicago: The Christian Witness Co., 1925.

Clarke, Adam. *Clarke's Commentary* VI. New York & Nashville: Abingdon Press, nd.

-------. *Memoirs of the Wesley Family*. New York: Lane & Tippet Publishers, 1848.

Clarke, J. B. B. ed. *An Account of the Infancy, Religious and Literary Life of Adam Clark*. New York: B. Waugh and T. Mason Publishers, 1833.

Dallimore, Arnold A. *A Heart Set Free*. Wheaton, IL: Crossway Books, 1988.

Excell, Joseph S., and H. D. M. Spence, eds. *The Pulpit Commentary, Psalms* III. London & New York: Funk & Wagnalls Company, nd.

Fletcher, John. *The Works of the Reverend John Fletcher*. 4 vols. Salem: Schmul Publishers, 1974.

Holy Bible. Authorized King James Version. Cambridge: University Press.

Jones, D. M. *Charles Wesley A Study*. London: Skeffington & Son, Ltd, nd.

Telford, John, ed. *Wesley's Veterans. Lives of Early Methodist Preachers Told by Themselves.* 7 vols. Salem: Schmul Publishers, 1976.

Tyerman, L. *Wesley's Designated Successor: The Life, Letters, and Literary Labours of the Rev. John William Fletcher.* Stoke-on-Trent: Tentmakers Publications, 2001.

Watson, Richard. *The Life of the Rev. John Wesley, A. M.* New York: W. Disturnell Publishers, 1834.

Wesley, Charles. *The Journal of Charles Wesley (two vols.)* Reprinted by Baker House, 1980.

Wesley, John. *The Works of John Wesley.* An edition of the complete and unabridged *Works* reproduced by the photo offset process from the authorized edition published by the Wesleyan Conference Office in London, England, in 1872. 14 vols. Grand Rapids: Zondervan Publishing House, 1958.

Wiseman, F. Luke. *Charles Wesley: Evangelist and Poet.* London: The Epworth Press, 1932.

Printed in the United States
128072LV00003B/124-183/P

9 781434 329813